COLLECTED WORKS OF ERASMUS

VOLUME 42

COLLECTED WORKS OF
ERASMUS

NEW TESTAMENT SCHOLARSHIP

PARAPHRASES ON ROMANS
AND GALATIANS

edited by Robert D. Sider

translated and annotated by

John B. Payne, Albert Rabil Jr, and
Warren S. Smith Jr

University of Toronto Press

Toronto/Buffalo/London

The research and publication costs of the
Collected Works of Erasmus are supported by the
Social Sciences and Humanities Research Council of Canada
(and previously by the Canada Council).
The publication costs are also assisted by
University of Toronto Press.

Canadian Cataloguing in Publication Data
Erasmus, Desiderius, ca. 1466–1536.
[Works]
Collected works of Erasmus
Contents: v. 42. Paraphrases on Romans and Galatians.
ISBN 0-8020-2510-2 (v. 42)
1. Erasmus, Desiderius, ca. 1466–1536.   I. Title.
PA8500 1974   876'.04   C74-6326-x

Collected Works of Erasmus

The aim of the Collected Works of Erasmus
is to make available an accurate, readable English text
of Erasmus' correspondence and his
other principal writings. The edition is planned
and directed by an Editorial Board, an Executive Committee,
and an Advisory Committee.

Contents

Preface

This is the first volume to appear in the series within the *Collected Works of Erasmus* (CWE) which is to be devoted to the New Testament scholarship of Erasmus, and it may be useful therefore to indicate the shape the series will assume. For this series, Erasmus' New Testament scholarship is defined as the *Paraphrases on the New Testament*, the *Annotations on the New Testament*, and those prefatory pieces which at one time or another accompanied the *Paraphrases* or *Annotations*. Erasmus' replies to criticism of these works will be published elsewhere in the CWE.

In both structure and format the series will reflect some important aspects of the original publication of Erasmus' New Testament scholarship, though modifications will be inevitable. An introductory volume (CWE 41) will contain the prefatory pieces, including the important *Ratio verae theologiae*. Thereafter the arrangement of the series will be determined in general by the chronological order in which Erasmus originally published the *Paraphrases* and *Annotations*. It is for this reason that the Editorial Board has changed the earlier plan (CWE 23 xvi) of publishing the *Paraphrases* and *Annotations* together. The *Paraphrases* and *Annotations* were not originally published together. The *Annotations* were first published with the 1516 edition of Erasmus' New Testament, while the *Paraphrases*, which constituted a quite separate undertaking, appeared over a period of years, beginning with the publication of Romans in 1517. Consequently, the series will be arranged in a sequence in which the *Paraphrases* will follow the introductory volume of prefatory writings, and the *Annotations* succeed the *Paraphrases*. The sequence of the volumes of *Paraphrases* will reflect as far as possible the order of their publication; the volumes containing the translation of the *Annotations* will be arranged in the traditional order of the Western canon of the Bible, the order in which they appeared in Erasmus' editions of the New Testament.

The *Paraphrase on Romans*, first of the *Paraphrases* to be published, therefore stands first in the present sequence. In their essay on the origin and character of the *Paraphrases*, the translators have shown the importance of Romans in the development of Erasmus as a biblical scholar. For this reason, too, it is appropriate that the *Paraphrase on Romans* stand first in our series. The *Paraphrase on Galatians*, published after the paraphrases on 1 and 2 Corinthians, breaks the strict sequence, but in the growth of Paul's thought, Galatians offered an early expression of the more systematic argument of Romans, and it will be convenient for our readers to have in a single volume Erasmus' expansion upon these two companion epistles.

The format of these volumes has also been designed with the practice and intent of Erasmus in view. Erasmus did not, for example, publish a biblical text to accompany his *Paraphrases*, although the one was clearly an expansion of the other. This series, too, will print the translation of the *Paraphrases* without an accompanying biblical text. In this way, the movement of Erasmus' thought can be followed without distraction. Though the *Paraphrases* may share in the nature of a biblical commentary insofar as they clarify the text, they are not, strictly speaking, commentaries, and for this reason the page should invite the reader first to trace the contour of theme and argument. If then he wishes to compare paraphrase with biblical text, he may consult for himself a suitable translation of the Bible: the running head of each page in the translation carries the reference to the appropriate passage in the New Testament. One modification of the Erasmian text has been thought desirable. The early editions of Erasmus' *Paraphrases* printed the text without paragraphs. Paragraphs have been added by the translators to promote facility in reading.

While the introductory volume in this series will contain a general essay on the New Testament scholarship of Erasmus, the first volume of the *Paraphrases* offers the reader discussions designed to facilitate orientation to the materials. These discussions are not, of course, exhaustive. In particular, the essays by Sir Roger Mynors and E.J. Devereux have been written within strict limits of length. While the cwe normally wishes to trace the *fortuna* of a work as far as possible, yet in discussing the influence of the *Paraphrases* boundaries had to be set. We are not yet in a position to determine precisely the influence of the *Paraphrases* on the life and literature of Britain and the continent. Moreover, translations of the Bible appeared not only in England; they abounded on the continent, and in the final analysis it may be very difficult to distinguish echoes from the *Paraphrases* and those from the Bible.

RDS

The *Paraphrases* of Erasmus: Origin and Character

In the *De oratore* Cicero represents Crassus as saying that although in his youth he made paraphrases of the works of Latin authors, he soon saw that this was a defective method inasmuch as the authors in question had already chosen the most appropriate expressions, thus placing him in the position of using the less appropriate. He therefore decided to translate freely the speeches of eminent Greek orators, enabling him not only to use the best words but also to coin expressions that would be new to Latin-speaking people. Quintilian, explicitly countering Cicero, says that although translation from Greek into Latin is one way of acquiring facility, paraphrasing Latin is not to be discounted. On the contrary, he urges the student to turn poetry into prose, prose into poetry, long declamations into concise statements and brief assertions into lengthy speeches, and believes that by so doing a student may improve as well as change the original from which he is working.[1] Erasmus very early developed an interest in both translation and paraphrase as a means of facilitating fluency in Latin.[2]

When we first meet Erasmus (in his letters) in the monastery at Steyn, he is already an accomplished Latinist. His prose is polished, and he is a competent poet as well. He is also, as we see him later – from his days as a theological student in Paris to the end of his life – a teacher of Latin eloquence to others. Erasmus has not told us how he acquired his own mastery of Latin, but as a teacher he firmly upheld the paraphrase as an effective method of learning the language.

Among Erasmus' early writings are some pieces written as aids for the instruction of his protégés when he was forced into the role of tutor in order to maintain himself in Paris from 1497. These were published many years later - after he had also become proficient in Greek and had incorporated Cicero's as well as Quintilian's ideas about the instructive power of that language into his method of teaching facility in Latin. In the *De copia* (first published in 1512), he writes:

We shall add greatly to our linguistic resources if we translate authors from the Greek, as that language is particularly rich in subject-matter and vocabulary. It will also prove quite useful on occasion to compete with these Greek authors by paraphrasing what they have written. It will be of enormous value to take apart the fabric of poetry and reweave it in prose, and, vice versa, to bind the freer language of prose under the rules of metre, and also to pour the same subject-matter from one form of poetic container into another. It will also be very helpful to emulate a passage from some author where the spring of eloquence seems to bubble up particularly richly, and endeavour in our own strength to equal or even surpass it.[3]

And in the *De ratione studii*, also published first in an authorized edition in 1512, he says:

And it is a highly beneficial exercise to translate from the Greek. Accordingly it is desirable for the pupils to receive the most frequent and careful training in this exercise. For as soon as the mind is trained to grasp meanings, then the vigour and peculiarity of each language is thoroughly appreciated and points of similarity and variance between ourselves and the Greeks are grasped. Finally, to capture the peculiar tone of the Greek one must deploy all the resources of the Latin language.[4]

The first of these two passages particularly reflects Quintilian's discussion, except that Quintilian counsels the paraphrasing of Latin writers, or even one's own writings, rather than those of the Greeks, thus distinguishing the training to be derived from translation and that resulting from paraphrase. Erasmus, on the other hand, links translation and paraphrase as parts of the same process. The second passage reflects Cicero's discussion of the advantages of translation from Greek to Latin. But Erasmus also emphasizes a notion characteristic of him in all his activities as a scholar: that the exercise is designed to train the mind to grasp *meanings*.

In his own first efforts at a translation from Greek into Latin intended for publication, Erasmus' practice was suprisingly conservative. He does not approve of the freedom Cicero exercised in translation or granted others and prefers 'to err in seeming to keep too close rather than be too free.' Nor does he paraphrase, a method he believes is conducive to hiding the ignorance of a translator who cannot otherwise make a text clear. Finally, he prefers to copy the style of the text of Euripides' *Hecuba* rather than render it in the elevated style of Latin tragedy.[5]

This was written in January 1506, when Erasmus felt himself still a novice and justified his position on that ground. In November 1507, however, when Erasmus issued Euripides' *Iphigenia* in Latin translation, his views had already altered somewhat, and in the direction of his advice to students. This play, he says, he has translated a little more freely and expansively, 'but again in such a way as in no degree to fall short of a translator's duty to convey the meaning.' He confesses that in his translations of both plays he has departed from the author's practice at one point: he has reduced the metrical diversity and licence of the choric parts. Why? Because in the choruses the Greeks so strove 'for novelty of utterance that they destroyed clarity of expression, and in the hunt for marvellous verbal effects their sense of reality suffered.'[6] Here Erasmus enunciates a principle which is to be fundamental to his paraphrase of Scripture: the form is intended to serve the meaning. The meaning is of primary importance; the form can be changed to serve that end.

Erasmus' interest in becoming an interpreter of Scripture was first awakened when he visited England in 1499 and heard John Colet lecture on Paul.[7] Colet urged Erasmus to lecture on parts of the Old Testament, but Erasmus demurred on the grounds that he did not know the languages in which Scripture was composed. Nonetheless, no sooner had he returned to Paris than he began to write his own commentary on Paul. In the autumn of 1501 he says in a letter that he has been carefully preparing an interpretation of Paul for some time.[8] And he asks a friend to send him Ambrose, Augustine, Origen, Nicholas of Lyra, 'or anyone else who has written a commentary on Paul.'[9] Just prior to this, Erasmus had begun his study of Greek, but it was not far enough advanced for him to continue his commentary on Paul. As he wrote to John Colet three years later (December 1504):

> Three years ago, indeed, I ventured to do something on Paul's Epistle to the Romans, and at one rush, as it were, finished four volumes; and would have gone on, but for certain distractions, of which the most important was that I needed the Greek at every point. Therefore for nearly the past three years I have been wholly absorbed by Greek.[10]

Many years later, in 1514, Erasmus returned once again to St Paul and his Epistle to the Romans. He describes in a letter to his English patron, Lord Mountjoy, an incident in which his frightened horse caused his spine to be twisted. At first Erasmus was unable to move; his servant had to take him from his horse. It was then that he 'made a vow to St Paul that I would complete a commentary on his Epistle to the Romans if I should have the good fortune to escape from this peril.'[11] Escape he did, in his own mind somewhat miraculously. Nonetheless, in a letter to Cardinal Grimani (to whom he subsequently dedicated his *Paraphrase on Romans*) in May 1515, he wrote that he meant 'to take up again the work I once started on St Paul.'[12] Whether he meant the work he had begun in 1501 or a new beginning he may have made in 1514 is not clear. In the dedicatory letter accompanying the publication of the first edition of his New Testament, he says that he prepared for that work 'by starting some time ago my commentaries on St Paul.'[13] In the 1516 annotations themselves he wrote that the points under question he discusses 'more fully in the commentary which I started some time ago on St Paul and with Christ's help shall finish shortly.'[14] It may well have been this comment that stirred a number of Erasmus' friends to encourage him to complete his commentary and to express their eagerness to see it.[15]

Erasmus published his *Paraphrase on Romans* in November 1517. But that this was not the intended commentary he had projected is attested in a letter of 24 October 1518 in which he writes that he has begun to publish paraphrases and soon, heaven willing, will complete commentaries earlier begun.[16] Moreover, in his letter to Johann von Botzheim in 1524, a catalogue of his works, he lists his *Commentary on Romans* as one of his books.[17] The comment in the 1516 edition of the *Annotations* that he hoped soon to complete his commentary on St Paul drops out in 1527, and a 1530 catalogue of his writings finds no mention of such a commentary. It appears, then, that as late as 1524 Erasmus still intended to write a commentary on St Paul and that he did not regard his paraphrases as the completion of that task.

We have seen that Erasmus abandoned his commentary on Romans in 1501 in order to master Greek and that he did not focus his attention on it again until an accident led him to reaffirm his earlier project. The way back to it was circuitous. In 1504 Erasmus discovered a manuscript of Valla's *Annotations on the New Testament* and brought it to Paris where he had it published (for the first time) in March 1505. These annotations awakened in him the idea of becoming a translator and editor of the text of Scripture itself.[18] In 1506, the same year during which he translated Euripides, he also translated the New Testament from Greek into Latin (a translation he used in the second edition of his *Novum Testamentum* of 1519). This work of editing the scriptural texts took precedence over his commentaries. For he published the first edition of his Greek New Testament (*Novum Instrumentum*) together with a Latin translation (more conservative than the translation of 1506) and annotations in March 1516. It was, as we have seen, while he was in the midst of completing this task that he once again turned his attention to Paul and expressed the desire to resume his commentary.

The reception of the text, translation, and notes on the New Testament may have played a role in turning his attention to the paraphrases and

commentaries. For his enterprise of dealing critically with the text of
Scripture in general and his translation of the New Testament in particular
brought a great outcry from theological circles. He may well have thought
that writing paraphrases of Scripture was both easier and more acceptable to
the carping critics. If so, his views were confirmed by the reception his first
paraphrase received. Two months after its publication he wrote: 'I am
especially pleased that men who are so well thought of should think well of
my paraphrase; I only wish I had always laboured in that sort of field. I
would rather construct a thousand paraphrases than one critical edition.'[19]
Two months later still, he writes: 'my paraphrase is praised throughout by
everyone. It is something to have produced even one small book that can
find favour with critics so prejudiced and hard to please. I only wish I had
confined myself to the sort of fields in which there was not a little more fame
to be had, and far less work.'[20] In both these passages Erasmus suggests that
by temperament and inclination he is more fitted to produce paraphrases
than critical editions.[21]

Erasmus thus seems to have begun the work of writing paraphrases
unself-consciously, as a kind of relief from the work of the critical editor.[22] In
only one passage prior to the actual writing of his first paraphrase does
Erasmus make a theoretical statement about paraphrases. Musing on his
critics (August 1516), he asks: 'Suppose I had expounded all the sacred
books by way of a paraphrase, and made it possible to keep the sense
inviolate and yet to read them without stumbling and understand them more
easily? Would they quarrel with me then?'[23] Written in the context of the
criticisms levelled at him for 'tampering with Scripture,' this passage
suggests that Erasmus made a clear distinction between paraphrase and
translation. Moreover, it suggests that he believed a paraphrase could, as he
puts it in later statements, actually make the text of Scripture clearer.[24]

This notion that the function of paraphrase is to improve the text by
making it clearer is fundamental to Erasmus. In the presentation of his
Paraphrase on Romans to Cardinal Grimani, he says that it has been difficult to
make Paul clearer by 'bridging gaps, smoothing rough passages, bringing
order out of confusion and simplicity out of complication, untying knots,
throwing light on dark places, and giving Hebrew turns of speech a Roman
dress.'[25] When it is later suggested to Erasmus that such things as these are
not merely clarifications but changes or interpretations, he remarks that his
interpretations do not preclude others.[26] This appears, however, to be more
an attempt to dodge the problem than to confront it. In presenting his
Paraphrase on Romans he says simply that he tries to say things differently
from the way Paul said them without saying different things.

A paraphrase, then, seeks to clarify the text by rephrasing what an author says in the paraphraser's own words. In this respect a paraphrase differs from a translation, in which one attempts to render the author's words themselves.[27] On the other hand, a paraphrase shares with a commentary the use of the paraphraser's or commentator's own words. But a paraphrase differs from a commentary in being a continuous narrative rather than an interrupted one. Quite often Erasmus blurs this distinction in his numerous assertions that a paraphrase is a kind of commentary or can be taken like one.[28] In his presentation of Romans, however, he distinguishes the two, asserting that he would not have had to exert much more effort to produce a commentary. This probably means that Erasmus understood a commentary as more akin to a critical analysis of the text both philological and theological. At the same time, he goes on to say that whoever rejects any change in the letter of Holy Writ may use his paraphrase as a commentary.[29] In other words, if anyone is offended because he seems to be *rewriting Scripture* instead of *writing about Scripture*, then let him remember that a paraphrase is *like* a commentary in the sense that it seeks to interpret (make clearer) what Scripture means, not to replace Scripture.

There are other differences between a paraphrase and a commentary as well. A paraphrase does not attempt to clarify all the difficulties of the text of the New Testament but only to enable a better understanding of the text in order to elucidate the philosophy of Christ.[30] Nor does a paraphrase summarize (or even mention explicitly) the opinions of previous commentators.[31] Since a commentary presumably would perform these latter two tasks, Erasmus may have thought of a commentary as combining what he did in his annotations and paraphrases or, perhaps, as more closely akin to his annotations, where he does deal with all the difficulties of the text and the opinions of previous commentators. At the same time, it must be remembered that he distinguished commentary from annotation when he announced in his preface to the *Annotations* that he has written 'short annotations,' not a 'commentary,' implying a difference between philological notes and continuous theological exposition.[32]

Finally, in his presentation of the *Paraphrase on Romans* to Cardinal Grimani, Erasmus asserts that one who is not offended by the fact that he has changed the words of Holy Writ in order to make them clearer may hear the voice of Paul himself. This implies that Erasmus has no clear awareness of the differences between Paul and himself as speakers in the paraphrase. It is as if he were not Erasmus speaking at all, but Paul speaking for himself, even though in words different from those used by Paul in his letters.[33] This impression is reinforced by the statement in a letter of 1522 that a paraphrase is a continuous commentary 'without change of person,'[34] and by the assertion in his dedicatory letter to the *Paraphrase on Luke* a year later that 'the more inexperienced reader should be advised that I nowhere speak in the Paraphrase.'[35] In response to his critics at the Sorbonne, he writes in 1532 that he tried in his paraphrase to understand a passage as the ancients understood it, and in accordance with the intent of Paul.[36]

We have seen that in response to his critics, Erasmus had insisted that his interpretations did not preclude others, nor did he claim any special authority for his interpretations. But he has another line of defence as well: that he is doing nothing different from what others have done before him, not only Themistius in relation to Aristotle (the legitimacy of whose work the critic might grant since Aristotle is not Scripture), but Juvencus in relation to Scripture, and indeed in part, Augustine and Jerome.[37] If, says Erasmus, I added nothing to what Scripture says, I would not be a paraphraser or an explainer (the two were for him synonymous). It is sufficient if what I add does not disagree with the sense of Scripture. At least I do not teach what is contradictory to Scripture, or explain Scripture from the sophistries of Aristotle or Averroes.[38]

There were a number of precedents for Erasmus' use of paraphrase. The most formative was undoubtedly Quintilian with whom, as we have seen, Erasmus was on familiar terms before he wrote paraphrases and whose method of paraphrasing he recommended to students. Two others whom he cites as precedents were mentioned in the preceding paragraph. Themistius (317-88), a pagan interpreter and teacher of rhetoric, paraphrased the works of Aristotle.[39] Themistius' purpose appears to have been quite similar to that of Erasmus. Like Erasmus, Themistius evidently saw the need to simplify and clarify the text, and he tried to make Aristotle available in simple language intelligible to the non-specialist. He wished to give force to an ancient tradition, and endeavoured to find a practical role for philosophy in the life of individuals and society.[40]

Juvencus, a fourth-century Spanish priest, wrote a metrical version of the gospels.[41] Erasmus took comfort in the fact that a Christian writer dealing with the most sacred of texts changed the form of the texts without bringing censure down upon himself. The fact that what Juvencus wrote was new in relation to the past forms of Scripture shows clearly that Erasmus is not undertaking something novel and worthy of rejection for that reason alone.

Several others are cited in the same connection, all in relation to sacred subjects. Jerome, of course, not only revised the text of Scripture but created a new version from the Hebrew original.[42] Arator (d c 550 AD) wrote an epic concerning the Acts of the Apostles in 2326 hexameters, interpreting Acts in an allegorical-mystical manner.[43] Gillis van Delft, a theologian at the Sorbonne (d 1524), wrote versifications of seven penitential psalms and of Paul's letter to the Romans.[44] Lefèvre d'Étaples, a friend of Erasmus, wrote a new version of Paul's Epistles (1512) which brought no great criticisms upon him.[45] Finally, Erasmus also cites Frans Titelmans, a Franciscan Observant who became a Capuchin and wrote paraphrases of the apostolic epistles. Titelmans, however, was not a model for Erasmus, since he published his paraphrases after those of Erasmus. Indeed, Titelmans made use of Erasmus' work, which is somewhat ironic, since Titelmans was a champion of orthodox scholarship against the humanists.[46]

But if Erasmus sought precedents for the form of paraphrase, did he seek them as well for the content of his own work? Although he says, as has already been pointed out, that it is not the task of a paraphraser to summarize the opinions of commentators,[47] this does not mean that the work of previous commentators does not inform his own. A perusal of our notes on the paraphrases on Romans and Galatians shows a number of points at which Erasmus' interpretations have been informed by others. Nor does Erasmus hide that fact. As we have noted, while working on his commentary on Paul in 1501 he asked his correspondent to send him the works of Augustine, Ambrose, Origen, Nicholas of Lyra 'or anyone else who has written a commentary on Paul.'[48] In connection with his paraphrase on 1 and 2 Corinthians, he says that he made use especially of Ambrose (Ambrosiaster) and Theophylact, though he followed their advice only when it seemed to him to agree with the Pauline sense.[49] For his paraphrase on Matthew he says he followed Origen, Chrysostom, and Jerome.[50] For his paraphrase on John he followed the most trustworthy doctors of the church, but not everywhere.[51] Later, in response to his critics, he denies that he has followed his own fancy and insists that the most reliable doctors of the church have been his guides.[52]

For the interpretation of Romans and Galatians, Erasmus' favourite interpreters are clearly Origen and Jerome, respectively. But Ambrosiaster, Chrysostom, and Theophylact also exercised influence on the interpretation of both letters, as did Pelagius on that of Romans. And yet, as he suggests in other instances, he is never slavish in his appropriation even of his favourites. We have observed (in the notes) several instances where his interpretation departs from theirs. His attitude is critical and eclectic: he chooses that interpretation which he thinks best fits the Pauline sense.

The influence of Augustine on Erasmus' interpretation of Romans and Galatians is notable by its absence, especially in light of the fact that these two letters deal with the contrast between letter and spirit, grace and law, and similar themes which were at the heart of Augustine's theology. Erasmus goes counter to Augustine's exegesis of original sin in Romans 5, his view of law in Romans 7 as applicable not just to pre-Christian man but to Christian man, his understanding of grace and free will (predestination) in

Romans 9, his interpretation of the encounter between Peter and Paul in Galatians 2.

In his annotations Erasmus makes occasional references to medieval interpreters, especially Nicholas of Lyra, Thomas Aquinas, and Hugo of St Cher. But most of these references are critical, and we have found no direct relation between their work and the paraphrases. The same is not true, however, of Erasmus' contemporaries. On the one hand, the influence of friends can readily be seen: Erasmus' interpretations bear comparison with the work of John Colet and Lefèvre d'Étaples, which preceded his own.[53] On the other hand, Erasmus was able to profit also from his critics, and many elucidations of paraphrases were made, or noted, in response to them. Noël Béda, Petrus Sutor, and Alberto Pio were his principal critics. Their criticisms may be found at appropriate points in our notes.[54]

JBP, AR Jr, WSS Jr

The Publication of the Latin
Paraphrases

How did the *Paraphrases*, as they grew from a modest quarto of 78 leaves to a best-seller in two folio volumes, find their way into the hands of the reading public? The following sketch, based mainly on the collections in Rotterdam and in the three principal English libraries, is doubtless incomplete, but the main lines of the picture can probably be trusted.[1]

THE SEPARATE EPISTLES

We start with individual issues of the Pauline Epistles. The paraphrase on Romans was finished, it seems likely, in the summer of 1517, and Erasmus thought of sending it to be printed by Johann Froben in Basel (Ep 732). There was reason, however, to suspect that Froben had too much in hand; so he gave it to another familiar firm, in Louvain where he was then living, the press of Dirk Martens. Martens therefore published the first edition in November 1517 in quarto (NK 846; A 786),[2] with a dedication dated 13 November to Cardinal Grimani (Ep 710). On 6 December Erasmus sent to Beatus Rhenanus, who was then working for Froben, a copy of the book 'with some revisions' (Ep 732), and Froben added a short preface of his own, altered the year-date of the dedication to 1518, and published it in January (R 1214). It sold well; he printed another quarto in November 1518 (with the dedication dated 1517), and an octavo in April 1519 (R 1215). A Strasbourg reprint in octavo, with no publisher's name, followed in October 1519, and is remarkable for the misprint RGIMANUM for GRIMANUM on the title-page, which is corrected in a special note at the end of the book.

Corinthians when it was ready was likewise sent to Martens, and was published in time for a presentation copy to be despatched on 19 February 1519 (Ep 918); the long dedication to Erard de la Marck (Ep 916) bears the date 5 February. This first edition, Louvain (Dirk Martens) in quarto (NK 844), undated but published in February 1519, had not been in circulation more than two or three weeks when the printer added at the end a six-leaf quire containing a new but unrelated piece, the *Apologia pro declamatione de laude matrimonii*, addressed to the members of Louvain university and dated 1 March 1519, which is lacking in some copies. Like Romans, Corinthians was immediately reprinted in Basel by Froben in March 1519 in quarto (A 789, B 1434), the *Apologia* following by itself in May; and there is said to be a Froben octavo of April 1519, which we have not seen. As before, there was at least one unauthorized reprint in Germany, at Leipzig by Valentin Schumann in quarto dated 1520 (R 1205), which omits the dedication.

Galatians followed as soon as Erasmus could find the time, though the exact date of completion is uncertain, and was first printed, like its predecessors, in quarto by Dirk Martens in Louvain, May 1519 (NK 895), with an undated dedication to Antoine de la Marck (Ep 956). A Froben quarto (A 787) followed in August 1519, ready for the Frankfurt fair in September; a quarto reprint at Leipzig by Valentin Schumann (A 788) also in 1519; and an octavo at Strasbourg by Johann Prüss in March 1520. But this time there was no independent Froben octavo; only a stout octavo volume of 496 pages, put out by Hieronymus Froben in January 1520 (R 1196, A 790), which contained Romans, Corinthians, and Galatians.

Timothy, Titus and Philemon perhaps came next; for in the *Apologia qua respondet invectivis Lei* (*Opuscula* ed W.K. Ferguson pp 253,256) Erasmus tells us that he was at work on the Timothy forty days before Christmas 1519. He also says that he gave this for publication to Michael Hillen in Antwerp instead of Martens, because Martens (who produced his edition of Cicero *De officiis* and the letter to Lupset, Ep 1053, in mid-December) was short of hands. Hence Allen dates the dedicatory letter to Philip of Burgundy (Ep 1043) provisionally in November 1519, and Hillen's edition (NK 0442) in November-December. An incomplete copy survives in the Cathedral Library at Aachen. On the heels of it came Ephesians-Thessalonians. This has a dedication to Cardinal Lorenzo Campeggi dated 5 February 1520 (Ep 1062); and in his headnote to that letter Allen suggested that the first edition, like those of the earliest paraphrases, was produced around that time by Dirk Martens in Louvain (NK 0439). This seems to be lost, and the earliest printing we have of this volume is Froben's of the two together in March 1520, a quarto (B 1445+1457) which we have not seen, and an octavo (R 1197-8, A 792+791, B 1446+1458). We put the Froben Ephesians-Thessalonians and Timothy-Philemon together because, though they have separate title-pages, in the five copies we have seen they have always been bound together, and with them normally the *Ratio verae theologiae* of February 1520 (R 1395, A 819, B 1692); this has the same number of lines to the page, and the way in which the signatures of the *Paraphrases* complement without overlapping those of the *Ratio* suggests that this was Froben's intention. No doubt there were reprints in Germany: we have seen an Ephesians in quarto by Valentin

Schumann in Leipzig dated 1520, bound with his Galatians of the previous year, and B 1447 vouches for Philippians.

The remaining Epistles were not slow to follow. Peter and Jude, with a dedication to Cardinal Wolsey (Ep 1112, conjecturally dated by Allen June 1520), was published by Dirk Martens in Louvain some time that year (NK 842). There was the usual quarto reprint by Froben in Basel, dated 1520 on the title-page and January 1521 in the colophon (R 1217, B 1438), and a Leipzig quarto by Valentin Schumann dated 1520 (R 1216, B 1437). James from Martens (NK 2958) followed in December 1520, the dedication to Cardinal Matthäus Schiner (Ep 1171) being dated 16 December. If he also published John in the following month, the dedication of which to the same patron (Ep 1179) is dated 6 January, it seems to have left no trace. In that same January of 1521, Martens completed the Epistles by publishing Hebrews (NK 2959), with a short dedication dated 17 January 1521 to Silvestro Gigli (Ep 1181). Froben's further activity will concern us in a moment. In the meantime, we note that Hebrews is said to have been reprinted in 1522 in Cologne; and there may well have been other reprints of these Epistle-volumes in Germany, of the existence of which we are unaware. We have seen, for instance, an octavo Timothy-Hebrews published by Johann Schoeffer at Mainz in August 1522 (A 795), and B 1531 vouches for a parallel volume containing the earlier Epistles.

FROBEN TAKES OVER

Hitherto the pattern has been consistent: a first printing in Louvain (except for Timothy-Philemon, which first appeared in Antwerp and perhaps for John), a second by Froben in Basel (as far as Peter and Jude) often in both quarto and octavo, and a scatter of reprints in Germany of which our present record is no doubt incomplete. Henceforward Froben's press will have the initiative. For one thing, it was in the autumn of the year we have now reached, 1521, that Erasmus migrated from Louvain to Basel; it must also have been clear by now that not many printing-houses were financially and technically equipped to meet the heavy demand that had developed for the *Paraphrases*. Dirk Martens and the German printers follow Froben's lead.

A word of warning. As the size of the whole work increased by the putting into one nominal volume of all the Epistles and the addition of Gospels and Acts, Froben provided each edition with a general title-page; but he also gave each section of the book an independent title, and so arranged the signatures of the quires that sections could be taken apart and bound separately, as they commonly were. As he puts it on the title of the Epistles of July 1521, he 'has divided the work in *tomi*, so that every man if he wishes may be free to cut it up into handy form (*in formam enchiridii*).' The librarian who has in his hands (say) an *In aliquot epistolas* complete with the title-page and contents and independent signatures and dated May 1522, may well be excused for not recognizing that it is really not a separate work, but only the second half (everything after Galatians) of the *In universas Epistolas* of that year. The tedious chronological summary that follows is an attempt to see the wood in spite of the trees.

Froben still had to round off his *Paraphrases* on the Epistles, and this he did in a thick octavo of 476 leaves (R 1199, A 797, B 1526) in time for the Frankfurt fair at Easter 1521. Hebrews was probably an afterthought: Martens' independent first edition had been published only in January; it is not mentioned on the title-page or in the list of contents, and occupies five quires dated March 1521 at the end of the book. This, or some part of it, is found bound up with Froben's *Ratio verae theologiae* of 1521, which looks, from the number of lines to the page and the choice of signatures, as though it had been designed as in 1520, for binding with the *Paraphrases*, though librarians and collectors in the course of rebinding sometimes split up these associations. This volume is repeated in July 1521 in an octavo of 492 leaves in all (R 1183 = 1200, B 1527), divided into eight parts with separate title-pages, each with a woodcut border. In February 1522 came a folio, part two of a volume of which the first part, dated March, was the first edition of the paraphrases on Matthew (R 1262+1219, A 740+794,[3] B 1469+1628); in May 1522 another stout octavo normally found in sections (A 796, B 1529), with which Froben's *Ratio verae theologiae* of June 1522 is sometimes bound. Froben's next octavo edition of the Epistles, dated 1523 (R 1222+1201, A 799, B 1499), is the second volume of a complete *Paraphrases*, and will be considered in its proper place. Sporadic reprints of the Epistles continue elsewhere. We have mentioned Schoeffer's of August 1522; those of Eucharius Cervicornus at Cologne in 1522 (B 1530) and Johann Knoblouch in Strasbourg dated 11 March 1523 (B 1536) we have not seen; and there is a Paris printing of 1523 by Pierre Vidoue for Conrad Resch at the Écu de Bâle in the Rue St Jacques (A 796, B 1534-5 with two states of the title-page, one of which has no printer's mark).

THE GOSPELS AND ACTS

We must now turn to the individual paraphrases on the four Gospels. These first appeared in Froben's list in folio (except for Luke), with an octavo edition bearing the same date; there are no more quartos. Matthew of course came first, in March 1522 (R 1262, A 740, B 1469) in a volume of which the second part consisted, as we have just seen, of the complete Epistles dated February. Also in March appeared an octavo (R 1263, A 741, B 990), with a dedicatory epistle to Charles v dated 13 January 1522 (Ep 1255) featured so prominently at the head of the title-page that librarians have been known to catalogue the book among Erasmus' *Epistolae*; a letter (Ep 1248) to Cardinal Matthäus Schiner, who had suggested the work, stands at the end, but is dated 14 December 1521. Later in 1522, perhaps for the fair at Frankfurt in September, what is in part at least a page-for-page reprint of it appeared (R 1270, B 995), which has no colophon and bears neither printer's name nor date. For a Froben book, this is surely very unusual; but its authenticity seems beyond question, for the title-border is that used by Froben in his *Colloquia* of 1522, and the Berne library possesses the copy of this printing which Erasmus himself sent to Hugo von Hohenlandenberg, bishop of Constance, on 18 November 1522 'by the hand of Johann von Botzheim, canon of Constance.'[4] Froben followed this up with another octavo, dated 1523 (A 745, B 904), which prints Charles v's letter of thanks dated 1 April 1522 (Ep 1270) on the verso of the title-page. But the Froben folio Matthew of 1524, and later reprints, are parts of the complete *Paraphrases in Novum Testamentum*, and will be considered in a moment.

How great was the market for these books can be gauged from the way in which other publishers joined in, several of them reproducing more or less closely the precise layout of the 200-leaf Froben octavo which they were copying. In 1522 we have editions in Antwerp by Michael Hillen in June (NK 2937; R 1264, B 988); in Augsburg by Sigismund Grimm dated 7 July (R 1265, B 989); in Cologne by Eucharius Cervicornus (not yet seen) and also by Johann Soter in July (A 744, B 1472); in Haguenau by Thomas Anshelm in October (A 372 = 742, B 991); in Mainz by Johann Schoeffer (B 1473). In 1523 in Paris by Pierre Vidoue for Conrad Resch (B 1476); in Strasbourg by Johann Knoblouch in January (A 746, B 997); in Venice by Gregorio de' Gregori for Laurentius Lorius dated 19 May (R 1266); in January 1525 in Nürnberg by Johannes Petri (B 1478), which we have not seen.

John came next. With a long dedication dated 5 January 1523 (Ep 1333) to the Archduke Ferdinand, brother of Charles v, it was published in folio in February 1523 (A 765, B 1482), and again in octavo in March (R 1225, A 766, B 1483) and April (R 1226, B 1484), and without month-date (A 767, B 1481).[5] There is said to be a Froben octavo of 1524 (A 769); but perhaps, like the firm's folio of that year and all their later editions, this is part of a complete *Paraphrases in Novum Testamentum* (see below). And again there are outsiders, though on our present knowledge not so many as for Matthew: in Antwerp by Michael Hillen in 1523 (NK 2960); in Paris by Pierre Vidoue for Conrad Resch, who says in a foreword that he has printed a thousand copies, in June 1523; two anonymous and undated reprints, c 1524, one ascribed to Sigismund Grimm and Max Wirsung in Augsburg (R 1236, B 1485) and the other to Eucharius Cervicornus in Cologne (R 1237, B 1489); in

[margin handwritten note: but my 1523 is a Feb octavo not necessarily]

Strasbourg by Johann Knoblouch in June 1525 (A 770, B 1490); in Alcalà by Miguel de Eguía dated 24 November 1525.

Then Luke, with a still longer dedication to Henry VIII dated 23 August 1523 (Ep 1381). Luke and Mark had to wait for their first appearance in folio until volume one of the first edition of the complete *Paraphrases* came out in 1524. The first edition of Luke by itself is Froben's octavo dated 30 August 1523 (R 1239, A 755), of which a copy was sent to the king with a covering note dated 4 September (Ep 1385). This was repeated later with 1523 on the title-page and 1524 in the colophon (R 1240, A 756); reprints of the first edition were produced in Basel by Thomas Wolff in December 1523 (R 1241), and anonymously (but in Cologne by Eucharius Cervicornus) in late 1523 or 1524. There may be others which we do not know of.

Of the four Gospels only Mark remained, and this was equipped with a dedication dated 1 December 1523 to Francis I (Ep 1400). Froben, who no doubt knew that Acts was on the way, had decided to market the *Paraphrases* in two formats, folio and octavo, and the second of the two folio volumes, containing the Epistles and dated 1523, was probably already published (R 1189, B 1500).[6] By the middle of December he had set up and printed Mark in its folio format as part of the first volume. But the other Gospels were perhaps not ready, and Acts was not yet to hand; so he must have decided to hold the sheets of Mark for the time being, perhaps intending to launch the complete volume at the Frankfurt fair in the spring of 1524. Erasmus, anxious no doubt to make an offering to his royal patron without delay, seems to have persuaded Froben when he came to print the preliminaries, which would normally be done last, to pull a title-page with the date 1523 instead of 1524, so that a complete set of sheets of Mark bearing that date could be rapidly bound up and despatched to Paris by special messenger with a covering note (Ep 1403). The volume, with an inscription dated in December, is still in the Bibliothèque nationale, and constitutes the first state of the first edition of Mark, normally 1524. That is also the date of the octavo (R 1253, A 750). This was followed as usual by several reprints in the same year in other centres: in Antwerp by Michael Hillen (NK 847); in Cologne by two without printer's name or date (one is now ascribed to Eucharius Cervicornus, the other is R 1254); in Strasbourg by Johann Knoblouch in December 1524 (R 1908). But all editions from 1525 onwards that appear separate are really parts of some publication of the complete *Paraphrases*, and will be mentioned later. Acts followed closely on Mark. It began with a dedication to Clement VII dated 31 January 1524 (Ep 1414), and a short account of the Apostolic journeys, *Peregrinatio apostolorum Petri et Pauli*; the letter sent with the dedication-copy, dated 13 February 1524 (Ep 1418), is still in the Vatican archives. The text appeared, like Mark, in two forms, a folio designed to take its place in a two-volume complete *Paraphrases* and an independent octavo (R 1169, A 778), the signatures of which look as if they were chosen so as to allow it to be bound without any chance of confusion after the octavo Mark of 1524. Erasmus tells us in Ep 1423 that three thousand copies were printed of both forms of Acts. This first octavo had its title-page set, like that of the 1524 octavo Mark, in italic type. It was followed later in the year by another Froben octavo (A 779) with the title-page set in roman. But there are two other Basel printings of 1524 whose relation to each other and to Froben is still uncertain. Both attract attention by declaring themselves on the title-page 'revised by the author' (*ex secunda Erasmi Rot. recognitione*), though Froben's first octavo was probably the source of both, as they adopt its system of signatures. One (A 780) follows these words with 'are to be had' (*habentur*) 'in Basel,' and concludes the title with a date, 27 June (*a.d. quintum calendas Julias*). So precise a date on the title-page would be hard to parallel in Erasmus editions. The other (A 781) says not *habentur* but *prostat* ('is on sale'), and also has a date on the title-page, 4 July (*a.d. quartum nonas Julias*). An odd pair, with a strong smell of counterfeit about both, assisted by the spelling ERSAMI on the title-page of the first; a salutary reminder, how little we know about the production of these unauthorized reprints. There were of course other reprints of Acts: in 1524 by Michael Hillen in Antwerp (NK 2957; R 1170) and by Eucharius Cervicornus (anonymous as usual) in Cologne; in 1525 by Johann Knoblouch in Strasbourg, which we have not seen, and another without place or printer (R 1171). 'By 12 April 1525 all the original issues were sold out;'[7] there may well have been a resetting of the folio Acts which has not yet been detected, before the regular pattern of issues set in, which was to last for forty years.

THE COMPLETE PARAPHRASES (FROBEN)

The first known evidence that the Froben firm intended to publish a complete corpus of the *Paraphrases* is the appearance of a stout octavo volume of 400 leaves dated 1523 and called *Tomus secundus* (R 1222+1201, A 799, B 1499), which contains all the Epistles, with a second title-page (*In aliquot epistolas*) after Galatians, so that a purchaser could bind the book conveniently in two parts. A corresponding full *Tomus primus* of that year would not have been possible, because Mark and Acts were not yet available; if it exists, it must be dated 1524, and the octavo John dated June 1524 (A 769) could be part of it. With the octavo, or not long before or after it, came the same thing in folio: *Tomus secundus* containing the Epistles, dated 1523 (R 1184, B 1500), and *Tomus primus*, which included as we have seen the first folio printing of Mark and Acts, dated 1524 (R 1267+1252+1227 = 1718,A 746A+749+757+ 765+777+799, B 1501). This was a considerable investment, and the firm kept it in their list for ten years. When stocks ran out, they reset Matthew, Mark (B 1502) and John (B 1503) without change of date (we have as yet no evidence for a resetting of Acts). They reprinted Luke with the date 1526 (R 1242, A 758), and John, according to Erasmus' own statement in Ep 2008, in the autumn of 1527; and B 1504, which we have not seen, may be a surviving portion of another reprint. In 1532 they brought out a new *Tomus secundus* (R 1185, A 732 = 800, B 1505), described as 'newly revised and corrected by the author himself.' This last volume carries the imprint of Johann's son Hieronymus and Nicolaus Episcopius, Johann having died in October 1527. Let him have his tribute of respect from all students of Erasmus and all who feel the importance of the publisher's calling.

Thereafter the format of the Froben publication, which was always organized as two volumes divisible into sections, alternated:

in 1534 an octavo (R 1255+1243+1229+1172+1186 = 1743, A 753, B 1506);

in 1535 the first volume ('now diligently revised for the last time by the author') and in 1538 the second volume in folio (R 1268+1256+1230 = 1720, A 747+752+760+772+782, B 1507-8);

in 1540 an octavo (R 1721, A 761+773+783, B 1509-10), the second volume dated 1539 on the title-page and 1540 in the colophon;

also in 1540 a folio which formed volume 7 of the *Opera omnia* (R 1116, A 309, B 11), repeated in 1541 (R 1188 = 1724, A 735, B 1513-14);

in 1548 an octavo (R 1189+1232+1247 = 1725, A 736 = 776A, B 1515-16);

in 1556 a folio (A 737, B 1517-18);

in 1557 an octavo (R 1190+1233+1248 = 1726, A 738, B 1519-20), and in 1566 there is said to have been another.

When one is faced with one of these editions in folio, one has to remember that a purchaser would see them as composed of separable parts, out of which sets could be made up in any way that supply might dictate. Thus Jean Grolier, the great French bibliophile (1479-1565) possessed a straight run of 1535-8, now in the British Library; the working set given to Corpus Christi College, Oxford by its first president, Erasmus' correspondent John Claymond, contained the Matthew, Mark and Acts of 1535, Luke of 1526, John of 1524 (the second setting), and the Epistles of 1532. The twenty or so sets we have examined, containing material from 1532 through 1538, exhibit eleven different mixtures.

THE COMPLETE PARAPHRASES (OTHER PRINTERS)
While the paraphrases on the books of the New Testament were still being published separately, they were reproduced, as we have seen, by a number of other publishers. As far as we know, no one save Froben produced a set of

them under a common title-page; how many printers did in fact bring out all six parts (four Gospels, Acts and Epistles) it is still hard to say, and some of the separate publications no doubt do not survive. The Cologne printer identified as Eucharius Cervicornus seems to have done so; from Michael Hillen in Antwerp no Luke or Epistles is yet recorded; from Johann Knoblouch in Strasbourg no Luke; from Miguel de Eguía in Alcalà there is evidence for all except Acts; from Pierre Vidoue in Paris, printing for Conrad Resch, we have seen only Matthew, John and Epistles, but perhaps he printed the rest; and the same may be said of the Venetian printer Gregorio de' Gregori, working for Laurentius Lorius, though we have seen only Matthew and Epistles.

Once the complete text had been launched as a whole by Froben, it found three belated competitors. In 1540 the Paris printer Pierre Regnault did the six parts in two volumes, in two issues: one with his own name and elephant trade-mark on the title-page (R 1259+1245+1231A+1174 = 1722, A 762+775+784+801, B 1511), and the other with the galley mark of Galéot du Pré (R 1258+1244+1231+1173, A 774). At the same time the Antwerp printer Martinus Meranus, working for Joannes Steelsius, produced Gospels and Acts, dated 1540 on the general title and 1541 in the colophons of the separable parts (NK 2961+4336; A 734), and Epistles dated 1540 (NK 843; B 1512+1549). In 1542 the firm of Sebastianus Gryphius in Lyons, then halfway through its five-and-thirty years' output of Erasmus' non-contro-versial writings, added the *Paraphrases* to its list in six separate octavo parts without general title, with a seventh for the *Peregrinatio apostolorum*, which, though only one quire of sixteen pages, appears now in library-catalogues as an independent work (R 1269+1260+1907+1231, A 763+804+802, B 1494). Of the *Peregrinatio* there were two settings of this date, one with the imprint reading, as it does in the other volumes, *Lugduni apud Seb. / Gryphium*, and the other *Apud Seb. Gryphium / Lugduni*; of the rest there may well be resettings which have not yet been detected. The set was reprinted in 1544 (R 1246+1175+1221, A 748+754+764+776+785+803, B 1479+1495+1144+1147+1542). Considering the size of Gryphius' trade, all the volumes seem harder to find than one might expect.

A volume of 466 leaves published in Cologne in 1555 by the Heirs of Arnold Birckmann with the title *Paraphrasis sive enarratio in Epistolas et Evangelia* (R 1275) contains the liturgical epistles and gospels for the Church's year, the biblical text in italic type and the relevant paraphrase in roman, with a preface addressed to the Christian reader.

And here the matter seems to have rested until 1668, when the 'Paraphrase hitherto for so many years sought in vain by the pious and the truly learned, copies having long since become unobtainable' (so the title-page) was reprinted in 1846 pages quarto by Georg Friedrich Grimm at Hanover, the editor being Hilmar Deichmann, pastor of the Ægidien-Kirche in that city (R 1727). As before, each part had its own title-page, in order to make it possible to bind them in groups, or to combine any one part with some other relevant work. There must have been some sale, but probably not so much as had been hoped for; for there were still sheets twenty years later, and these were reissued in 1689 with a new title-page, '*Annotationes in Nov. Test.* impensis Nicolai Förster,' in Frankfurt (R 1728). An octavo edition by Haude and Spener, Berlin 1778-80 (R 1729), followed the seventh volume of Leclerc's edition of Erasmus' *Opera*, Leiden 1703-6.

RABM

Sixteenth-Century Translations of Erasmus' New Testament Commentaries in English

There are really two separate stories to sixteenth-century English translation from Erasmus' New Testament commentaries, each of which has a special importance. The first is about small translations of parts out of context, made always in response to current religious or moral questions. The second is about the complete translation of the *Paraphrases*, made and finally published through the influence of Catherine Parr, Henry viii's last queen, and actually forced upon all parish churches in an effort to infuse the English Reformation with even more Erasmian thought.

The first English translation known was a private abstract of Jude made in 1530 by John Caius of Gonville Hall for a 'deare friende' whom he felt it would benefit.[1] Though it seems lost, it can probably be assumed on the basis of its text to be a response to the spread of reformed thought and the Royal Divorce question. Two years earlier William Tyndale had remarked that the preface *Pio lectori* of the *Paraphrase on Matthew* contained arguments for the translation of the Scripture into vernaculars;[2] in 1534 one of his followers translated it, and it was published under the Royal Privilege,[3] possibly in connection with Convocation's appeal for an authorized English Bible.[4] And also in 1534 Leonard Cox submitted a translation of the *Paraphrase on Titus* to Thomas Cromwell, offering to translate as well the first and second Epistles to Timothy.[5] All three were intended as propaganda for immediate use, as they all treat the Christian's obligation to obedience in the state; but only the Titus was printed, with a vigorous preface by Cox to point out 'how moche and howe straytly we be bounde to obey next God our kyng' and how blessed England was in the marriage with Anne Boleyn.[6] Each of these books had a specific purpose, to use the name of Erasmus to argue a case, with little or no concern for the context of Erasmus' thought.

There was only one early translation from the *Annotationes in Novum Testamentum*. It was made c1549 by Nicholas Lesse, at the urging of a friend who had been told about Erasmus' treatment of divorce in his annotation on 1 Corinthians 7. Both men must have felt that the widespread public discussion about the Marquis of Northampton's remarriage in 1548 might be stopped or mitigated by the publication of *The Censure and iudgement of the famous clark Erasmus.*[7]

The complete translation of the *Paraphrases* forced on all parish churches and less well educated clergy in 1548 was a more complex matter than these simple appeals to Erasmus on issues of the day. It involved several translators, a group of printers, a difficult sequence of issues and editions, and a set of political pressures and circumstances about which we cannot possibly know everything. It is certain enough that the idea of a translation to guide English Scripture readers into less contentious paths began with Catherine Parr, who became Henry VIII's last queen on 12 July 1543. By the autumn of 1545 she had assembled translations of the whole of Gospels and Acts, offering her patronage to translators and printers, and was awaiting an opportunity to have the work published. Matthew and Acts were anonymous, and may indeed have been partly the queen's own work, judging by the editor's later praise for 'noble weamen' who were able 'to endicte or translate into the vulgare toungue for the publique instruccion & edifying of the vnlerned multitude.' Luke was translated by the very skilled Nicholas Udall, former headmaster of Eton. Mark was done by one Thomas Key, at the suggestion of the king's physician George Owen. And John was translated by Princess Mary with the help of her chaplain, Francis Malet. Indeed, when the queen wrote Mary in September 1545 to ask her to send her the translation, she suggested that it should even be published under her royal name, 'aut potius incerto authore.'[8]

After the text had been assembled, with translators' prefaces implying strong hopes for patronage, the queen gave Udall all five sections for editing, correcting, and 'addyng, digestyng, and sortyng the texte with the paraphrase,' which he did in a manner that later brought sharp criticism from Bishop Stephen Gardiner.[9] The Scripture text was that of the Great Bible, a monopoly of the printers Edward Whitchurch and Richard Grafton, both friends of Udall and former clients of Thomas Cromwell. All three had been in trouble after Cromwell's fall from power. Somehow or other all three came under the patronage of the gentle and devout queen.

On 29 May 1545 the two printers issued the newly approved Primer – 'to be taught lerned & read: and none other to be vsed' – under a special licence which gave both the king's 'grace especial,' and Grafton the new title of Printer to the Prince of Wales.[10] In April 1547, a few months after the old king's death, Grafton became King's Printer, but significantly did not receive the normal stipend, which was still to be paid to Thomas Berthelet, his predecessor. On the other hand, Grafton's patent strengthened the position, for it gave him authority to arrest those violating his monopolies.[11] On the same day he and Whitchurch received a privilege on all service books and books of sermons, with imprisonment at the king's pleasure for those violating the patent, and a septennial privilege for all their other publications.[12]

On Sunday 31 July 1547 the new *Injunctions*, printed by Whitchurch and Grafton, were read. Among other things they ordered all parish churches to have 'within one twelfe monethes, next after the saied visitacion, the Paraphrasis of Erasmus also in English vpon the Gospelles,' to be set up for public study, with the cost divided equally between the parish and the parson or holder of the advowson. Clergy under the degree of BD were also supposed to buy Latin and English New Testaments and the *Paraphrases*, 'and diligently study the same, conferring the one with the other.'[13]

Though both printers had long experience with publication of large books, they seem to have run into difficulties, and on 17 December were granted Writs under the Privy Seal that gave them virtual power of seizure of printing equipment, paper, ink, and even skilled workmen 'for the spedy furtheraunce of our workes onely.'[14] These Writs, with the evidence of constant reprinting of the *Paraphrases, Homilies, Injunctions*, and the *Book of Common Prayer*, suggest that the Stationers – or the guild that existed before the Stationers – insisted that the patentees would have to spread the wealth by limiting the number of sheets that could be printed from one setting of type; for there was ample information about the number of copies that would be needed, some 40,000, according to Gardiner.[15] It is also possible that the delays occasioned by such an enormous press run of each sheet would have delayed publication of any of the material for up to three years, and that Grafton and Whitchurch decided on their own to keep reprinting, but the former suggestion seems to me more plausible.

Whatever the difficulties were, the earliest printings of the *Paraphrases* probably appeared early in 1548, with the date given as 'the last daie of Ianuarie. Anno Domini, 1548,' a date retained for further issues and for four complete reprintings.[16] The retention of the date was normal enough for religious books, and indeed was required by law.[17] But clearly five complete settings and printings of a book of about 1300 pages must have been spread over approximately two years. Though the imprint attributes the book only to Whitchurch, its typography indicates that help was given by Grafton, as might be expected, and by their usual associate Nicholas Hill,[18] and probably a variety of neighbours.

In the autumn of 1548, as printing of the first volume went on, Whitchurch himself began assembling translators for the rest of the *Paraphrases*, though the *Injunctions* had only demanded the Evangelists.

Without the moderating influence of Catherine Parr the second volume became more Protestant in tone than the first had been. Myles Coverdale, who had worked with Whitchurch and Grafton on the Bible, became editor, and the volume was expanded to include Tyndale's *Prologue to Romans* and a paraphrase on Revelation by Leo Jud. Coverdale himself translated Romans, Corinthians, and Galatians; Whitchurch's friend John Old did Ephesians, Philippians, Thessalonians, Timothy, Philemon, and the Canonical Epistles, for which he was rewarded with a Warwickshire living by the Duchess of Somerset. Old also sought out Leonard Cox, and persuaded him to revise his old version of Titus. The numerous prefaces show beyond doubt that work began in the autumn of 1548, and that the book was probably in press before everything was complete; one of Old's prefaces is dated 15 July 1549, just under a month before the publication of the whole volume.[19]

Coverdale's preface shows that Whitchurch intended selling the book under the twelfth Injunction, to priests under the degree of BD, though he may have been hoping to get the *Injunctions* revised to include it for parish churches. There was only one complete printing of *The seconde tome or volume* in 1549, complicated only by second printings of Romans, Galatians, and Colossians, which were no doubt the result of sheet shortages. The total press run must have been only a fraction of that of the first volume.[20]

Revised editions of each volume appeared in 1551 and 1552 respectively, the former with an alphabetical subject index by Udall and the latter with one by Thomas Norton.[21]

When the accession of Queen Mary in 1553 returned Gardiner to a position of power, some steps may have been taken to discourage use of the *Paraphrases*, even though the queen had been one of the translators.[22] Gardiner heartily disapproved of the book that Erasmus had written 'aboue 26 yeres a goo, when his penne was wanton,' considered the translator 'ignoraunt in Latten and Englishe,' felt that the enforced circulation of the book would bring the printers 'rather aboue xx.m pound then vnder,' and that the whole book would cause subversion in religion.

> I waxe euery day better learned then other, and finde euery day somewhat to impugne the Paraphrasis and homilies, not by wit or deuise or other subtitly, but plain sensible matter, if I may be hard.[23]

A sampling of records shows that most churches followed the Injunction, paying prices between ten shillings and about thirteen, depending on the quality of the binding, and that the charge was divided as stipulated between church and parson or proprietary. Several Oxford Colleges that held advowsons have records of the expenditures; All Souls, for example, paid 'xij^s viij^d pro Erasmi paraphrasi' for its own chapel in 1548, and also 'v^s vj^d pro dimidio pretij Erasmi paraphrasis' for a less well bound copy for one of its parishes.[24] There seems little point in a large survey of parish and diocesan records on such purchases; a handful of records shows clearly enough that the book was sold at a consistent price range through a period of three or four years, the cost divided. It was not reprinted after 1552, however, and though the Elizabethan *Injunctions* of 1559 again demanded the *Paraphrases* it is difficult to see where they could have been obtained. By 1583 the *Paraphrases* patent was insignificant enough to be given up by the Queen's Printer Christopher Barker, along with other monopolies that were no longer profitable.[25]

The extent to which the English *Paraphrases* were read, as distinct from sold, is a difficult question. Its interpretations reflect Erasmus' beloved *consensus ecclesiae*. It would be hard to tell whether an attitude or view found in a contemporary book came from Erasmus or directly from his sources, just as one can seldom be certain whether a phrase came from the *Adagia* or from the classic text from which it was taken. Nevertheless, it is probable that the *Paraphrases* were in fact widely read and had a considerable influence on religious thought in sixteenth-century England.

EJD

Translators' Note

The Latin text of Erasmus with which we have worked is the Leclerc edition of the works of Erasmus, *Desiderii Erasmi Roterodami opera omnia* (LB), published in Leiden, 1703-1706. Volume seven contains the *Paraphrases*. In establishing our text of Romans, we have collated the Leclerc edition with the original Louvain edition of November 1517, the Froben slight revisions of November 1518 and April 1519, the collected edition of the Pauline letters of 1521, and the collected editions of all the paraphrases of 1532 and 1534. The Leclerc edition of Galatians has been collated with the Froben editions of 1519, 1520, 1521, 1523, 1532, and 1534.

In the paraphrases on Romans and Galatians as in the other paraphrases, changes were of two kinds. The first consists of corrections of printer's errors and minor stylistic improvements. Erasmus alludes to these several times and even published some emendations in one of his apologies in 1529.[1] The second were more substantive changes, usually additions to the text. Though there were a few changes of this kind in 1521, the most notable were made in 1532. In the 1532 edition there are major revisions in which Erasmus approximates ideas of the Protestant reformers. One can easily detect the greater prominence of grace and faith as trust as well as the elimination of an emphasis on free will in the exposition of Romans 9. These changes can be read in different ways, either as reflecting the degree to which Erasmus believed his views could accommodate those of the reformers for the sake of Christian unity or as betraying the influence of the reformers or as revealing both the influence of the reformers and a bending of his views for the sake of the peace of the church. The question remains an open one, and the changes are so noted that the reader may form his own judgment while he may refer to works mentioned in this volume proposing one or another solution.[2]

The paraphrases on Romans and Galatians are appropriately brought together in the same volume since they are united by several common themes: sin, law, grace, justification, righteousness. Erasmus perceives the dominant theme of both letters to be the contrast between the carnal and spiritual law, the carnal and the spiritual righteousness. He equates the carnal law and carnal righteousness with ceremonies, the spiritual law and spiritual righteousness with faith *and* a virtuous life. When he refers in the paraphrase on Romans 1:5 and 10:12 to 'faith alone' as the basis of justification, he interprets Paul to be repudiating ceremonial works, not all works of the law. His exposition of this theme follows closely the patristic commentaries, especially those of Origen, Ambrosiaster, Jerome, and Pelagius, as the reader can readily discern from the notes.

In this translation, we have striven not so much to achieve literal accuracy as to interpret the intent of Erasmus. We could not ignore the effect of style, for in the *Paraphrases* Erasmus was highly conscious of the art of style. He sought quite explicitly language appropriate to the dignity and special idiom of Scripture.[3] Upon this he imposed the skills of rhetoric: he enjoyed parallelisms and antitheses, the enthymeme and the rhetorical question, and he frequently enlivens his page by accenting the dramatic setting of narrative or argument. More problematically, from the point of view of the translator, he sometimes indulges in plays on words and ambiguities, difficult if not impossible to render in English, and we have been obliged at points to indicate this fact in the notes. In addition, Erasmus occasionally spins out his thought in sentences too long for easy comprehension. He was encouraged to do so, no doubt, both by the desire to develop parallel and antithetical ideas, often finely nuanced, and by the necessity, in a paraphrase, to expand the original scriptural text, sometimes – for example, in Romans 1:1-6 – following the Pauline sequence of thought unbroken over several verses as in the Greek. In many cases we have replaced Erasmus' sentence structure with normal English patterns to facilitate understanding. Always we have striven for the dignity in English which Erasmus desired for his Latin.

The translation of the *Paraphrases* also raises acutely the problem of theological language in Erasmus.[4] On the one hand, Erasmus appears to choose words of central theological significance often with an eye more to stylistic variety and rhetorical effect than to a reflective consideration of their precise meaning. For example, we have found it sometimes virtually impossible to make significant distinctions in the many different words for 'sin' (besides *peccatum* also *vitium, commissum, culpa, noxa, admissum, flagitium, scelus, error, transgressio, crimen, delictum*). As there is a great variety in the words for human sin, so also is there a rich diversity of expressions for God's goodness, generosity, kindness, and gentleness (*bonitas, beneficium, beneficentia, benignitas, munificentia, benevolentia, lenitas, mansuetudo, humanitas*).

Several terms deserve comment here. The word *justitia* is used with regularity in the paraphrases on Romans and Galatians to refer, we believe, to the condition of innocence as opposed to guilt before a moral or legal standard. We have chosen to render this by 'righteousness,' a word familiar in a theological context to English readers.

Erasmus was himself well aware of the ambiguity of the important theological word *gratia*. As he indicates in an annotation on Romans,[5] the word may mean either 'gift' or 'favour.' In his paraphrase on Romans 1:7 he renders it explicitly with the former meaning. On the other hand, in his paraphrase on Romans 8:28 he himself uses the word *favor* in place of *gratia*. We have generally rendered *gratia* simply with the English equivalent, 'grace.' But in some places we have preferred to translate it as 'favour.'

Likewise, as he shows in a 1527 annotation on Romans 1:13, Erasmus was quite conscious of the double meaning of 'faith' (*fides-πίστις*) in Paul, 'belief' (*credulitas*) or 'trust' (*fiducia*), the latter closely connected with hope.[6] In some instances of its use in the paraphrases on Romans and Galatians, *fides* seems to have the meaning of belief,[7] whereas in others it is less clear how he intends its meaning. It is probable that often he does not have in mind a precise sense for the word but that either or both connotations may be present. Even in the former instances, where the context seems to indicate the meaning of belief, we have chosen to retain the ambiguous rendering, 'faith.' In 1532 Erasmus seems to wish to indicate that both meanings are present in Romans 3:22 when he adds *ac fiduciam* to *per fidem*. In his paraphrase on Romans 4, which portrays the faith of Abraham, Erasmus generally uses *fides*. However, in one instance he uses instead *credulitas* ('belief')[8] and in another *fiducia* ('confidence') as the ground on which Abraham was considered righteous.[9] In 1521 he changes one case of *fides* to *fiducia* as the merit on account of which Abraham was considered justified.[10] In his paraphrase on Galatians 2:15-16 he uses both *fides* and *fiducia* to describe the gift of salvation.

We mention finally, by way of further example, the difficulty of rendering the word *commendatio*, of which Erasmus is particularly fond. The word seems to refer generally to the 'ground of recommendation.' He uses the word both in a positive context to speak, for example, of *fidei commendatio* (the 'commendation' of faith) and in a negative context, for example, of the 'commendation' of circumcision. As a rule, we have not rendered the word consistently by a precise English equivalent, but have employed a circumlocution appropriate to the immediate context.

In short, in a generally uncharted field, we have tried to proceed with caution, considering that Erasmus' first intent was not to construct a new theological language, but to give to the argument of St Paul a fresh and expansive vitality that could play its part in the renewal envisioned by the 'philosophy of Christ.'

JBP, AR Jr, WSS Jr

PARAPHRASE ON ROMANS

*In epistolam Pauli Apostoli
ad Romanos paraphrasis*

DEDICATORY LETTER

TO THE MOST REVEREND[1] FATHER IN CHRIST
MY LORD GRIMANI[2] OF VENICE, CARDINAL OF ST MARK'S,
FROM ERASMUS OF ROTTERDAM, GREETING

Those who find it surprising, most reverend Father in God, that Paul the Apostle, who was a good linguist, should have written to the Romans in Greek rather than Latin, will wonder no more if they remember, first, that at that date the use of the Greek language was almost as widespread as the Roman rule, and secondly that the Romans themselves at one time had such a passion for Greek literature that it was held up to ridicule by the satirists. Scaevola in Lucilius,[3] mocking Albutius as unusually pro-Greek, greets him with '*Chaere* praetor at Athens,' and in Juvenal[4] some character is indignant because he cannot stand Rome turned into Greek. Not but what the Apostle's Greek is such that a pure Greek speaker can hardly understand him, on account of the admixture everywhere of Hebrew idiom. Even had he written in the most perfect and pure Greek, great difficulties for the reader would have remained, because he was writing for men who were still raw and recently converted to Christianity, and so he touched on some mysteries instead of going into them, and provided indications rather than explanations, 'serving the time.'[5] Now however that Rome is entirely Christian, so that it is the capital and chief seat of the Christian religion, and Latin is spoken all the world over by everyone who acknowledges the authority of the Roman pontiff, I thought I should be doing something worth while if I could make Paul speak to men who are now pure Romans and adult Christians, not only in the Roman tongue but more intelligibly; if, in fact, he could talk Latin in such a way that one would not recognize the Hebrew speaking but would recognize the Apostle. He was accustomed to vary his style, but never lost the apostolic dignity.

I will not set forth here how much this small work has cost me, such as it is, for I am sure that no one who has not made the experiment himself in similar subject-matter would find it easy to value or to believe the difficulty of bridging gaps, smoothing rough passages, bringing order out of confusion and simplicity out of complication, untying knots, throwing light on dark places, and giving Hebrew turns of speech a Roman dress – in fact, of altering the language of Paul, the heavenly spokesman, and so managing one's paraphrase that it does not become a *paraphronesis*, a caricature. One must say things differently without saying different things, especially on a subject which is not only difficult in many ways, but sacred, and very near the majesty of the Gospel; one works on slippery ground where a fall is very easy, and yet one cannot fall without grave peril. One thing only I will say, in honesty rather than arrogance: the labour would not have been greatly increased if I had essayed to publish a full-dress commentary[6] on the epistle. I shall think, however, that my efforts have been richly rewarded, if I can feel that as a result Paul has become somewhat more attractive and certainly more accessible to your Eminence, and through you to the rest of Rome, to whom it is right that he should be most attractive and most accessible. For I know well how many people have been deterred from reading him hitherto by the strangeness of the language, and how many more by the difficulty of disentangling and understanding what he says, wrong though it is that any inconveniences should deter men from such fruitful reading. It is the distaste or the despair of such people that I have tried to remedy by this enterprise of mine, so balancing my work that he who rejects any change in the letter of Holy Writ may use it as a commentary, while he who is free from such superstition may hear the voice of Paul himself.

Let Rome prepare a welcome, therefore, for the first or at least the greatest teacher of her religion. Let her embrace the herald of her ancient fame, let her return the love of one who loved a city he had never seen. Happy indeed the change in the style of her prosperity! Long ago under imperial despots she offered worship to dumb images; now under Peter and Paul she presides over the earth. Long ago the handmaid of every superstition, now she is the great mistress of the true religion. Jove on the Capitol has made way for Christ, who alone is best and greatest;[7] the emperor for Peter and Paul, immeasurably gifted each of them in his own way; that solemn famous senate for the College of Cardinals, revered all the world over. If she is stirred by arch or pyramid, the relics of her ancient superstition, how can she resist the monuments of revealed religion to be found in the books of those apostles? She marvels at Hadrian's statue or Domitian's[8] baths; let her embrace instead the most holy epistles of Peter and Paul. If she loves to read in the works of a Sallust or a Livy the ancient fables of early days, how she was exalted from small beginnings to a world dominion that was soon to fall, guided by vultures,[9] much more ought she to love the writings of apostles and evangelists, in which she can recognize from what rudiments she rose to a dominion over the church that shall never fail, guided by Christ. Among the Jews not a trace remains today of their temple, once so sacred; so too the Capitol of Rome, which foolish prophets[10] long ago promised should be eternal, has left so few remnants that one cannot even point out where it stood.

If she admires the tongue of Cicero, of which it were hard to say whether it did more good than harm to the republic, why does she not enjoy still more the eloquence of Paul, to which she owes the greatest part of her salvation and religion? She was always greedy for praise, and now she has this great and famous herald of her glory, for what triumph so great as to be praised in the words of an apostle? O Romans, Romans, learn what Paul did for you, and you will understand what the glories are that you must maintain. Listen to his warning voice, lest you fail to know what you must shun. He praises faith, which nowhere else has kept more spotless. He speaks of obedience, which made you early exchange superstition for religion. He grants you affability, whose companion often is credulity; this was the reason why false apostles tempted you into Judaism;[11] but with that ease of manners went prudence, which caused a swift repentance. He marks your proud spirit and therefore warns you so carefully against pride and insolence, calls you from luxury to sobriety of life, from lust to chastity, from brutality to toleration, from strife to concord, from war to peace. Such is your true Roman character, from which it would be disgraceful to descend. Beware lest you, being Rome, degenerate into Babylon.

St Jerome[12] tells us that even in his day there was still evidence of the religious spirit praised by Paul. 'Where else,' he says, 'do such zealous crowds throng round the churches and the martyrs' tombs? Where does the Amen echo like a peal of heavenly thunder, till the idols' empty temples quake? Not that the Romans hold a different faith from all the other churches of Christ, but because in them is greater devotion and the simplicity that leads to belief!' In truth a splendid tribute from Jerome! But what would he say now, if he could see in that same city all those churches, all those cardinals, those bishops? If he could see all the princes of the world seeking answers from this one infallible oracle of Christ; men gathering in crowds for the sake of religion from the utmost corners of the globe; no man thinking himself truly a Christian until he has seen Rome and the Roman pontiff, as if he were some earthly deity upon whose nod,[13] for yes or no, all human affairs depend; and finally, if he could survey the city of Rome under Leo the Tenth, with the storms of war laid to rest, a flourishing home of literature no less than of religion; the one place that combines so many leaders of the church, so many men distinguished for learning of every kind, so many lights and glories of the world, that Rome seems the earth in little rather than a city? Nor need we pray for anything from the higher powers, except that she may forever answer to her reputation, that good fortune in her may forever be surpassed by piety and majesty outstripped by virtue. And this will come to pass, if she tries with all her might to express the spirit and the saintly life of Peter and Paul, under whose patronage and protection she reigns. But nowhere can a more express and lively image of them be found than in their own writings.

Meanwhile they will more gladly welcome this fragment of Paul, eminent Father, if it is offered to them by the hand of one who, like you, is a wonderful patron of all learning, and especially of such as is concerned with knowledge of the tongues; though at the same time you are so conspicuous for your high character that even among so many great luminaries you outshine them all, not so as to cast them in the shade but adding to persons gifted and illustrious in their own right a new wealth of light and glory. My respectful best wishes to your Eminence.

Louvain, 13 November 1517

THE ARGUMENT OF THE EPISTLE OF PAUL TO THE ROMANS BY ERASMUS OF ROTTERDAM

To make the subject clearer, I must now explain briefly the argument of the epistle.[1] And let me begin with the name itself. I am aware that Jerome,[2] in the commentary which he wrote on the Epistle to Philemon, was of the opinion that the apostle was first called Saul; but that he adopted the name Paul as a kind of memorial from the proconsul Sergius Paulus, whom he won to Christ, as we read in Acts 13.[3] There are others who like to think that he was called Saul while he still followed Judaism, but that after he changed his religion he changed his name as well. And yet the first of these theories is rendered less probable by the fact that Luke, in the chapter just cited, writes, 'Saul, who was called Paul, filled with the Holy Spirit,'[4] thus showing very clearly that he had two names before Sergius Paulus had been converted. The second opinion is clearly refuted by the fact that, not only in several other passages, but even in the same chapter, he is called Saul, even though now preaching the gospel of Christ. Luke writes: 'The Holy Spirit said to them: Set apart for me Saul and Barnabas.'[5] Consequently, the opinion of Origen[6] seems to me closer to the truth, who points out that in the books of the Old Testament some men were designated by various names, such as the one called Jedidiah[7] who is elsewhere called Solomon; and the one called Uzziah[8] in some places, who is called Azariah in others. Likewise, in the gospels, he who in Luke is called Levi[9] calls himself Matthew in his own gospel.[10] So also Paul had a double name, although he himself in his own epistles never calls himself Saul, but always Paul, perhaps because the name Paul was more familiar to the ears of the Greeks and Romans to whom he wrote. For the name Saulus seems to have been altered from the Hebrew Saul, just as the Greeks turned Joseph to Josephus.[11] Nevertheless, Paul means 'wonderful' in Hebrew, if we think it is permissible to seek the etymology of Greek and Roman names in other languages. Jerome[12] himself, while at times condemning other men who seek such etymologies, permits himself to do so in this instance, I suppose because the matter is not really serious. Certainly the word means 'peaceful' in Greek, 'paltry' in Latin. In

Hebrew Saul means 'demand'; and if we believe Ambrose,[13] it means 'disquietude' or 'temptation'; but the Greek version is Σαῦλος.[14] So much for the significance of the name – indeed, almost too much for this argument. Moreover, he dictated this letter to Tertius his scribe, as the latter also testifies at the end of the letter, adding: 'I, Tertius, who wrote the letter in the Lord, send my greetings to you.' It is clear that the letter was sent from Corinth through Phoebe, a woman of Cenchreae. Now Cenchreae is the port of Corinth,[15] located not far from the city. But if the occasion is also asked for, it is clear that he wrote this letter after he had written the two letters to the Corinthians (which, in the opinion of some, explains why in this letter particularly there shines forth the evidence of a piety which had now been complete and established) at the time when he had already travelled through Achaia (where Corinth is located) and its neighbour Macedonia as far as Illyria. And he had not only preached the gospel of Christ far and wide, at least in those places where none of the other apostles had preached, but also, following the advice of Peter,[16] he had collected some money from his people for the help of the poor and was now getting ready for his journey to Jerusalem. His intention was to go from there to Spain after delivering what he had received. On the way to Spain he planned to journey to Rome[17] and, in passing, greet the Christians there, about whose faith and religion he had heard, although he had not yet seen them.

Their experience was somewhat different from that of the Galatians. For the Galatians, at first correctly instructed by Paul, were afterwards deceived by the fraud of pseudo-apostles and were drawn back into Judaism. The Romans, on the contrary, first badly instructed by pseudo-apostles, came to their senses as soon as, in accordance with their own good judgment, they understood the deception. And they persevered in what they acknowledged to be right. For in the early stages of the young church there were those who believed that the grace of the gospel ought not to be propagated immediately among heathen nations devoted to the cult of images and demons, since they thought such grace had been promised especially to the descendants of Abraham and the Jewish people. It is clear that even Peter was not totally hostile[18] to this opinion, since he had to be warned in a vision that he should admit Cornelius the centurion.[19] For this reason he soon encountered trouble at Jerusalem, when those who had been converted to Christ from Judaism complained because he had had association with the uncircumcised. And among these converts it is probable that there were also some apostles. For we read this in Acts 11[:1ff]: 'Now the apostles and brothers who were in Judaea heard that the gentiles also had received the word of God. So when Peter went up to Jerusalem, those who were among the circumcised criticized him, saying: "Why did you go to uncircumcised men and eat with them?"' Again, there were those who, although they did not think that the gentiles should be absolutely prohibited from partnership in the gospel, believed nevertheless that they should not be admitted unless they were circumcised according to the Jewish rite. They were assuming that Christ needed the support of the Mosaic law, and at the same time they wished to transfer the glory of the gospel to their own race. And in Acts 11[:19] it is recorded that those who fled into Phoenicia, Cyprus, and Antioch because of the persecution that followed the death of Stephen, preached Christ to no one except to the Jews. Again in Acts 15[:1ff], certain Jews came to Antioch, preaching publicly against Paul and Barnabas that there was no hope for salvation unless they were circumcised according to the rule of Moses. And so great a tumult was stirred up through these men that it was determined in assembly that Paul and Barnabas, together with their adversaries, should go to Jerusalem, and that the dispute should be settled by the judgment of the apostles and the elders. And there, with some people sharply resisting once again, especially the Christians of the pharisaical party, to which Paul also had belonged, a Synod of apostles and elders was gathered together, and it was determined by the authority of Peter and James that the gentiles should not be burdened with the Mosaic law so long as they abstained from eating animals which had been strangled, from blood, from meat offered to idols, and from immorality. However, this concession to the unconquerable superstition of the Jews was made out of consideration of the times, as is proven by the fact that we have seen these three prohibitions long since removed and completely abolished.[20]

From the same source arose that controversy at Antioch between Peter and Paul, when the apostle to the gentiles, discerning that his own people were in danger because of the hypocrisy of Peter, publicly refuted him, as he himself notes in his letter to the Galatians, chapter 2[:11-21]. Moreover, in Jerusalem at the instigation of James, in order that he might clear away a rumour now spread among the Jews that he seemed to be drawing back from the Mosaic law, he shaved his head together with the others, and having been purged according to the Jewish rite, he offered a gift in the temple, as Luke records in Acts 21[:17-26]. In this text it seems that James, even though he had previously virtually liberated the gentiles from the burden of the Mosaic law, nevertheless was of the opinion that observance of the law by Jews was required at least to the extent of placating those who had not yet advanced far enough in the truth of the gospel to be able to reject totally the rites of their fathers.[21] For thus James[22] says in verse 24: 'And all will know that the things which they have heard about you are false, but that you yourself also live in observance of the law.' This was the reason, in my opinion, that he shaved his head according to a vow at Cenchreae as recorded in Acts 18[:18]. He circumcised Timothy, as recorded in Acts 16[:3] because of a similar necessity: Timothy had been born of a Jewish mother but of a gentile father. So great was the task of making a Christian out of a Jew.[23] For a certain stubbornness is peculiar to this nation, and no nation was ever more tenacious in holding to its own religion, as Josephus, in polished style, informs us in his apologetic work, the *Jewish Antiquities*.[24] In addition to these things, the Jewish nation was peculiarly hateful at that time to all the nations of the world, and they in turn cursed all nations as impure, profane, and impious, considering them unworthy of association and believing their own temple to be polluted if some uncircumcised person by chance entered into it. So great was the arrogance associated with the cutting off of a little bit of skin.

Therefore, since there was no hope that the Greeks and Romans would accept the commonly[25] hated law, and since the Jews protested with an incredible stubbornness, Paul, understanding that there was a danger that the fruit of the gospel might in large part perish from such a destructive dissent and that the glory of Christ might be obscured by intermingling with the name of Moses, takes special pains everywhere to annul and to reject the ceremonies of the law and to transfer to Christ alone all hope for obtaining salvation. He scolds the Galatians sharply (but nevertheless lovingly) because they were drawn to Judaism;[26] and in the same way, he prepares and fortifies the Romans so that they might not become careless and be trapped by the pseudo-apostles (who, as he knew, never ceased in their efforts), but would persist instead in the right teaching which they had begun to embrace. For there was at Rome a huge number of Jews, either because they had been taken there by Pompey,[27] or because the province of Judaea, whose superstition is again and again branded in the writings of Juvenal, Horace, and Seneca,[28] now belonged to the Romans. Paul also had a great deal to do with the Jews after he came to Rome, as Acts 28[:17-22] testifies.

And so by a wonderful plan, this unique craftsman aims his message at both Jews and gentiles in his eagerness to entice everyone to Christ through every possible means. He wishes that, if possible, no mortal at all should be lost to the commander under whom he is serving. Thus, now he rebukes one group, now the other, now again he encourages and supports them. He checks the arrogance of the gentiles, showing them that neither the law of nature nor the philosophy by whose profession they are swollen up is of any use in preventing them from falling into every kind of disgraceful crime. On the other hand, he restrains the arrogance of the Jews, who by trust in the law, had destroyed the chief point of the whole law, namely, faith in Jesus Christ. He teaches them that the ceremonies of the law have now been rendered obsolete through the radiant gospel of Christ, of which the shadows of the law had provided only an outline. Now all were repealed: rest on the sabbath day, the injury of circumcision, recurrences of the day of the month, holidays returning three times every year, the choice of foods, the filthy baths repeated again and again on particular days, the murder of innocent beasts, the religion of a temple which has been defiled with incessant slaughter. Paul teaches further that these shadows of reality have vanished away from the shining light of truth; that the true sons of Abraham are those who imitate the faith of Abraham; that those are truly Jews who profess Christ; that those are truly circumcised who have a mind purged from filthy desires; that true righteousness and perfect salvation are conferred on an equal basis upon all, without the help of the law, through the gospel and faith alone in Jesus Christ; that even though salvation was at one time promised especially to the Jews, the prophets were not silent about the fact that if they should reject these promises the proclamation of Christ would be extended to the gentiles; and finally, that true righteousness comes to no one through the Mosaic law (which they were observing in accordance with the flesh)[29] but through faith. He teaches all these things through the example of Abraham and through the various testimonies of the law itself. And in this way, having removed the arrogance and taken away the self-confidence of both races, he makes all equal with respect to evangelical faith; and while he rejoices in the salvation of the gentiles, yet he laments the blindness of his own nation with a paternal love, even though he had encountered the extraordinarily stubborn hostility of that nation at every turn. The reproach of their blindness, harsh when taken in isolation, he softens by saying that not all have been blinded and that some time in the future the whole nation of the Jews would come to its senses, challenged by the faith of the gentiles.

In passing he puts forth many and various doctrines: foreordination (or rather, predestination), foreknowledge, the elect, grace and merit, free will, the divine plan inscrutable to us, the law of nature, the law of Moses, the law of sin. Varied indeed are the sources of his allegories: he depicts Adam as two men, one by whom we are born mortal according to the flesh; the other by whom we are reborn to become immortal. He depicts two men, the internal and the external. The internal man is obedient to the spirit and to reason; the external man is subject to desires and passions.[30] Sometimes he calls the internal man 'spirit,' the external man at one time 'body' or 'limbs,' at another time 'flesh,' sometimes 'the law of sin.' He speaks of two kinds of death, one of the body and another of the soul, and a third, by which we die to sin and to the passions which accompany sin. Likewise he describes three kinds of life: one by which we live according to the body, a second according to the mind, and a third according to righteousness and sin. He speaks of a double servitude or freedom: one by which we are emancipated from sins and become the servants of innocence; or, in turn, one by which we are freed from righteousness and serve sin. There are two kinds of Judaism, two kinds of circumcision, two kinds of descendants of Abraham. There are two parts of the Mosaic law:[31] one carnal, the other spiritual – the body and soul, as it were, of the law. Baptism is twofold. In the first kind, we are cleansed from our former sins by a sacred bath, and in the second we die with Christ, having renounced the passions of the world. There is a double burial: a bodily burial in which Christ was buried for three days; and a spiritual burial by which we are freed from the vices of the world and rest quietly in Christ. There is a twofold resurrection: one which preceded in Christ and will follow in us; and another in which we are restored to life from our former sins and progress from virtue to virtue, in this respect practising as far as possible the future life. There is a double righteousness, that of God and that of men. There is a double judgment, that of God and that of men. There is a double glory or praise, one according to God, and another according to men.

Having examined these things, he passes on to the moral sphere, especially exhorting his readers to mutual concord, using the example of bodily members. For inasmuch as peace cannot exist where there is arrogance or envy, he pleads that by mutual indulgence they may nourish and cherish a mutual love. He begs the Romans that for the time being they should bear the weakness of the Jews which remains from the long habit of the law. On the other hand, he pleads with the Jews that they should not envy the gentiles who have been received into the fellowship of the gospel, but rather that they should emulate their faith and freedom. And since the same God, the same Christ, the same grace, the same reward belong to all, all should coalesce in one body. And no one should arrogate anything to himself, but if anyone excels with respect to some gift, he should devote this to the help of his brother. On the topic of morality, his discussion ranges widely. He teaches them how they ought to behave towards unbelieving Jews or towards somewhat superstitious Christians (or as he himself calls them, weak Christians); how they should behave towards those superior to them, those below them, those equal to them; how they should behave towards emperors and magistrates who are heathen, but who all perform their own duties in one way or another; and how they should behave in prosperity, how in adversity. Then again he softens the sharpness of his admonitions by praise of the Romans, and he commends his own authority among them, calling to mind how much further he has advanced in the gospel of Christ than others. He declares how great is his desire to see them, and he expresses the hope of coming to them. He explains why he is compelled to delay his coming, praising the spontaneous liberality of the

Macedonians and the Corinthians towards the poor brethren, tacitly and modestly challenging the Romans to emulate them.

He fills the final chapter almost completely with salutations, not lifelessly heaping up the names of many people, but admirably by adding his own word of acclaim to each one. Finally, since he knew deeply both the shameless cunning of the pseudo-apostles and the simplicity and affability of the Romans, again and again he admonishes them to beware of being deceived by the flattery of the pseudo-apostles. However, although a great many of these things were more specifically appropriate to that age, in which the church, composed of Jews and gentiles and subject to heathen rulers, was gradually taking shape, but still not fully formed, nevertheless there is nothing from which some salutary instruction cannot be derived, and applied to these times as well. Take, for example, his discussion of the escape from superstition, which is a breeding ground of discord and maintains the appearance of piety in such a way that nothing is more opposed to the real thing. Other examples are his discussions of the foolish trust in worldly philosophy and in the works of men;[32] the merit of faith; the avoidance of arrogance; tolerating the weakness of those who are less learned on some matter; prompting concord by mutual obedience; enduring rulers (no matter how evil they may be) and ungodly bishops, lest public order be disturbed; conquering wrong with kindness; not judging what does not pertain to you; understanding charitably whatever can be done with a good conscience; guarding against insidious flattery; and other things of this kind in which our common life is involved even today.

But the difficulty of this letter equals and almost surpasses its utility.[33] And this seems to me to be the case for three reasons in particular. First, nowhere else is the order of speech more confused; nowhere is the speech more split by the transposition of words; nowhere is the speech more incomplete through absence of an apodosis, about which Origen[34] complains time and again, as he struggles and labours everywhere in difficulties of this kind. Whether this should be attributed to Tertius, in his role as interpreter or as recorder, or to Paul himself, I leave to others to judge. Paul plainly acknowledges his inexperience in discourse, though he begs his ignorance to be excused. Furthermore, so far from aiming at a discourse composed by human skill, he actually thought that he ought to avoid it, lest it detract in any way from the glory of the cross.[35] And for this reason Origen[36] thought that it was superfluous to search for polished composition in Paul. Jerome[37] sometimes takes Paul's side in defending the skill of his discourse, and at other times he denies its skill, frankly confessing that some of its faults could be attributed to the corrupted speech of Cilicians. Augustine[38] even singles out ornaments of the rhetoricians and artificially polished phrases[39] in Paul's letters. In fact, even in Acts Paul shows he is a master of speech,[40] and in 1 Corinthians[41] he speaks in tongues more than everyone else. For although, as Jerome[42] testifies, the entire east spoke Greek at this time, nevertheless it is reasonable that among the Celts the purity of the Roman language was not the same as it was at Rome; and in the same way, it is probable that there was not a little difference between a Cilician speaking Greek and an Athenian. Another factor which contributed to these difficulties of the language was Hebrew, the idioms of which Paul is constantly bringing in, speaking Greek in such a way that nonetheless you sometimes recognize it as Hebrew.

The second cause of difficulty, in my opinion, is the obscurity of things which are hard to put into words; because of them, no other letter is handicapped by more frequent rough spots or is broken by deeper chasms. So much is this the case that he himself, having abandoned something which he had started to say, is compelled to exclaim at one point: 'Oh depth of riches!'[43] And furthermore, as a prudent man he so touches upon certain mysteries as to display them as though through a window only, accommodating his speech to the situation of the times and to the capacity of those to whom he writes. Paul knew and saw certain things which it was unlawful[44] for one to say, and he knew to what extent milk and to what extent solid food[45] were needed. He knew the stages of growth in Christ, and what had to be applied to each one. On the basis of a similar judgment, the apostle Peter, when he was going to speak about Christ before an assembly of untaught people, calls him a man and avoids the word God.[46]

I believe that a third reason is his frequent and sudden change of masks, while he considers now the Jews, now the gentiles, now both; sometimes he addresses believers, sometimes doubters; at one point he assumes the role of a weak man, at another of a strong; sometimes that of a godly man, sometimes of an ungodly man. The result of all this is that the reader, wandering about as though in some kind of confusing labyrinth or winding maze, does not see very well whence he has entered or how he may leave. Origen,[47] in my opinion not less truly than elegantly, compares Paul to a man who leads a stranger into some very powerful ruler's palace: a confusing place, owing to various kinds of winding passageways and to the recesses from the rooms. However, from afar he displays certain things from a most abundant treasury of wealth; he brings some things closer, but is unwilling that others be seen. Often, moreover, after having entered in through one door, he exits through another, so that the stranger himself wonders where he has come from, where he is, or what way he should go out. Even the apostle Peter acknowledges this in his second letter,[48] testifying that there are certain things hard to comprehend in the Pauline letters, which those who are not very learned and not very strong might distort to their own ruin. We for our part have attempted to remove the difficulties to the best of our ability, except for certain words which are so peculiar to the language of Paul that they cannot be expressed in more than one way; these for example: faith, grace, body, flesh, member, spirit, mind, feeling, to build, and others of this kind which, although it was not possible to change outright, we have striven to soften as much as possible. But now let us hear the man himself, speaking like a Roman to the Romans, no, rather to all, in terms quite blunt and clear.

THE PARAPHRASE ON THE
EPISTLE OF PAUL
THE APOSTLE TO THE ROMANS

BY ERASMUS OF ROTTERDAM

Chapter 1

I am Paul, though formerly Saul, that is, I have become peaceful, though formerly restless,[1] until recently subject to the law of Moses, now freed from Moses, I have been made a servant of Jesus Christ. Not that I am a deserter or forsaker of my former tradition, but I have been summoned to the duty of this mission, and I am now more happily separated than I was before, when as a champion of the pharisaical sect, I wandered about in error, impiously pious, ignorantly learned.[2] But now at last I am truly worthy of the name pharisee,[3] inasmuch as I have been set apart and chosen by Christ himself to undertake a task far more glorious, namely, the preaching of the gospel of God. This gospel is by no means new but one long ago promised by him through the oracles of his prophets which also now appear in books – no ordinary books, but holy, and of inviolate faith. This is the gospel concerning his Son who was born in time of the lineage of David according to the infirmity of the flesh, but was also revealed to be the eternal Son of the eternal God according to the Spirit which sanctifies all things. Moreover, he was revealed as such by very many other proofs[4] and especially by the fact that, when, by rising from the dead, he had overcome death, he himself became the prince and author of the resurrection for all who have been reborn in him, Jesus Christ our Lord.

Through him I have obtained not only this grace, which observance of the law could not have conferred, but also the duties of an apostle,[5] in order that, just as the other apostles have spread the gospel among the Jews, so I might preach it among gentiles of every race to prevent them from being overwhelmed by the burdens of the law but to submit to the faith preached to them concerning Christ and to rely upon this, not upon the empty wisdom of the philosophers.[6] You too are among the number of these gentiles as far as race is concerned; not by race but by adoption you have been admitted into the authority and name of Jesus Christ, in order that the names of sects or regions may not separate you any longer, since the adoption is common to all. For all of you at Rome who are beloved of God and have been called from your former wickedness to holiness of life, I wish grace and peace. Not the grace for which this world is accustomed to pray in its usual way, but a true and a new grace, that is, the free gift of the truly justifying faith of the gospel. And I also wish that as a result of the complete abolition through grace of the sins of your former life, you may have the peace of a conscience now free from anxiety and a steadfast friendship with God. These two things neither the strength of human wisdom affords, nor the observance of the Mosaic law; instead they originate for all from the unique generosity of God the Father and of his Son, our Lord Jesus Christ.[7]

And on account of you all do I especially give thanks to God the Father, who through Christ his Son has richly bestowed this upon you, that though you were hitherto unbelieving, now your faith is celebrated and proclaimed throughout the whole world. Because of the love I bear you, I naturally cannot fail to find this most pleasing. For I have as my witness God the Father himself – whom I worship[8] with my spirit, not with gross[9] corporeal ceremonies, now that I have been freed from the law of Moses[10] and preach the gospel of God's Son (for this is the worship most pleasing to him) – God is my witness that always and without ceasing I make mention of you in my prayers, beseeching him that, if it is at all possible, I might obtain at last my long-standing desire to make (if he so wills) a happy and safe journey to you. For indeed, I am possessed by a great longing to see you, not for my own advantage, but that I may impart some gift to you – not the fleshly gift of Moses but the spiritual gift of Christ – in order that you may be even more resolved in what you have undertaken, or rather, in order that there may be a mutual encouragement to each of us, while I rejoice with you in your faith and you in turn rejoice with me in mine. And so it will come about that mutual exhortation will corroborate and support at the same time both your faith and mine. It has been by no means my own fault that this has not yet come about. On the contrary, I would not wish to hide from you, my brothers, that I have often intended to make a visit to you but have been unable to do so up to the present time due to obstacles which have fallen in my path. I was especially eager to visit you for this reason, that I might reap some harvest among you also, just as I have previously done among other nations. This task of preaching the gospel has been entrusted to me by God, nor am I obligated to any particular nation; but just as God is equally the God of all, so the gospel of Christ extends equally to all. By the gospel I mean justification through faith in Jesus Christ, the Son of God, whom the law promised and prefigured.[11] And so I owe this work not only to the Greeks but also to the barbarians, not simply to the wise and learned but also to the uncultured and illiterate, to anyone, whoever he may be, who does not reject it and turn away. Therefore, at least as far as I am concerned, I am eager to preach the gospel to you also who live in Rome.

For the majesty of imperial Rome does not deter me from this, nor do I think that I ought to be ashamed of performing my task if I preach the gospel of Christ. For just as to the impious and unbelieving the gospel seems silly and worthless, so to whoever believes it is the power of God capable of conferring salvation on the believer and truly quieting his conscience,[12] which neither the traditions of the Jews nor your philosophy nor your wealth is able to do. Although this power is equally effective for all, nevertheless, as the Lord commanded, it was offered first to the Jews for the sake of honour; soon, through preachers of the gospel, to be spread among the Greeks and all the nations of the world, so that all equally might acknowledge their own unrighteousness and seek the righteousness of God, whether they be Scythians or Britons.[13] Far, indeed, from salvation is he who neither understands his own sickness nor knows where to seek a remedy for it. For formerly, different people had different views of what righteousness depended upon; but now the righteousness, not of Moses, but of God himself, is disclosed to all through the gospel of Christ. This righteousness does not depend on the superstitious cult of idols or on the legal ceremonies of the Jews. Rather it comes from faith,[14] as long as men acknowledge that God is now offering what formerly he had promised through the mouth of his own prophets. For instance, Habakkuk[15] prophesied: 'My righteous man shall live[16] by faith.'

For although up to this time most mortals have sinned with impunity, assuming that God overlooked their sins, now he reveals his own anger openly from heaven, anger which has been justly kindled against all men who are in any way ungodly and unrighteous, even those who are exempt from the law of Moses. For they have not applied the truth however they have come to know it to pious and holy living, but they have persisted in their sins. And although they have understood more than the masses who are ignorant of God, nevertheless they have been no less impious than those. God, indeed, as he wholly is, can by no means be known by human intelligence; and yet these have attained the limits of human knowledge, although even this they owe to God. For they could not have attained it if God had not revealed it to them. Indeed, if God did not reveal this in the books of the prophets in which he seemed to be speaking only to the Jews, he has certainly revealed it in the miracle of this whole structure of the world. For even though God himself is invisible, nevertheless by the intellect he is seen in this world so marvellously created and so wonderfully administered. Granted that the world has had a beginning and will have an end, nevertheless from its workmanship is seen the power of the creator, a power which neither knows any beginning nor will have any end. In fact, the creation demonstrates his very divinity by which he was always in himself complete even before the founding of the world,[17] so that they have no pretext for their own impiety.[18] For although they acknowledged that God exists, nevertheless they failed to honour him as God, as the sovereign of all. And they did not give thanks to him as the author of every good, to whom they should have credited that very knowledge by which they became swollen with pride. But they have become puffed up by the vapour of empty glory and, in their vanity, have been deceived by their own cogitations. Their foolish hearts have been darkened by a cloud of arrogance. And they have become foolish and unlearned because they boasted that they were wise and learned.

See then how far they have gone in blindness and foolishness. They have defiled the majesty of immortal God with the counterfeited image of mortal man, and not only of man, but even of birds, beasts and serpents. And on account of this unnatural worship of God, he has allowed them to rush headlong into the gratification of the desires of their own hearts, and to sink into such foulness and filth that they have mutually brought shame upon their own bodies and polluted themselves with shameful acts. Nor is it without justice that those, who because of their pride of heart so perversely worshipped the known God, fell into these monstrous vices, inasmuch as they worshipped a false statue fabricated by art in place of the true God, and absurdly venerated and worshipped created things and have honoured these more than him who created all things, bringing dishonour upon God who alone ought to be praised and who alone deserves this kind of honour from mankind for all eternity. Amen.

God, I say, was offended for these reasons, and he has allowed these to sink into filthy and shameful desires. For not the men alone but also their women, forgetful of their own sex, have changed the natural use of the female body into one which is contrary to nature, following the example of the males,[19] who as I have said, having abandoned the natural use of women, burned for one another with mutual desire to such an extent that the male committed abominably foul acts with a male. And in these ways the outrage committed against God has fallen back upon them, a reward which their madness deserved. For just as it did not seem good to these to acknowledge the known God and to keep him before their eyes, so in turn God has allowed[20] them, blinded by their own darkness, to turn aside into a false way of thought to the point that they have perpetrated such deeds as are extremely[21] unworthy of men. And yet in other ways as well they are steeped in every kind of wickedness: fornication, covetousness, cunning,

everywhere polluted with envy, murder, contention, deceit, malice, possessed of an evil character, gossips, backbiters, haters of the divine power,
overbearing, arrogant, proud, inventors of wickedness, disobedient to
parents, devoid of understanding, confused, lacking all sense of piety,
ignorant of covenants, unmerciful. Although they know that God exists and
also that he is supremely just – so that those who perpetrate such disgraceful
deeds are necessarily worthy of death – still, they not only themselves do
these things but even assent to others who do them, and so become the
authors of sin among the ignorant.

Chapter 2

Nor is it of much consequence that the philosophers condemn these crimes
by words, and that the magistrates prohibit and punish them by law. For
anyone who imitates something gives his assent to it.[1] Therefore, you have
no excuse, whoever you are, if while gratifying your own pleasure, you pass
judgment on another. On the contrary, while you judge another you
condemn yourself by this very act, since as a judge you commit the same
crime of which you find another guilty. And since you are guilty of the same
sin, you pronounce judgment upon yourself while you pronounce it upon
another. Men can be tricked; you will perhaps escape the judgment of those
who deliver verdicts on the basis of conjectures and the appearance of truth
but who do not perceive the secrets of the mind. God, however, to whose
eyes all things are visible, will render his verdict, not according to
appearance, but according to the truth, against those who do the disgraceful
deeds we have just recounted.

   Do you so greatly flatter yourself, O man (whoever has a conscience
should be assured that he is being addressed), that while you judge those
guilty of such sins you think you are able to escape the judgment of God,
even though you yourself commit the same sins? And when you, a man,
punish another man, do you think God will not punish you? And will you
escape from the judgment of God when men are not able to avoid your
judgment? Does the gentleness of God give you hope of escaping punishment? Do you hold him in contempt because of his immense and abounding
goodness, or because he is very patient and defers punishment? Do you
think he closes his eyes to transgressions, or that he actually favours evil
deeds? You do not understand that this divine gentleness toward you, far
from promising freedom from punishment to sinners, entices and invites you
to repent and return to your senses, so that you may be overwhelmed by his
kindness and at last become dissatisfied with yourself. However, you
yourself are turning the gentleness of God toward you into the full measure

of your own condemnation. No amount of reasoning can soften your obstinate mind[2] and cause it to repent; you despise and reject God when he calls you to better things,[3] and you hide away and heap up for yourself a store of divine anger. And although this anger may not make itself manifest for the moment, nevertheless it will be felt eventually: without doubt on that terrible day when God's tenderness is at an end. The impious will be punished with a severity corresponding to the stubbornness with which they have rejected the gentleness of God when it called them to better things. At that time the just judgment of God will be disclosed in the sight of all. For he will by no means judge in the manner of men, either erring or playing favourites, but he will be absolutely incorruptible, a judge who knows everything, and will give a reward to each according to his deeds: eternal life to those who now rely on the promises of the gospel and[4] persevere in pious works. They do not seek the vain and fleeting advantages of the present life but rather eternal life in heaven. To these he will give eternal glory in place of temporary disgrace, honour in place of contempt, immortality in place of the despised life of the body.[5] For others, who have stubbornly and perversely preferred to yield to unrighteousness rather than obey the truth, there will be a reward worthy of their deeds, that is, divine indignation and anger, and hence suffering and anguish of mind.

This punishment awaits equally all mortals who have sinned, but in the first place the Jew and the Greek, so that the first in punishment may be those to whom the kindness of God was first offered. On the other hand, glory, honour, and peace will be repaid equally to all who, through faith,[6] have lived well, but in the first place to the Jew, then to the Greek, finally to all barbarians.[7] For God is no respecter of persons as judges of men usually are, but he treats all men equally and justly. Consequently, whoever have sinned outside the law will likewise perish outside the law, and whoever have sinned under the law will be judged by the law. For you are not counted righteous in God's eyes just because you have heard the law: do not flatter yourself on that score, Jew! But those who express and fulfil the law by their deeds and habits are the ones who will be considered righteous in God's judgment. God cherishes and approves meritorious action even if there should be no law, and he turns away from those even more who, although they have the law, do not obey it. There is no one, however, who is entirely without the law. For when the races foreign to the law of Moses do of their own accord under the guidance of nature the things which are ordered by the law, even though they are instructed by no prescription of the Mosaic law, they themselves are a law unto themselves, because they express the substance of the law, engraved not on tablets but on their own minds. Whatever among them is usually done before a tribunal of justice is done in their hearts; your conscience gives testimony for or against you, and your thoughts, contending with one another, alternately accuse and defend you. Accordingly, God will someday judge these, when what now goes on secretly in the depths of their hearts will be spread open under the eyes of all. For he to whom nothing is secret will pronounce the sentence. But God will exercise this judgment through Christ his Son, now Lord and[8] Saviour, in the future the judge of the whole human race. This, indeed, is a part of the gospel which I am proclaiming to you, so that no one should suppose that it is a tale or a dream.

How is it therefore, Jew, that you are self-satisfied on account of the law? Consider: you take pride in the name of Jew; you rely on the privilege of the law established by God; you boast that God is the author of your religion; you know his mind and will from sacred literature which derives from him; you are thoroughly trained by the teaching of the law, so that you yourself discern what is to be avoided, what to be sought, and what among good things are to be preferred. Moreover, you are confident of your ability to lead the blind and to bring light to those who live in the shadows, in other words, to be a teacher of the simple, and instructor of those who have little wisdom, because the law has enabled you to possess the form and the rule of life and the norm of truth. Should all of this give you preference over the heathen under the grace of the gospel?[9] I do not think so; on the contrary, because you have the law, you will have an even worse case before the judgment seat of God unless you base your life upon the law in which you take pride. And so the knowledge of which you boast will be cast back against you.

Why then do you boast about yourself to me, parader of the law? You who teach another, do you not teach yourself? You who proclaim that one must not steal, do you yourself commit theft? You who warn that adultery must be avoided, do you yourself commit adultery? You who curse the worship of idols, are you defiled yourself with sacrilege? You who praise yourself and boast among men about the law given you by God, do you transgress the law and bring dishonour and disgrace upon God the author of the law? Do you pervert the source of your own glory among other men and turn it into a disgrace before God to whom alone all glory is owed? What else is that but to dishonour God, as far as you are concerned? – for no dishonour reaches God. About such things formerly even the holy prophets complained, specifically Isaiah and Ezekiel.[10] They said: Through you the name of God is ill spoken of and tainted with insults; through your fault it is held in disgrace among the nations devoted to idols; for while you boast in the name of God and the law, you live impiously.

For it is not enough to have been born a Jew, or to have been received into the religion of the Jews. But circumcision will be profitable to you to the extent that your actions are in accordance with the goal which circumcision was intended to fulfil, and to the extent that you practice in your life what you profess in your ceremonies. Otherwise, if you transgress the law your circumcision will confer nothing, since before God your circumcision will be considered as no circumcision at all. For just as circumcision is changed into uncircumcision for you unless you also carry out the other ordinances of the law which are conducive to a good character, so the uncircumcision of the heathen will not at all count against him; on the contrary, God himself will regard him as circumcised if, though he has no knowledge of and neglects the ceremonies of the law, he achieves what is the essence and goal of the law, namely, a sound and pure life; and if he trusts and[11] obeys Christ who is the fulfilment of all laws. Indeed, not only will he be equal to you, he will even be preferred in this respect, that by his very ignorance of circumcision he is considered better than you. And therefore his innocence will reveal your impiety as more damnable because he, a stranger who has not acknowledged the law, nevertheless fulfils the end and intention of the law by his life, while you, relying on the words and syllables of the law and having acknowledged the law by the mark of circumcision, cry out against Christ and thus[12] violate the central point of the whole law.[13] In the eyes of God, who judges not on the basis of the marks of the body but on the basis of the piety of the soul, you have lost the name of Jew unless you carry out the commitment of a Jew. For he is not a Jew who carries around the characteristic mark of Judaism on his body, and he is not circumcised who has a little bit of foreskin cut off. But he in truth is a Jew who is one inwardly and in his heart. God alone examines the hearts of all and judges accordingly. He is truly circumcised whose heart rather than genital member has been circumcised, who relies not on letters engraved in stone but on the spirit and intention of the law. For one whose flesh alone has been circumcised can indeed boast among men that he is a Jew; but one becomes a true Jew only when his mind has been purged of sin[14] and is inclined toward Christ. God acknowledges and approves him, without doubt, even if mortals deny him his due praise; and to be approved by God's standard is unshakable happiness.

Chapter 3

But here someone will say to me: If the whole matter depends on a pious life and innocent character and on faith in Christ, what then is left to the Jew by which he excels the heathen? Or what was the advantage of being circumcised at all if piety and faith make the uncircumcised equal to the circumcised, or if circumcision actually makes worse the case of a Jew who sins? As far as the grace of the gospel is concerned, the position of the Jews is not at all better than that of the gentiles. But yet in some respects[1] it is indeed an advantage to belong to the Jewish race. For first on this count they may justly boast, whether because to them especially the words of God have been entrusted or because to them in particular the law and the prophets were handed down or because to them only God saw fit to speak. In the first place it is a wonderful thing for this nation to have been given this honour by God. Secondly, he who holds the promises of the law appears to be much more prepared for the faith of the gospel,[2] and he who holds the image of the truth is the nearer to it; for the law of Moses and the oracles of the prophets are indeed a step toward the evangelical teaching of Christ.

Now it is not detrimental to those who believe, if some who are unfortunately in bondage to the letter of the law have refused to believe the gospel. Will their unbelief render the faithfulness[3] of the divine promises null and void, so that God should become offended, in our human fashion, and break his agreement, thus fulfilling for no one what has been promised equally to all? By no means! In reality the promise will be fulfilled for all except those who have rejected it when it was offered, so that now no one can find fault with the faithfulness of the one who made the promise. Thus God is revealed as truthful who, since he cannot lie, is prepared to fulfil whatever he has promised.[4] On the other hand, the lie begins with those very ones who, through their own fault, are cheated of the promises of God. God cannot be deceived and he cannot deceive. But man, inasmuch as he is man, is capable of both. For even the mystic Psalm of David[5] testifies that the reliability of God is absolutely sure. He says: So that you may appear just and truthful in what you say, and be vindicated, as often as men accuse you of being a false promiser, when they suspect that my wickedness will prevent you from fulfilling the promises which you have made to the house of David. I myself did not deserve to share in the promise; but nevertheless there is this advantage, that your faithfulness and truth become all the more attested and commended to mankind through my sin, if it is observed that you have not changed your judgment even when you have been offended by so great a crime.

But here it may occur to someone: If our unrighteousness makes the righteousness of God more commendable and esteemed, what must we conclude? That God is unjust, who wishes sin to exist in order that his own righteousness might all the more shine forth? (These are the words, not now of myself, but of the impious) – God forbid that such a thought should ever enter the mind of the pious. For how will God be the supreme judge of this world if he is unjust? Now if God has so managed things that I am a liar in order that his truth may be rendered the more conspicuous through my lying and that my disgrace may be changed into his glory, why is my sin imputed to me, and why do we not rather think as those slanderous men falsely charge, interpreting my words as if I said: 'Let us do evil that good may come of it,' since indeed by our unrighteousness the righteousness of God has been made more commendable. But may God turn this thought away from pious minds. For those are justly and deservedly condemned for their unbelief, for this reason: they cannot charge God with their sins, for they themselves of their own free will are the authors of those sins; and similarly, no thanks is due to them if God of his own goodness turns to his glory the sins which they themselves commit by their own degeneracy.

But to return to the matter at hand: What shall we say? Are we Jews superior to the gentiles? Not at all. Certainly not insofar as the grace of the gospel is concerned, even if we seem to have preference through the privilege granted by the Mosaic law. For we have already cited evidence to show that Jews and Greeks alike are all subject to the same fault. Concerning the gentiles indeed, this is too obvious to be denied. Concerning the Jews, however, even their own Psalms bear witness.[6] For thus it is written in Psalm 13[14:1-2]:[7] 'There is no one who is righteous. There is no one who understands or who searches out God. All have failed, all alike have become unprofitable. There is no one who practises righteousness, there is no one, I say, not even one.' Again in Psalm 5[:9]: 'Their throat is an open tomb, they have used their own tongues for deceit, the poison of asps is under their lips.' And again in Psalm 9[10:7]: 'Their mouth is full of curses and bitterness.' And with these witnesses Isaiah agrees [59:7-8]: 'Their feet are swift to shed blood; in their paths are ruin and misery, and the way of peace they do not know; there is no fear of God before their eyes.' It cannot be pretended that these things do not pertain to the Jews. For it is obvious that whatever the law says has special reference to those to whom it has been given, and for this reason it considers them more[8] guilty. And this of course has been done for no other purpose than to stop up equally the mouths of all mortals, and to demonstrate that the whole world is equally guilty before God, since the law of Moses, when observed according to the letter,[9] has no power to make any one at all righteous and innocent before God as judge; for unless you are righteous in his eyes, to be considered righteous by men is useless.

But you will say: what then is the use of the law if through it no one attains justification? It was useful at least to this extent, that through it everyone more clearly recognizes his own sin. To understand one's own sickness is a considerable step on the road to health.[10] Moreover, just as parts of the law were [given] previously to reveal human sin which had previously been less evident, so now through the gospel, righteousness has been revealed which does not need the support of the Mosaic law, although the law and the prophets have given witness to it. Righteousness, I say, not of the law but of God, and this not through circumcision or through the ceremonies of the Jews[11] but through faith and trust[12] in Jesus Christ, through whom alone true righteousness is conferred, not only upon the Jews, or upon this or that nation, but without distinction upon each and every one who has faith in him.

For just as this disease is common to all, and all alike have regressed to a point where they are not able to boast before God about their own righteousness, so justification must be sought by all from the same source. It is certainly not paid back to us as a reward earned through the observance of the Mosaic law or even through the observance of the law of nature. Rather it is given freely by the divine goodness, not through Moses but through Jesus Christ by whose blood we have been redeemed from the tyranny of sin. To be sure, the Jews formerly had their own means of propitiation,[13] clearly a shadow and type of the future; but God has now revealed that Christ is the true propitiation for all, in order that we, formerly hostile on account of our sins, now might be reconciled to God, not (as with the Jews) through the blood of beasts, but through the most holy blood of Christ himself, which washes away all the sins of all people. In this way he reveals his righteousness to all men, while through the Son[14] he pardons the errors of their former life with the intent that they afterwards do not fall back again into sin. He does not forgive because they have merited it, but because he himself has promised[15] [forgiveness]. Nor did he endure sinners until then because he was ignorant of their sins or approved them, but to make known his righteousness at this appointed time, so that it might be clear that he is by nature and of himself truly righteous, and that he is the one and only author of human righteousness. And this he is without respect of persons for all who have faith in the gospel of Jesus Christ.

Tell me, therefore, you Jew, where is your[16] boasting? Of course this boasting was taken away from you after the divine will made all the races of the world equal with respect to the gospel. Salvation and righteousness are conferred also on the gentiles. Through what law then? Through that old Mosaic law which prescribes ceremonies?[17] Not at all, but through a new law which demands nothing except faith in the Son of God.[18] For we believe what in fact is the case, that in the future anyone at all will be able to attain righteousness through faith,[19] even if he does not observe the prescriptions of the Mosaic law. That law was peculiar to the Jewish nation, but this favour of the grace of the gospel[20] proceeds from God himself to all. But is God the God of the Jews only? Is not the same God equally the God of the gentiles? It cannot be doubted that he is common to gentiles and to Jews equally.

Moreover, since God is one and the same for all, it is proper also that the gift of God be common to all. And so it is not the case that there is one God who justifies the circumcised leading him from faith in the law which promised a Saviour,[21] to the faith in the gospel which exhibited the promise;[22] and another God who justifies the uncircumcised, calling him from the worship of idols to a common faith.

But here some Jew will say: How can this be, Paul? If what you say is true, that now all things are accomplished[23] through faith, you make the law of Moses utterly idle and useless to the Jews. Perish the thought! We are so far from abolishing or destroying the law that we are actually confirming and establishing it, preaching that what the law had promised for the future has now been accomplished, and announcing him towards whom the whole law pointed as its goal. For something is not abolished when it is restored to a better condition – no more than when fruit follows the blossoms that fall from the trees, or when a body takes the place of a shadow.

Chapter 4

Besides, if someone continues to hold doggedly onto the law of Moses in its present gross and carnal condition and in his confidence in this holds out to others the hope of obtaining salvation, I shall confront him with not just any Jew, but Abraham himself, the founder of circumcision, in whom the whole tribe of Jews takes special pride and about whom they boast as the father of their race. Although Abraham, so far as family relationship is concerned, is the father of the Jews, he is not less for this reason the father of all those who resemble him by a likeness of faith, that is, who resemble him by a spiritual, not by a bodily image. For circumcision, which, as I said, was first revealed in Abraham, is like a pledge and a kind of sign of the whole Mosaic law, and, so to speak, a special symbol by which Jews are Jews. Let us, then, consider what Abraham obtained and on what grounds he obtained it.

First, sacred literature testifies that praise for righteousness came to Abraham. But if this praise came to Abraham on account of circumcision or other rites of this kind which the law of Moses commands to be kept, he indeed has something to boast about before men, but not likewise before God. Why before men? Assuredly because his praise would have resulted from corporeal things on the basis of which men make judgments. Why not before God? Because it was not based on a commendation for faith which commends us in God's eyes. But Abraham obtained praise for righteousness before God himself.[1] Therefore, he did not obtain it from observing the precepts of the law, but from the same faith through which the same praise ought now to be solicited by all Jews and likewise by all gentiles – I should say, by all true sons of Abraham. My words would have no weight if sacred literature did not declare this most clearly. For thus you read in Genesis 15[:6]: 'Abraham believed God, and this belief was imputed to him for righteousness.' God promised Abraham that his posterity would equal the stars in number, although his wife was barren and no heir had appeared up to that time. Without hesitation, Abraham had faith in the one who made the promise, not considering what was promised but who the author was. And immediately because of the merit of trust² he was considered righteous, not from circumcision which he had not yet received, but from his belief – and considered righteous not before men, but before God, who was the only witness to this transaction, and from whom he received credit for his trust as righteousness, although he had not fulfilled the righteousness of the Mosaic law. For it is properly said that credit is entered on account or received when the money has not actually been paid but nevertheless is considered as paid due to the kindness of the creditor.

Now Abraham the patriarch himself did not receive praise for righteousness by the merit of circumcision; he received it prior to circumcision by the commendation of his faith. Why then would the Jew, to whom this law was given for a time, trust in the ceremonies of his law – much less the heathen to whom that law has not been given? For to the Jew, subject to the ceremonies of the law, if some reward is paid for observing the law, it seems that what is owed is being paid as though by contract, rather than by the favour of the one who gives, while if some punishment is inflicted for not observing the law, it is inflicted as justly due. For just as the slave who performs his duty receives his due reward, so the one who forgets his duty is punished with whips. But as for the gentiles who do not know the ceremonies of the law, or even the Jews who abandon the servitude of the law for faith in Christ, these no longer labour as though by rule, but purely and simply trust in Christ who bestows as a free gift perfect righteousness even on the impious, all of whose sins he has taken away by his death. To these, I say, after the example of Abraham, faith offers this, that they are considered righteous, commended not for having observed the law, but for faith alone,³ to which no one is compelled but all are invited. Thus, it becomes a matter of free will, not of servitude, that we believe in Christ;⁴ and a matter of grace, not of something owed, that we are included in the number of the righteous through him.

David also agrees with us, that kingly prophet and prophetic king, after Abraham the principal glory of the Jewish people, and in whom Christ, the one and only source of our righteousness, has been promised to us especially. For in Psalm 31[32:1-2] he in the same way describes this blessed state of man which is now revealed through the gospel, showing that it does not come through the works of the Mosaic law, as a payment, but from divine beneficence, by which we are drawn to faith in Christ. He says: 'Blessed are those whose iniquities have been forgiven and whose sins have been covered over. Blessed is the man to whom the Lord has not reckoned his sin.' You are being told that iniquities committed against the Mosaic law are forgiven. You are being told that sins perpetrated against the law of nature are covered up. You are being told that no kinds of sins at all are imputed to the man who has already gained a state of blessedness through Christ. And yet no reference is anywhere made to observing the law.

And so the Jews' descent from Abraham and David is not sufficient grounds for them to exclude the gentiles and claim for themselves alone either this blessedness described by David or the praise bestowed on Abraham for his righteousness. And yet, they may respond to me: This happiness which has been promised – does it pertain only to those who are circumcised and who are consequently subject to the law? Or does it pertain equally to those who know neither circumcision nor the ceremonies of the law? Certainly they themselves admit that faith was credited to Abraham for righteousness. Now, since he is the head of the whole Jewish people, the rest of the nation ought to be judged according to this standard. For it would not be right for the descendants to claim for themselves a right which the ancestor of their nation did not have. It is clear that Abraham was called righteous, but they should explain why he was so called. Was it because a small bit of foreskin had been cut away or rather because of his faith without any commendation for circumcision? It is obvious that praise for righteousness did not come to Abraham on account of Jewish circumcision, since at that time he was not yet circumcised nor commanded to be circumcised. First came his belief that from his own seed Christ would be born, through whom all nations would gain this blessedness and the praise given to him for his righteousness, and for this belief he was considered righteous. Then circumcision was added, not to confer righteousness but to serve as a kind of symbol and mark before men, not before God, to enable them to be recognized as the sons of the man who, not yet circumcised, believed in God, and while still uncircumcised had pleased God by faith alone. If as one circumcised he had believed and had been called righteous, the felicity of this title might have been thought to belong to the circumcised alone. Now, on the contrary, before he had been ordered to be circumcised, he was pronounced righteous by the commendation of his faith.

Circumcision followed, however, not as begetting the righteousness, which he had already obtained, but in part as a kind of type of true circumcision, that is, of an innocence which would follow in those who were going to believe in Christ. This true circumcision is not accomplished by a sharp stone which cuts away the foreskin from the glans, but by the spirit which cuts away all the perverse desires of the mind.[5] In part also circumcision was a kind of sign and pledge by which confidence in the promise made to Abraham might be established, a promise not to be fulfilled immediately in Isaac who merely foreshadowed Christ, but to be realized in its own time in Christ the Son of God;[6] so that at length Abraham the first example of faith might be understood as the father of all who, in imitation of him, believe in Christ,[7] whether or not they are circumcised in the flesh. And just as faith was credited to him as righteousness, so faith might be counted as righteousness for these also as the genuine and legitimate sons of Abraham. And thus he might be the father of the gentiles, but in a sense which does not exclude the Jews, provided the Jews do not pride themselves on this score, that they trace their descent from the circumcised Abraham, bearing merely bodily marks as proof of their relationship. Much rather, they must imitate the faith of Abraham, by which God considered him righteous even before his circumcision. The most dependable proof which parents can claim of their children's legitimacy is the emulation by the children of their parents' virtues. For when men renounce their own offspring and deny that those are children who degenerate from the character and nature of their ancestors, how much more will God separate bastards from legitimate sons by the same test!

Moreover, not by the observance of the Mosaic law (which had not yet been revealed), nor by the merit of circumcision (which, as has been said, he had not yet received), did Abraham deserve to be honoured by God with the great promise that either he or, by inheritance, his descendants, would have dominion over the whole world – not by these but by the commendation for his faith, by which he merited the name of the righteous man.[8] Thus, there is no basis for the Jews' hope that they will obtain the privilege of the divine promise solely on the pretext of circumcision or the law. For the promise cannot be transmitted to the descendants by any other means than that by which it was brought to birth for the author of the race himself. For if the inheritance of the earth promised to the descendants of Abraham belongs on the basis of the law to anyone who happens to be born under the Mosaic law, God's faithfulness seems to have been made of no effect and his promise seems to be empty, since it is agreed that what God promised to Abraham does not come to anyone by the help of the law.

For the law of Moses is far from being able to fulfil such exceptional happiness; in fact, it spurs the eternal deity to even greater anger and indignation, while it provides the occasion for a graver offence. Faith, on the contrary, makes the ungodly righteous. For where offences and indignation exist, there is no inheritance to be passed on to sons. But if you should ask in what way the law brings about anger rather than righteousness, I will tell you. You cannot make accusations against someone without first outlining the terms of the penalty which the law imposes. Moreover, the Mosaic law prescribed a great many things regarding circumcision, the sabbath, new moons, discrimination among various kinds of food, the dead, suffocation, blood, washing.[9] All these prescriptions are of such a kind that even if they are observed they do not confer that saving righteousness. Nevertheless, anyone who transgresses them is guilty and liable to punishment.

However, inasmuch as this law is binding on the Jews only, while the promise to Abraham was the inheritance of all nations, the promise of God cannot reach all through the carnal law. Therefore, it follows that the inheritance comes from faith, so that it may be seen as a matter of grace and unowed kindness. Thus will be established the faithfulness of the divine promise by which the hope of this happiness has been held out to all the descendants of Abraham. I call his descendants, however, not those who are merely related to Abraham through the kinship of the law, but much more those who imitate the faith of the parents. For it is right that a kinship of faith, through which he who became a friend of God merited the promise,[10] should have more weight than a kinship of the law, which begets offences and makes defendants. Therefore, the Jews boast foolishly of this father as if he were only theirs, when actually he is the father of us all who embrace faith in Christ, whoever we are and from whatever nation we come. God himself also testifies to this in Genesis 17 [:5] when, augmenting the name, and calling him Abraham in place of Abram, he says: 'I have established you as the father of many nations.' Certainly what God spoke must be true. But how, tell me, will Abraham be the father of many nations if he belongs only to the nation of the circumcised? On the contrary, just as God belongs to all of those who trust in him, likewise he wished Abraham, who was a type of God as Isaac was of Christ, not to be the father of this or that nation in particular, but a father common to all nations which the affinity of faith had united to him. Moreover, Abraham could not be deceived by his credulity, inasmuch as he trusted the promises of God, who not only is able to grant fertility to the barren but can even give back life to the dead. Thus, later, when Abraham had been ordered to kill his only son Isaac, in whom alone hope of his whole posterity had been placed, he still did not at all doubt the trustworthiness of the promiser. For he knew that Isaac could be called back into life by God and that God admits to this happiness things which are nothing at all in the opinion of mortals, treating them as if they were something.[11] The Jews think that they are alive; they think they amount to something; they detest the gentiles as if dead and worthy of nothing good. But the summons of God accomplishes more for the gentiles than their own ancestry accomplishes for the Jews.

And the old man's faith, so genuine and so firm, was worthy of favour. Relying on the promises of God he entertained a sure hope about things for which the powers of nature offered no hope, acknowledging and witnessing by his acts to both the trustworthiness and the omnipotence of the promiser. For he did not doubt, although he himself was worn out and had a barren wife, that nevertheless he would be the father of many nations and the originator of a posterity so numerous that it could be equal to the multitude of the stars. For after God had led him into the country and had pointed out to him the heavens filled with a countless density of stars, he said: Just as you are not able to count these fires, so the descendants which will come forth from you will be innumerable.[12] Although this seemed not at all probable or realistic at that time because of the weakness of age, nevertheless, though he was weak in strength of body, he was not weak in the vigour of his faith, and he did not begin to search for proofs that this could or could not happen as doubters would do; nor was he concerned that the strength of his body had already been spent and that he was incapable of begetting children, inasmuch as he had now entered his one hundredth year.[13] He did not consider the age of his wife whose reproductive organs also had now withered through age, so that even if he himself had not yet failed in his ability to reproduce, still she was unfit for childbearing. None of these difficulties, I say, entered into his mind. He did not mistrust; he did not hesitate, but relied on the promises of God with his whole heart, as strong in faith as he was weak in body. Despairing of his own strength, he maintained a most certain hope from the strength of the promises, and claiming nothing for himself in this matter, he transferred all glory and praise to God alone. By his own unshaken trust he attested at once that God was truthful – since he was unwilling to deceive anyone, and omnipotent – since he was able to fulfil whatever he had promised, however much this exceeded human strength. He who has no need anywhere of service from us especially delighted with this glory, and on account of this it was imputed to Abraham as righteousness, as it says in Holy Scripture.

But the statement that faith was imputed to Abraham as righteousness must not be considered to have been written on account of Abraham alone. For Holy Scripture is concerned with more than just the glory of Abraham. Holy Scripture is also concerned with preparing a model[14] for us, who are the descendants of Abraham, and with making it clear to the whole world that just as Abraham gained this – that he was regarded as righteous before God – through commendation for his steadfast confidence apart from the protection or support of the law, so we must seek this with absolutely no[15] regard to the observance of the law. Abraham was called righteous because he believed God. For no other path to righteousness lies open except that we too believe in the same God who has fulfilled for us in Jesus Christ our Lord what he promised Abraham through the prototype of Isaac.For God raised Christ from the dead, proving that Abraham had not vainly believed, that it was God who gave life even to the dead, and who calls back those things which do not exist just as if they did. We ought therefore to attribute the righteousness and innocence we have received not to Moses, but to Christ, who voluntarily surrendered himself to death so that through faith[16] he might as a pure favour wash away our sins. And likewise he rose from the dead and lived again in order that we might refrain from deeds belonging to the dead and that we might not sin hereafter, doing the same deeds again on account of which Christ had met death. He died, I say, in order that he might slay sin in us, and he rose from the dead so that we who once died through him to our former sins, and were then raised again along with him and through him to a new life, might live henceforth for righteousness,[17] a righteousness we have received through his kindness.

Chapter 5

For since sins alone produce enmity between God and men, now that we who were impious and sinful have been made righteous – and this not through the Mosaic law which increased our offences the more, nor by the merit of our own deeds, but according to the example of our father, Abraham, by commendation for our faith – we have made our peace[1] with God the Father, to whom Abraham also was made a friend by the worth of his faith. And this has come about not through Moses but through the only Son of God, our Lord Jesus Christ. Christ, by washing away our sins with his blood and death, and reconciling God who was previously hostile to us because of our sins, has opened an approach for us, so that through the intervention of faith we might be led without the assistance of the law or circumcision to this grace of the gospel.

In this faith we stand firm, and not only do we stand eager and resolute,[2] but we even boast that we have both peace with God and a most certain hope spread before us. Our hope is that through the perseverance of faith we will enjoy at last the glory of God. And we do not envy the Jews if they boast about their circumcision. We will not repent of our faith which bears a far richer fruit. Nor will we repent of our glory, for the hope of this glory sustains and encourages us in the meantime. If it does not yet appear and if it must be reached by bearing many things, nevertheless even these very afflictions we count to our glory and praise. We endure them, as a badge of honour, for they open up for us the way to immortality. Since indeed we have taken up this new example from Christ and received from him an excellent doctrine, namely, that the virtue of endurance is strengthened by bearing evils, we become, by endurance, like gold from the fire, better tested and approved by God and men. Again, the more we have been tested by evils, the firmer is the hope of reward which is born in us. And indeed, there is no danger that this hope will deceive or forsake us, so that among the ungodly we should be ashamed[3] that we have believed. For even now we hold a most certain guarantee and pledge, namely, the wonderful and unheard of love of God toward us, which has not only been displayed publicly, but has also been engraved in full measure on our hearts and compels us to love him in return.[4] This comes to us through the Holy Spirit who has been given to us in place of the cold letter of the law as a pledge of the promise.

For unless God had deeply loved us with a kind of supreme tenderness, never would his only Son Jesus Christ by the will of the Father have come down to the earth, assumed a mortal body,and died for us; especially since at that time we were still very weak,[5] subject to our sinful desires, which the law could stir up but could not restrain. Yet such as we were, he deeply loved us in the hope of our salvation, indeed, he even loved the ungodly and those who serve idols. And he so loved us that he willingly submitted to death for our sake; there could be no clearer or more extraordinary evidence of love than this. And yet among men you would scarcely find anyone so much a friend that he would rescue an honest and deserving friend[6] from danger by his own death. But let us grant that someone might be found who would not refuse perhaps to undertake death for a good friend; still, God has surpassed all examples of human love, because he handed over his Son to death for the impious and the unworthy.

But if he has offered such kindness toward the ungodly and those who have done wrong, how much more will he also grant this to those now purified and reformed[7] and reconciled by the blood of the Son, that we do not sin again and fall back into his wrath, to be condemned all the more severely because to the sin of impiety we have added the evil of ingratitude. Christ died for us for a time, but he also rose again and will live forever. Just as he died for us, so he rose again for us. But if his death accomplished for us so much that, although previously we were faced with an angry and hostile God, afterwards we began to obtain his favour and kindness, much more will his life accomplish this for us, that we should not fall back into our old enmity. His death has taken away our sin, his life will protect our innocence.

His death rescued us[8] from the power of the devil, his life will preserve his Father's love toward us. These proofs of the divine love toward us are so evident that they render us fearless and offer us a sure hope that we will be safe from the wrath to come; moreover, they give us so much joy that it is a delight even to boast. Not that we take pride in our own merit, but we give thanks to God the Father, to whose kindness we owe this complete happiness. He wished to bestow this upon us, not through the law or[9] circumcision, but through Jesus Christ, his Son, by whose mediation we return to his favour. Thus it is clear that the whole of this benefit should be ascribed to none other than God himself and his only Son.[10]

And it was provided by the wonderful and secret plan of God that the way by which our well-being was restored would correspond to the way in which we had suffered ruin. Accordingly, through Adam alone, who first transgressed the law of God, sin crept into the world, and sin dragged along death as its companion inasmuch as sin is the poison of the soul.[11] And so it happened that the evil originated by the first of the race spread through all posterity, since no one fails to imitate the example of the first parent.[12] Just as sin originated through one man, so through the one Christ, in whom we are all born again through faith, innocence has been introduced, and life the companion of innocence; and this felicity, proceeding from the one source of the new race, flows down to all who belong to Christ by the relationship of faith and who follow eagerly in the footsteps of innocence by a blameless life.

Moreover, as soon as sin had once crept into our world and had seized the whole race of mankind, it could not be defeated either by the law of nature or by the Mosaic law, although laws were helpful to this extent, that those who sinned were now seen as guilty and as deserving punishment. Now just as sin is not imputed to boys in whom the law of nature does not yet have a place, since they are not yet old enough to discern right from wrong,[13] so also it was not imputed to the heathens if they violated the law of Moses. Therefore, prior to the law which revealed transgression, sin was not completely absent because of the law of nature, but people took liberties and sinned with virtual impunity as if they were bound by no law. And so, since he had not yet come who would take away the sin of the world and defeat the tyranny of death, death, which had entered the world through Adam, reigned with impunity also over those who had not wickedly sinned against God's precept as Adam had done.

Even then Adam was a type and figure of Christ who would come much later, not because he is in every way like Christ, but because to some extent he did display the image of Christ. The similarity consists in the fact that each was the first of his generation, but Adam of the earthly generation, Christ of the heavenly. There is also a similarity in the fact that from each something spread to all proceeding as from a source, but the earthly Adam was the origin of unrighteousness and death, the heavenly Adam the beginning of innocence and life.

And yet, even though they were similar in some respects, nevertheless they were not at all equal. Since in itself the act of saving is more powerful than the act of destroying, Christ has far more power to save than Adam had to destroy, and the obedience of Christ was much more effective in conferring life than the transgression of Adam in bringing on death. The goodness of Christ altogether conquers the wickedness of Adam; thus no one should attribute so much to the sin of the first parent that he doubts whether saving health can be restored. For if the author of sin so far prevailed that so many are liable to death on account of the deeds of one man, God's benefaction and his gift of kindness will the more prevail and will abound toward more men, a gift which he freely bestows upon us through one, likewise a man, Jesus Christ, the author of innocence. Through Christ God not only abolished the tyranny of death and sin, but he bestowed righteousness in place of sin and the sovereignty of life in place of the tyranny of death in such a way that, by the kindness of God, Adam's loss was worked out to our advantage.

Again, though destruction has been brought in through the sin of one man, Adam, and salvation through the innocence of the one Christ, nevertheless the two are not alike. For in fact destruction began in such a way that the sin of one man was spread to all his descendants, thus finally rendering all guilty;[14] conversely, the kindness of God is so bestowed that all the sins of all people which now have been heaped up and firmly established are at once abolished by the death of Christ. And not only are past sins abolished, but righteousness is freely bestowed also. But if the one sin of one man was so effective that it bound all under the tyranny of death and that those who sinned following the example of the first parent similarly bore the yoke of death, nevertheless the overflowing kindness of God bestows still more. Thus without doubt those who, following the example of Christ, embrace innocence and righteousness,[15] not only are freed from the tyranny of sin and death, but, now that life rules supreme, also rule through him, the one and only source of all our felicity. Therefore, it is fitting that just as through the offence of one man sin crept into the world and rendered all subject to death, so through the righteousness of one man we are made righteous and sharers in life, since his righteousness has been extended to all who believe and submit to the kingdom of life. For just as one man, Adam, by his failure to submit to the precept of God, dragged very many[16] into sin as imitators of the transgression of their ancestor, so one man, Christ, who obeyed God the Father even to the point of suffering on the cross, will render many righteous as followers of obedience.

But let us return to what we had begun a little earlier. If in the plan of God it had been determined to remove sin in this way and to confer righteousness and life, what was the point of introducing the law when it would confer nothing? And yet certainly the law conferred this much: that through it the kindness of God toward us became more clear and evident. For the more sin looms up and howls, the more the kindness of God, who frees us from sin, shines forth. The law revealed the tyranny of sin while struggling in vain against it. Its tyranny was powerful and effective, but the kindness of God was more powerful still; and we feel his kindness all the more in proportion to the harshness of the tyranny of death which we have experienced up to now. And we certainly owe to the law our understanding of God's goodness. It was a result of this goodness that, just as the devil gained the tyranny through sin, and brought upon all of us the death of our souls (which is the truest form of death),[17] so, thanks to God's bounty, innocence gained sovereignty and confers upon all life, whose author is Jesus Christ. It is he alone, our Lord and leader, about whom we boast, free now from servitude to death, under whose command we fought a little while ago.

Chapter 6

But because we have said that sin abounded through the law and that this was useful because through it the kindness of God abounded even more, let no one seize from this an opportunity for persisting in sin and think to himself: 'If sin reveals and magnifies the grace of God toward men, it is expedient to sin again and again so that grace may abound more and more.' Let such a wicked thought be far from pious minds. I have been speaking about the sins of our earlier life which God has turned to our advantage. But once we have been liberated from the tyranny of sin [and brought over] to the reign of innocence, let us by no means desert our liberator and go headlong into the old tyranny. Life and death are in conflict with each other to such an extent[1] that they destroy each other in turn, and they do not exist together at the same time on the same basis. And so, since as soon as we begin to live for Christ we are dead to the devil,[2] how is it fitting that we should still live for the devil to whom we are now dead? If we live for Christ we do not live for the devil. If we live for the devil, we are dead to Christ. But now we live for Christ and are dead to sin, which he crushed by his own death.

For since we have obtained the baptism of Christ, it is not fitting for you to avoid what that baptism either effects or denotes.[3] For when we are baptized in the name of Christ, together with him we die to our former sins which have been abolished by his death, and not only do we die together with him, but we are also buried with him, and this through the same baptism. Hence, just as Christ, who never lived for sin but died for our wickedness, was called back to eternal life, not by human strength but by the power of the Father, so we have been awakened through Christ from the death brought by sins. Dead to our former sins and living now the new life, let us follow in the footsteps of piety, always progressing from virtue to greater virtue.[4] For since we are grafted to the body of Christ through baptism and in a way are transformed into him, whatever we perceive [as] having been performed in him who is our head we, who are the members of his body,[5] must either imitate wholly, or hope to do so. Christ has risen, he ascended into heaven, he sits at the right hand of the Father. These things have already been accomplished in Christ; and they are what we must hope for at last, if only we emulate, and, as it were, practise them as far as we can. Consequently, if having received baptism we die to our former sins and wicked desires, and thus represent the death of Christ as we are able, it is right that henceforth by avoiding shameful things and by engaging continually in pious deeds, we also imitate the resurrection of Christ.

Meanwhile, we imitate Christ's death[6] in this manner, not by actually seeking death or doing violence to our bodies, but, as you very well know, if we so completely lose feeling for all our former desires that we seem dead to them. Let us imagine that according to our double origin there are two men in us,[7] the one old and more base and reflecting the earthly through likeness to Adam, the other new and eager for heavenly things as one who traces his origin from the heavenly Christ. Now this old man in us has, so to speak, been killed; he was lifted up on the cross together with Christ, and that whole desire for perishable things has been extinguished. It is the universal force of these perishable things which one might rightly call 'the body of sin.' But this body dies in us to our benefit whenever we kill our harmful passions and no longer are the slaves of sin. Now, whoever truly imitates the death of Christ in the manner described is received into the number of the righteous; he has ceased to be subject to sin, from whose tyranny he is now free. Therefore, if, as I have now often said, we have died together with Christ in his death and have been freed from our former sins, we believe that by the kindness of this same Christ we shall henceforth live together with the living Christ if our conduct is innocent and blameless, and we shall so live that we shall never again fall back into death. And in so doing, we shall reproduce the image of Christ as far as possible. For Christ did not rise again in such a way that he permitted death once more to have authority over him, but he lived again henceforth to be immortal. The death that he died to sin was a death once for all; but the life he now lives, he lives to God by whose power he has been called to immortal life.

Therefore, following the example of Christ, consider that you, too, have died once for all to sin. Your former sins and desires have been snuffed out, and you have become new. So reflect that, as those brought back to life, you are living a life immortal to God by whose kindness you have obtained innocence. No one lives to God except one who is alive to piety, righteousness, and all the other virtues. For since we are incorporated into the body of Christ and have been made one with him, it is necessary that the members correspond to the head. But Christ is the head. Since he ever lives to God, it is fitting that we likewise should live to God through the same Jesus Christ our Lord. Just as Christ has once for all been raised from the dead and does not suffer again any tyranny of death, likewise you must struggle so that sin, once destroyed, does not recover its lost tyranny over you and renew the authority of death.[8] For that is what will happen if you give in to your impious desires, by which the devil entices you into your former servitude. Your members have now been consecrated to Christ; do not allow them henceforth to serve at the devil's command to do unrighteous deeds, for the devil has been conquered by Christ. No, rather you should take care from now on so to conduct yourselves in every aspect of your existence that it will be clear from your whole life how, together with Christ, you have left behind things which belong to death and have been transformed into newness of life. This you will accomplish if hereafter your members, that is, all the powers of body and mind, fight not in the service of the devil on behalf of sins, but in the service of God on behalf of righteousness. For it is right that our entire selves should be in the service of God in whose army[9] we have once for all enlisted, and that we have nothing to do with the devil from whose allegiance we have broken away and whose yoke we have shaken off. Nor indeed is there any danger that sin will drag you back against your will into the former servitude inasmuch as now you are subject, not to the law which used to stimulate your desires instead of restraining them, but to the grace of God. Just as this grace was able to free us from the tyranny of sin, so now it can enable us not to return to the tyranny of sin.

But far be it from anyone so to interpret my words that, because I have said you are free from the law, you think you may sin with impunity since the law has been annulled; or think that the grace of God, which has forgiven your former sins, has given you licence to sin in the same way in the future without punishment. On the contrary, we must abstain even more from

sins, because we are no longer compelled to do good deeds by a command-
ment of the law in the manner of a slave, but we are stirred as sons through
kindness and love to do so. Servitude has been changed, not abolished
outright. When you ceased to be slaves of the law, you began to be slaves to
Christ – to serve whom is the height of felicity. Now in part it is left to you to
decide which one you wish to embrace,[10] for you cannot hold on to both at
the same time. You were free to decide not to become the slave of anyone; but
once you have voluntarily subjected yourself to the authority of the Lord
and have begun to obey him, you ought to obey him alone to whom you have
made yourself a slave. Accordingly, to those who devote themselves to sin,
and surrender themselves to its service, death is the fruit of servitude. On
the other hand, those who devote themselves to Christ must obey him, but
they obey him to their own good. For although they will make no gain by
their obedience to Christ, they will obtain righteousness for themselves, that
is, the harmony and concord of all virtues. However, I rejoice with you and I
am grateful to Christ for this reason, that although formerly you were slaves
in this most terrible servitude, dedicated to graven images and to foul
desires, now you have left the tyranny of the devil and have given
yourselves into the command of Christ freely[11] and sincerely. In the future
you will live not according to the will of the passions or of law, but according
to the new form of evangelical teaching to which you have been brought over
from your previous errors, and brought over in such a way that you have
passed outright to a different authority. Thus you are freed from the
dominion of sin, but brought over from it that you may serve righteousness
and do the commands of God. But let it not be thought hard that you are
commanded to serve virtue. Just as the nature of sin is far different from the
nature of innocence, so the reward is far different too. Consequently, if we
consider the matter closely, we clearly must serve God much more diligently
than we serve the devil. For whoever is a servant to sin serves the devil. He
serves God who is the servant of innocence.

Meanwhile, however, I will not demand from you what by right I could
demand. I shall accommodate my speech to the infirmities of certain persons
in whom the spirit has not yet grown to maturity, and the passions threaten
still to sprout again. I ask only that you rank righteousness as highly as you
did sin. Just as previously you surrendered your members to serve filth and
sin so that you sank from foulness to foulness under the power of desire and
became increasingly defiled, so now it is right that in the same way you
present your bodies to the service of righteousness, for you have voluntarily[12] declared that you are under its jurisdiction. Continually advancing from
virtue to virtue, you should always make yourselves more pure and faultless
than you were before. For it seems entirely unfair that Christ should not hold

even such jurisdiction over you as the devil formerly held, and that you should not offer the same allegiance to mistress righteousness as you did to tyrant sin. Even if something could in one way or another be alleged as a pretext for excusing your former life – namely, that as long as you were involved in paganism, seeing that you were slaves of sin, you seemed strangers to righteousness and did not owe anything to God to whom you were not yet dedicated – now there is nothing which can be alleged as an excuse.

But if the right itself, by its very nature, does not stir you enough, let those of you who have experienced both kinds of servitude consider how very different are the fruits of the two kinds of obedience. Remember that when you were serving sin you obeyed like slaves the most obscene desires. What reward, I ask, did you obtain? Sins themselves bring their own punishment with them insofar as they immediately defile and contaminate, and they corrupt by such shameful and disgraceful deeds that now, after you have come to your senses, as though waking up from a drunken fit of vices, you are ashamed of yourselves, and your mind is repelled by the very thought of your former pleasures. You see that these immediate wages must not be pursued. And yet beyond this recompense, the devil's ultimate reward to those who serve him is eternal death. But in the meantime a life so lived is not really life, but the most loathsome death of all.[13] Now see how happily servitude has been changed for you who have been freed from the tyranny of the devil and have begun to be servants of God. Of course you observe how unequal they are as lords. But if you want also the reward: first, instead of living in foulness and impiety, you are living in innocence, purity and holiness, which alone is true life. Next, when the time of brief servitude is completed, the highest reward of immortality awaits you. Now compare the devil with this God, holiness with filth, immortal life with eternal death. For plainly, the matter stands as I said a moment ago. The reward of the devil is death,[14] with which he repays a foul and miserable servitude. Those, on the other hand who serve God with all their might have immortality repaid to them, not as a due reward but as a benefit from a kind Father. And this comes not through Moses but through Jesus Christ our Lord; for the Father has wished that whatever he has chosen to bestow upon us should be credited to Christ, not to any law or circumcision.

Chapter 7

For Christ has freed us not only from sin and death but also from servitude to the law, which had been given only for a time. He has freed not only the gentiles, who were not subject to this law, but also the Jews themselves who had previously been subject to the law of Moses. That this is so can be learned, if you like, by the testimony of the law itself. Meanwhile, I call upon you Jews, who, since you maintain the prescriptions of the law, cannot be ignorant that a man subject to any law (as you formerly were subject to the Mosaic law) is under obligation to the law just so long as that law lives,[1] that is, maintains its strength and force. If the law should be rejected or repealed, he ceases to be subject to it. For in our obligation to the law, nothing else has to be observed than what the law orders, as in the obligation of a woman married to a man. For a woman married to a man and subject to the authority of her husband is bound to the man as long as the man lives. But as soon as he has died, the woman is released from the bonds of this marriage, and after the death of her husband she is thenceforth subject only to her own authority. Accordingly, if a woman attempts to marry another man while the husband still lives, under whose authority she once came, she will be considered an adulteress who has left her husband from whom she could have been freed only by death. On the other hand, if she waits until her husband is dead, she is free of her obligation to him and is now under her own authority; then she has the right to take another husband if she wishes. It is true a master's authority is passed on to his heir, and a slave, when his master dies, changes masters, but not his status. But a husband's authority over his wife is not likewise passed on to another man; it does not extend beyond the husband's life. If the husband were immortal, the wife would always remain obligated to him.

Now the law of Moses, inasmuch as it foreshadowed Christ by means of figures and ceremonies, was given only for a certain time. When the light came forth the shadows yielded, and when the truth appeared the likeness of truth departed. And because the Mosaic law was mortal (so to speak) it is not surprising if it is now dead. Consequently, as long as the time of the law lasted the law was in force, and it had authority over those who had submitted to it. You, however, have nothing to do with the Mosaic law since that law is now dead to you, and you in turn are dead to it – even if it were alive. For after Christ – who is the truth – appeared, the whole Mosaic law was repealed, certainly as far as the letter of the law is concerned. But since you are incorporated into the body of Christ, joined to him as the bride to the bridegroom and liberated from your old bonds, you have submitted to the authority of a new bridegroom – an *immortal* bridegroom,[2] for he rose once for all from the dead and will live forever. Henceforth, you must not think about a new marriage or divorce. (In any case, what an affront it would be to such a husband if you continued to receive aid from your former husband!) Instead, just as you have produced some kind of fruit from the law as from a husband, a fruit not unworthy of the husband, in the same way now that you have found a happier marriage, you must endeavour to bring forth fruit worthy of the father-in-law God and the bridegroom Christ. For as long as we were subject to the gross and carnal law as to a husband, the law seemed to rule over us as though with the authority of a husband, while desires, more fierce thanks to the opportunity provided by the law, were so strong in our bodies that we were dragged into sin in the manner of slaves. Thus we begot unhappy offspring from our unhappy union bringing forth whatever was born only for its death and destruction. But now that we have been liberated from the lordship of the law, under which we previously lived – though actually, insofar as we lived in sin, we did not live at all but were dead, and yet we were held in that law for the time prescribed – it is not right still to hold to this carnal husband, that is, to the letter of the law. Rather, we should serve a new bridegroom, one who is heavenly and spiritual, not through antiquated letter, but through the new spirit which we have received from him as a token of marriage.

But I fear that it will occur to some slanderer to suppose that I condemn the law itself as the author of sin, since I said that as the servants of the law we have fallen headlong into sin and death. For he will say that just as it is characteristic of righteousness to produce life, so it is characteristic of sin to produce death; if the law brings forth death, either the law itself could appear to be sin or at least in league with sin. God forbid that anyone draw this conclusion. The law is not the author of sin; it is the revealer of sin.[3] Sin lay hidden and deceived us, in a way, before the law existed, while everyone acquiesced in his own desires[4] and thought that whatever especially pleased him was permitted and that it was right to desire anything he found delightful. Therefore, I indulged myself and would not, for example, have known that the desire for another man's property was a sin, had not the law forbidden me to desire it. And indeed the law was brought in with the intention of restraining sins. But due to our sin, the results were quite the opposite of the intention. Inasmuch as the law revealed sin and did not add strength to enable us to fight back against our vices, it happened that the lust for sin took advantage of this opportunity and was all the more aroused, for human nature is more inclined to those things which are prohibited.[5] Thus, since before the law was revealed I had no knowledge of certain sins while of others I did have knowledge (but understood that I could do them, as they had not been prohibited), my mind felt relatively slight and sluggish temptations to commit sin. For we love those things more indifferently which we are permitted to have whenever we please. But so many forms of sin were revealed by the disclosure of the law that a whole troop of passions was aroused by the prohibition and redoubled its efforts to incite us to sin. Thus, by this means sin received strength and vigour. Before there was a law sin was sluggish and virtually dead. But I in the meantime lived as if outside the law, or rather I thought I lived – as if it were permitted to sin with impunity. But, when the precept forbidding me to sin intervened, sin not only was not restrained but actually seemed to gain new life and to receive new vigour. But while sin was gaining new life, I who seemed before to be alive, now died, recognizing through the law that I was guilty, and sinning nevertheless. And the result was that what had been established for the support of life became death for me, not however by the fault of the law, but by my own fault. For since the inclination to sin was innate in me, my sick mind, eager to sin, seized the opportunity provided by the law. And so the devil,[6] using a good instrument in a wicked way, seduced me into sin, taking the opportunity provided by the law, and through sin he struck me down so that I found myself a prisoner and in the power of another. Consequently, there is no reason here for us to accuse falsely the law which has been given by a good God, and thus sets forth holy, just, and good precepts. For whatever prohibits evil must be good.

But again someone might object: 'Since like produces like, if the law is good how has it produced death in me which is certainly evil and is the usual product of sin?' This objection would be rightly taken if the law had produced death in us. That, however, as I said a moment ago, is far from being the case. For it is not the law which begets death in us; sin itself more truly has been the cause of our destruction. Sin is such an evil that it changed a thing good in itself into a curse. Thus it became more evident how abominable a thing sin is by whose fault things which are very good fall into the worst state. And the precept of the law provided the opportunity for this to happen but was not responsible for it happening. The law is spiritual, as we all know, and it invites us to goodness; but for its failure to bring about what it is striving for, I myself am responsible (to take myself as an example). For I am carnal and inclined to evil and thus subject to and bound by sin through the long habit of sinning,[7] like a purchased slave bound to his own master, so that I myself do not know what I ought to do, so blinded have I become by my own vices. For I do not do that which mind and reason keep telling me is good. Although I long for the good by mind and reason, nevertheless, conquered as I am by desire, I do instead what is shameful – though I hate it for its shamefulness. Thus, even the wicked understand that no blame is to be laid upon the law. For if I am enticed by perverse desire to commit what mind and reason condemn and shun, certainly I witness that the law is good which has forbidden the things I myself condemn with the better part of my mind. The law must be good, for it prohibits those things which I know to be evil even while I do them in obedience to the flesh.

But someone will say: 'Why then do you not obey your mind, if it agrees with the law calling you to goodness and deterring you from what is shameful?' To reply: one should imagine that I am two men in one (inasmuch as now, to make my point, I have put on the mask of a man still subject[8] to vices and passions), one a carnal[9] and gross man, and another more pure and less gross. The first of these I call the external man, the second the internal man. The one, subject to passions, is inclined to vices; the other, retaining some seeds of goodness, strives in one way or another toward goodness and, insofar as he is able, protests and resists in the midst of vices. Now we really take our identity from our better part. Whenever, then, my mind, consenting to the law, strives toward the good, and yet does what is contrary to goodness, I do not seem to be the one doing what I do. For who would do what he does not wish to do? But the power of sinning and the inclination to vices is implanted in my grosser nature, so that although I will the good,I do what is shameful. Now if anyone wishes to judge me in terms of this baser nature, I confess that there is nothing good in me. For no matter how much I desire what is good according to the impulse of my reason, still the ability to fulfil what I approve is not present. As long as the desire alluring me to evil is stronger than reason encouraging me to good, I do not do what I desire, that is, the good; but rather I do what I condemn, that is, evil. But if one does not seem to do what he does against his will, when I do what I do not wish to do according to the better part of man, it does not seem to me that I do what I do, but rather the power of sin itself implanted in the grosser part of me. The law does not remove this baser self from me; nevertheless, if at any time I attempt to obey the law, it forces me to acknowledge that my evil is deeply implanted and impressed upon my mind. For indeed the power of goodness which I see in the law draws one to itself. But from the opposite side, I discover another law in the members of the outward man, opposing the law consonant with reason. Now when reason calls in one way, desire in another, the worse in me gains control, the better is conquered. For the inclination to sin is so deeply fixed in the flesh, and the habit of committing wrong is so powerful (as if now a part of my nature), that like some unwilling and struggling captive I am dragged into sin.[10]

Oh, unhappy man, tied to such a troublesome servitude! Who will deliver me from this flesh, subject to so many passions, so many vices, so many struggles, and always leading me on to death? Is it not right for one to cry out in this way who is pressed down by so hard a necessity? Hence, we certainly owe the more to the kindness of God towards us. He has snatched us from such great evils, not through the law of circumcision, but through Jesus Christ our Lord. If this had not happened, I myself also, although I am one and the same man, would be torn apart in the same way, so that with my mind I would be a servant to the law of God insofar as I desire goodness, while with my flesh I would be a servant to the law of sin, insofar as the allurement of sin conquered me.

Chapter 8

But if there still remain some remnants of former servitude in some Christians, they will overcome these by a pious zeal and will not be dragged against their will into any serious sin for which those deserve to be condemned who, through faith and baptism, have once been incorporated into Jesus Christ.[1] We have ceased to live by the will of carnal desires and passions now that the law of Christ – which is spiritual and the bearer of life, more efficacious, and conquering – has liberated us from the law of sin and from death, the companion of sin. The law of Moses could not bring this about insofar as it is carnal and consequently powerless; therefore God looked to our salvation with a new plan. For (as I have said) just as in one man there are two men, the carnal and the spiritual, so in the one Mosaic law there are as it were two laws,[2] the one base and carnal, the other spiritual. The first part of the law was conveyed by Moses, and just as it is not perpetual, so it has too little power to fulfil our salvation. The other part of the law is spiritual, effective, powerful, and immortal, which Christ, like a second Moses, delivered to us. It was appropriate, furthermore, for flesh to destroy flesh, sin to conquer sin, and death to overcome death. Therefore God, eager for human salvation, sent his own Son. Even though he is a stranger to all contagion of sin, nevertheless he was dressed in the same flesh in which other sinners are clothed. For he assumed the nature common to all and lived as a sinner among sinners.[3] Indeed, he was crucified as a criminal among criminals. To such an extent did he adopt the mask of sin, so to speak, that through the form of sin he first conquered sin, then destroyed it, made a victim for our sins. And since he died in this way in accordance with the flesh which he had put on, he subdued death, which used to be our master through the passions of the flesh and the carnal law; and he brought it about that for the future the flesh of the law would be abolished and that the better part of the law, which we have called spiritual, would take its place. The latter does not produce wrath as the former did, but it confers true righteousness on those who live, not according to the letter of the law in the manner of Jews, but according to the spirit of the law like men born again in Christ. In the Jews, a kind of shadow of righteousness had been traced out; in us a true and perfect piety has been realized through Jesus Christ. When the object of one's zeal has been changed, this is proof of a new kind of life.

We see that those who persevere in the old Judaism, inasmuch as they are still carnal, value highly the things which are carnal. Those, on the other hand, who have been incorporated into Christ have begun to be spiritual, and disregarding those things which pertain to the flesh, they are seized by a passion for those things which belong to the spirit. Now what each person especially cares about depends upon the kind of person he himself is. We are mortals according to the flesh. But the immortal Christ has called us into life since he himself is our life. Moreover, that carnal law of the Jews when observed only according to the letter[4] is opposed to Christ and draws us away from Christ. Consequently it produces death, for it fights against the one who alone is the author of life. For the Jews, by their zeal and enthusiasm for their law, killed the author of righteousness and life. On the other hand, those who have rejected the letter of the law and who follow things which are spiritual find life in Christ. They do not engage in a fight to the death over lifeless and trivial observances, but pursuing things which pertain to love, they have peace with all men. Superstition is quarrelsome, true piety is quiet and tranquil. And it is not surprising if the man who has no peace with God cannot get along with men. For adherence to the carnal law (which God wished to become obsolete through Christ so that the spiritual law might follow) is nothing else than rebellion against God. For this state of mind, inasmuch as it disagrees with the will of God, cannot help fighting against God who calls us to very different things. Consequently, let no one think that it is a small danger to lean on the letter of the law and to persevere in it. We please men in vain unless we please God. But those who doggedly hold on to the Mosaic law according to the carnal understanding do not please God, nor can they please him unless they reject the flesh and go over to the side of the spirit. No matter how many new moons and sabbaths the Jews may urge, they will not attain what they promise themselves.

These things do not apply to you who are spiritual and have nothing to do with the carnal law, provided[5] you so live that the Spirit of God sees fit to dwell in your heart. For one who is merely baptized[6] still belongs to the flesh unless he drinks in the Spirit of Christ and is breathed upon by his Spirit. We are joined to Christ not by ceremonies but by the Spirit. One who is void of the Spirit is alien to Christ. But if Christ is in you, since he is nothing other than purity, truth, temperance, and other virtues,[7] what place is there for vices in you? One who has Christ must imitate him. He has died in the flesh, as we said a moment ago, but he lives an immortal life. We imitate Christ[8] if the body, that is, that baser part of ourselves which tempts us to deadly things by the attractions of desire, is dead and free from all passion for sinning; and if the spirit lives, that is, the better part of ourselves, enticing us to the good, carrying us off by its own force to those things which belong to righteousness.[9] And so if the Spirit of God, who raised Jesus Christ from the dead, truly dwells in you, he will not be idle. The Spirit is full of life and effective. According to your capacity he will likewise effect in you what he effected in Christ. He raised Christ from the dead and does not allow him again to die. Likewise, after your perverse affections have been abolished he will call you back into life from sin which is true death. God will do this through his Spirit, the author of life, which dwells in you.[10] Therefore we are alive to this Spirit, we are subject to the Spirit, and we must obey the Spirit rather than the flesh to which we are now dead. For we ceased to owe anything to the flesh after we began to be one with Christ. Therefore, far be it from us to live henceforth in accordance with the desire of the flesh which ought rather to serve the Spirit. You have been called into life. Moreover, if you have been living according to the flesh you are hastening to death; on the other hand, if by the strength of the Spirit you kill the desires of the flesh, you will live since those desires are dead. The rule of the Spirit is not hard. It challenges us to great things, but as those who are willing and eager. For it breathes into us the strength of love for which nothing can be difficult, nothing can be unpleasant. Just as the body lives by its own spirit, so the soul lives by its own spirit. If the spirit of the body is faint, the whole body is sluggish; if it is vigorous, the whole body is lively.

And so all those who are impelled by the Spirit of God are sons of God. Sons imitate and reflect the character of their father and eagerly do of their own accord what they feel will be pleasing to him. Servants, because they are not joined to their master by nature, are restrained by fear and perform their duty when threatened with punishment. That is the case with the Jews, who are seduced by servitude to the law. Once freed from this servitude, you do not fall back again into the same servitude and so find yourself coerced through fear. Instead, you have received the Spirit of God, through whom you have been adopted into the number, not of servants, but of the sons of God. The Spirit furnishes us with this confidence so that we cry into the ears of God the word which parents most like to hear, addressing him as 'Father, Father!' We would not dare to beseech him with this word unless we were confident that we are his sons and that he is our kind Father. For we are not under compulsion but live of our own free choice according to his pleasure. In any case, he would not have imparted his Spirit to us unless he considered us his sons. Therefore, this pledge, so to speak, and symbol of paternal love, gives confidence to our spirit that we are the sons of him who gave the pledge.

But if we are sons, not servants, then certainly we are also heirs. We are heirs indeed of God, from whom as the source all things flow; and as co-heirs with Christ, incorporated into his body, we have begun to have the same Father as Christ, through whom we have attained the right to a common inheritance. However, the possession of this inheritance becomes ours only if we travel toward it on the same road by which Christ himself reached it. Christ attained the possession of the good by bearing evil, he came to power through obedience, he came to glory through dishonour, he attained immortality by death. We must therefore suffer with him so that we may enjoy these gifts with him, we must obey so that we may reign with him, we must bear the insults of the world so that we may be glorified with him, we must die with him for a time so that we may live with him forever. This is the law by which one gains this inheritance: since the inheritance is immortal and so great that it transcends all the capacity and judgment of the human mind, if all the afflictions of this life were heaped upon a single person they would be light if they paid for the reward of future glory which is procured through them, and so to speak, bought in return for troubles.

Now granted that we already have a pledge of this happiness so that we ought not despair, nevertheless it is not yet perfect and complete because this body is subject to death and sorrows. In the meantime, we are allowed a kind of secret taste of our future happiness, inwardly through the Spirit; but our full happiness will be revealed at the resurrection of our bodies, when we will leave behind the pain of this whole mortal existence and reign forever with the immortal Christ. Meanwhile, the whole structure of the world awaits this time, as if longing for the day on which the glory of the sons of God will be brought to light after their number has been completed. For while they are still weighed down with a mortal body and are afflicted by hunger, thirst, death, sorrows, and various other evils, even the world itself seems to participate in some way in human misery. This is because earth, water, air, the very celestial bodies,[11] and finally even the angels[12] themselves, were created especially to serve the requirements of men. Consequently the world itself is not going to be free until perfect freedom comes to the sons of God. In the meantime the world endures servitude unwillingly. For even in things without a mind there is a certain native craving for perfection. It endures, however, out of obedience to him by whose will it has been given over to this servitude, and it endures more patiently because it understands that it has not been given over forever, but on the condition that as soon as the sons of God have been fully liberated from every taint of mortality, then even the world itself will cease to be subject to the inconveniences of mortality. For we see that all the elements of the world are altered by so many transformations and are subject to so many corruptions – that the sun and the moon (apart from the fact that they labour almost in vain to restore things which are always transitory), feel their own defects, and the stars fight with the stars. Moreover, there can be no doubt that the whole crowd of angels, contemplating our calamities from above, are moved by a kind of pious compassion toward us and, as far as they can, grieve for us in our misfortunes. Thus, does not the whole cosmos[13] groan with us and as though in childbirth desire an end to its labour and pains?

It ought to seem less surprising that this happens to other things when we, too, who, after the advent of the Saviour,[14] were the first of mortals to be breathed upon by the Spirit of Christ (and this not in an ordinary way), are still subject to so many evils (partly on account of the various necessities of this life and partly on account of the wickedness of the impious) that very often among ourselves we groan and are compelled daily to feel grief for the misfortunes that come from without. In our prayers we long for that day when the whole body of Christ, complete in its members, will be delivered from all troubles and finally exchange its base and carnal being for its spiritual and immortal being. In the meantime we bear whatever evils afflict us through the hope of the happiness promised by Christ. Although we have received a pledge of our salvation from Christ, nevertheless he did not grant us full salvation here, but wanted us to wait for it in the age to come. In truth, our perfect salvation is dependent on future events of which we have received a certain hope. However, hope is not of things present and visible before our eyes, but of those which are not yet seen. For who has ever been said to hope for what he sees with his eyes? Here we would not be praised for our faith or hope if all the things which Christ has promised to us were now visible. But precisely in this way are we rendered acceptable to God by our faith[15] if we discern with the eyes of faith things which cannot be seen with the eyes of the body, and if we meanwhile persevere in our sorrows and wait with persistent hope for what has been promised.

In the meantime, suffering in the flesh is painful, but perhaps it is useful for us to suffer in this way. Our spirit is sympathetic and fights against the weakness of the body, but the Spirit of God breathes upon us, sustaining our flesh in its weakness and through hope giving us the resolution to bear all things, pointing out clearly what we should desire in our prayers or what we must pray to avoid. Now we ourselves according to human feelings, do not know what we should desire or how to ask for it. Consequently, it is not rare that we pray for pernicious rather than health-giving things. I can testify to this from my own experience. Once when I was bearing an affliction of the body only with great difficulty, I persistently implored divine help, asking three times that Satan, by whom I was then afflicted, might depart from me. My request was denied, because it was not expedient for me to obtain it.[16] What I was given brought health, not pleasure. Indeed God does listen to the prayers of those who belong to him if only they pray not according to the desires of the flesh but according to the wish[17] of the Spirit acting in us in hidden ways.[18] Even if we ourselves are silent the Spirit solicits God for us, and he does this not in a human way but by indescribable groans.[19]

Sometimes the human spirit prays with great sighs to avert external affliction, or prays for bodily conveniences, thinking that trivial things are of most importance. But that heavenly Spirit which is incorporated into the hearts of the pious demands things which, if they are absent, are to be desired with unspeakable groans; if they are present, they bring true and perfect beatitude.[20] If you want others to do something for you, you have to use speech to make your request, because they do not know what you want unless they have learned it from you, nor do they sufficiently perceive what is good for you. But God, who searches out even the inmost depths of the heart and looks deeply within us, knows even when we are silent what the Spirit longs for. As often as the Spirit intercedes for the saints, grieving for their afflictions, it intercedes not according to human feeling but according to the will of God. It desires only what contributes toward our eternal salvation, it desires only what contributes toward the glory of God. One who desires these things from the bottom of his heart, even if perhaps he errs in his choice, nevertheless does not err in his intention. Therefore God gives generously, not what is demanded, but what is more conducive to fulfilling the true intention behind your prayer.

We need not fear that we may be overcome by the magnitude of evils and fail, for we consider it most certain that no matter which of these evils befalls the pious, all things turn out for the good; so great is the favour of God toward those whom he has chosen by his fixed will and plan and has called into this happiness. Ours is the attempt but the outcome depends on the decree of God.[21] Those whom God has chosen have not been chosen at random. He knew those who belong to him long before he called them. He not only knew those whom he called, but by an unalterable decision,[22] he had determined that they would be grafted into the body of Jesus his Son and be transformed into his likeness. In defeating flesh and death Christ triumphed and entered upon immortality so that the members may likewise hope for themselves what they see already accomplished in the head. Thus, through one Son God would produce many sons for himself, among whom Christ Jesus would be the head and leader and, as it were, the first born, sharing his own rights also with others. To make firm our faith that he will bring to completion what he has once begun, God has now called through the gospel (and not in vain) those whom, before the beginning of time, he had known and chosen, and about whom he had already published an announcement of his intention in the oracles of the prophets; and having called them by his kindness, he changed the evil into the good, the guilty into the innocent. There remains only the glory! And this glory has reached us now as well, in large measure, unless you think it is not magnificent enough to be free from sin, to flourish in the glory of innocence, to have pure affections, to be incorporated with Christ so as to be one with him, to have his Spirit as a pledge, to be the heir of God and the co-heir of Christ. When all this befalls us, how can we have doubts that the rest will be fulfilled in its own time?

Since all this is true, how can anyone even speak about despair? You see how many proofs God has already used to show his love and kindness toward us. If God stands by us, what could any adversary do? What power will human spitefulness have when God protects us? Or what should we not now expect from a God well disposed to us who, although we were not yet reconciled, did not spare his only Son but offered him alone for us all? He emptied him completely and cast him down so that he might lift us up; he made him to be sin so that we might be freed from sins; he handed him over to death so that we might be restored to life. Consequently, since he gave his Son in whom all things exist, does it not follow that along with the gift of his Son, everything else belonging to the Son was given us as well, since God has made us co-heirs with Christ? Or rather, what will he not bestow on us, after giving his Son, who is more important than any living creature? There is no danger that God will turn from us and change his mind toward us through the work of a false accuser. For who would dare to introduce an accusation against those whom God himself has chosen by a predestined and unalterable judgment and whom he counts as his own? Will he listen to a slanderer charging those whom he himself has freely forgiven all sins? God, the judge of all, has absolved us from the guilt of our former life and considers us just. Now who will condemn those who have been absolved? And yet we must beware lest we fall back into our former sins. Christ is one whose love toward us is so unusual that he even died to save us; in fact he rose from the dead for us in order that he might not fail his own followers. This great advocate, who is also judge, is seated at the right hand of God the Father (to whom he is equal in every respect),[23] and he pleads our cause before God. Since by the death of the Son the Father has absolved us from all guilt, and since we are so dear to the Son, what should we fear from the devil in the future, or from anyone who is an agent of the devil, who either accuses or condemns us?

Since we have been laid under obligation to God and Christ by so many acts of kindness and so many pledges, who will ever tear us away from their love, so that we do not return the great love they have shown us? Any storm of human wickedness? Suffering or distress? Hunger or want? Shipwreck or some similar sudden danger? Persecution by the impious or the sword threatening death? That mystical author of Psalms foresaw long ago the things which would happen to the pious in this world when, inspired by the divine Spirit, he prophesied [Psalm 44:22]: 'Because we are handed over daily unto death on your account, we are regarded as sheep destined for the slaughter.' However harsh these things may seem, still there is no reason why they should frighten us. They can happen, but they cannot overwhelm us. Indeed, the more heavily they weigh on us, the more they will encourage our love towards Christ and the love of Christ towards us until everywhere we come away victorious, not at all by assisting ourselves, but by the protection of the one to whom we owe everything. For Christ so loves us that he will not allow us to be conquered. We are mindful of the kindness of Christ toward us and will not be shaken by the insults of evil men from returning the love of Christ.

But up to the present I have called to mind only ordinary things. Now I will tell you something even more bold, for I have been most certainly and especially convinced of it. More frightening were the dangers which could have arisen from invisible realities and attacked the mind, not just the body; for if we no longer attach importance to the body, we cannot be frightened by dangers which threaten it. But we need not fear anything from this direction since neither any common angel (though more powerful than any man), nor some pre-eminent one among the angels, whom they call principalities and[24] powers, neither any height nor any depth (that is, whether they attack from above or below, whether by the appearance of goodness or its opposite – even if wonders come forth from heaven or the terrors of hell threaten us),[25] neither present nor future dangers (whether the danger threatens us now, or whether its threat is aimed at the future life), even if – to be brief – there is anything worse than these, whether it is here now or appears anywhere in creation, whether visible or invisible, however strong and powerful, it will nevertheless be unable to draw us away from the love by which we are bound to God through Jesus Christ his Son, our Lord.

Chapter 9

Would that even all the Jews might abandon their Moses and be converted to Christ. The Jews now persuade themselves that it is sufficient for gaining salvation if they are sons of Abraham and possess the law once given to them by God. However, none of this will profit them unless they show themselves worthy through faith[1] of being drawn and cherished by God. But Christ, even though promised by the law and received by the gentiles, is stubbornly rejected by them. And I would not say this out of hatred of my people, even though they are everywhere hostile to me. Christ (who knows all things) is my witness that what I say is true; my conscience (whose counsellor and examiner is the Holy Spirit) is my witness that I tell no lies. The destruction of certain ones who are perishing by their own fault distresses me in a greater measure and wears me down with perpetual sadness. So far am I from hating Jews that I would choose, if it were permitted me, to buy their salvation with my own destruction, and I myself would not refuse to be rejected by Christ if only those to whom I have been joined by a relationship of nation and race would likewise be united with me in the faith of Christ.

And just as they are Israelites by race, I wish that they would truly become Israelites by understanding the truth; for they of all people had the best reason to embrace the one whom the law had promised. This is the nation which God formerly singled out from the others and chose peculiarly for himself; he considered other nations as though illegitimate and favoured this one as genuine and true sons. Glory and dignity are the special possessions of this nation, because they rejected images and worshipped the true God. In their possession are the authority and privilege of the law which was established by God. In their possession are pacts and agreements entered upon with God. In their possession are the worship and sacred rites according to God's order. In their possession are the oracles of the prophets long ago predicting the advent of Christ and promising the happiness about which I boasted a moment ago. These trace their ancestry from those famous men who were most pleasing to God, the luminaries and founders of our nation – Abraham, Isaac, Jacob, and others – and from their stock Christ saw fit to be born according to the flesh. In this respect, at least, they are, whether they like it or not, already close relatives of Christ, who is by far more outstanding than the fathers by whose titles they advertise themselves. Indeed, no matter how pious those famous men might have been, nevertheless they were nothing more than men. But Christ is a man in such a way that at the same time he is also God,[2] not the God peculiar to this or that nation, but the God of the whole world, and a God who is one with the Father. He is in command of all, and all these things are carried out by his inscrutable wisdom. Because of such an unusual love for the human race, praise and thanksgiving are owed to him alone for all eternity.[3] Amen.

All the more must the impiety of certain Jews be denounced. For in slandering the Son they are also insulting the Father who wished to be exemplified through the Son.[4] And yet their impiety is not so strong that God fails to fulfil what he promised he would fulfil by the oracles of the prophets. This happiness was promised to the Israelites and to the posterity of Abraham. However, it was not promised indiscriminately but only to those who were truly the descendants of those men. For not all who are descended from Israel are true Israelites. Only those who through firmness of faith are strong and unconquered in their struggle against the troubles of this world (troubles which God uses to test our piety of mind) truly fit the name of Israelite, that is, of one powerful with God.[5] And not all who have sprung from the blood of Abraham are necessarily the sons of Abraham so that they might claim for themselves the inheritance of the promise, but only those who display the faith through which Abraham deserved this happiness which was to be given to his descendants. But look and see whether the word of God does not reveal this clearly, when he promises, saying, 'Through Isaac shall your seed be named.'[6] It was promised to the seed of Abraham that through it all nations would be populated. But he does not wish all of the descendants of Abraham indiscriminately to be called his seed, unless they are in Isaac who is the son of faith and was a type of Christ. Isaac was born, not according to the common method of birth, but from a father who had faith in God despite his sterility, and from an old woman who was likewise barren. Thus the power of God and the faith of the father gave birth to Isaac more truly than did the flesh.[7] What, therefore, does he intend when he says: 'Through Isaac shall your seed be named,' except to explain clearly that not all those who have been born from Abraham according to the flesh are automatically sons of God and consequently inheritors of the promises, but those belong to the seed of Abraham who are people of faith, inasmuch as it was through faith that Abraham deserved the promise of God.[8] But if God made a promise of this sort: 'My promise will extend to any who have been born from you,' then anyone who was a descendant of Abraham by blood might rightfully claim this glory for himself. But in fact, when he said: 'About this time I will return and Sarah shall have a son,'[9] he meant the one and only son of faith whom God had especially chosen by his will, not from the commendation of circumcision – for the child had not yet been born – but on account of the merit of the father's faith. After this, children were born to Abraham from other wives and yet through the name of Isaac alone was the blessing promised to Abraham.

But what happened in the case of Isaac and the other children of Abraham likewise happened in the case of Jacob and Esau. If the inheritance of this blessing happened through a blood relationship alone, then it belonged more to Esau (since he was the elder) than to Jacob. Isaac was the common father of both, the same mother conceived both in a single union with her husband. They were carried at the same time in the womb of the mother and brought forth into the light together; nevertheless God acknowledged one as legitimate and disinherited the other as a bastard, saying: 'Jacob I have loved, but Esau I hated.'[10] What therefore distinguished these twins from one another? Not fleshly relationship, not observance of the law, not circumcision. For when they had not yet been born and before they had done anything at all, either according to the law or contrary to the law, it was said: 'The elder shall serve the younger.'[11] Why did God act in this way? What did he wish to be revealed to us by this event? Clearly he wanted no one to claim the right of this promise for himself by trusting in circumcision or the law, unless through his faith he shows that he is to be reckoned among the elect and to be such as Isaac and Jacob were. For it is the election of God that makes sons of Abraham, not blood relationship. But if God rejects and turns away from the Jews as formerly he turned away from Esau, it will be of no value to have descended from the stock of Abraham. Again, if God admits gentiles by the merit of faith to this inheritance, it will count not at all[12] against them to have no physical relationship to Abraham, since God acknowledges their legal adoption as sons.

And let no impious person[13] distort the things we have said and contend that blame should not be ascribed to men but to God, who arbitrarily rejects or chooses those who have merited or were guilty of nothing. Far be it from anyone to harbour such a thought and to interpret in this way what God says to Moses in Exodus [33:19]: 'I will have mercy on whom I have mercy, and I will have compassion on whom I have compassion.' So then,[14] it is not by willing or by exertion that salvation is attained, but by the mercy of God, for in vain do we desire, in vain do we strive, unless a willing God draws us to him. Moreover, he draws to himself whomever he chooses, even those who have merited nothing, and rejects those who are guilty of nothing. However, it does not follow that God is unjust to anyone, but that he is merciful toward many.[15] No one is condemned except by his own guilt. No one is saved except by the kindness of God. Thus, he thinks those worthy whom he wishes, but in such a way that if you have been drawn to him by his mercy,[16] you have reason to give thanks; but if you have been abandoned to your own obduracy,[17] you have no reason to complain. For God does not harden human minds to hinder them from believing in the gospel of Christ; but to illuminate the magnitude of his kindness and to reveal the glory of his power, God uses the stubbornness of those who, through their own obduracy, refuse to believe. For that is how we should interpret what is said to Pharaoh in Exodus [9:16]: 'But this is why I have raised you up: to show you my power and to make my name resound throughout the earth.'

From words of this kind the ungodly seizes the opportunity and says: 'If he has mercy on whomever he pleases, and hardens whomever he pleases, how can he afterwards blame us? Since it is impossible to resist the will of God, let him charge it to his own account rather than to ours if we sin.' Listen now to my reply. No one resists the will of God, but the will of God is not the cause of your destruction. He did not harden the heart of Pharaoh in such a way that he himself caused Pharaoh's stubbornness, but although he knew the tyrant's arrogance was worthy of sudden destruction, neverthe-less little by little he used heavier punishments against him by which

Pharaoh might have been corrected if he had not resisted by his own ill will. But the divine leniency provoked his impious mind even more. God, therefore, turned Pharaoh's evil into his own glory.[18]

I could say more things on God's behalf, but God hates all arrogance. However, what is more arrogant than a man (than which nothing is more lowly) disputing with God as if he were contending with an equal? For who would tolerate it if a clay vessel expostulated with its maker and said: 'Why have you formed me in this way?' What clay is in the hands of the potter, we all are in the hands of God. So says the Lord himself through the prophet Isaiah.[19] He forms whatever pleases him, making one vessel for a lowly function, another for a noble function. No matter what the reasons for his actions may have been, the potter is answerable to no one, and it is not proper for the clay to demand from him the reason for his decision. The clay in itself is nothing other than clay. If the potter forms an elegant drinking-cup from clay, whatever honour attaches to this belongs to his own artistry. If the potter forms a chamber-pot, no injustice is done to filthy and worthless clay. Therefore if God abandons someone in his sins, thus he was born, there is no injustice. But if he calls someone to righteousness, his mercy is a free gift. In the case of the former, God reveals his own righteousness so that he may be feared. To the latter he discloses his own goodness so that he may be loved. It is not the part of a man to require a reason from God for his decision – why he calls this one later and that one earlier, why he accepts one who has done nothing to deserve it and abandons a man who has incurred no guilt.[20] A man is far more lowly in comparison with God than is clay in comparison with its human craftsman. If it is monstrous arrogance for the clay to argue with its creator, is it not greater arrogance for a man to dispute about the purposes of God which are so far above us that we are scarcely able to grasp a shadow or a dream of them?[21] Begin to believe and cease to debate, and then you will understand more quickly.

And the potter can make a mistake, God cannot. It is enough for you to believe that God, since he is omnipotent, can do whatever he wishes. But at the same time, since he is the best, he does not desire anything but the best. He ought not to be blamed if he uses our evils for a good purpose. On the contrary, this itself is a proof of his supreme goodness, that he turns another's evil into good. God has not made you into a filthy vessel. You have defiled yourself, and you have devoted yourself to ignoble purposes.[22] After this, if God through his own wisdom makes use of your evil for saving the pious and for glorifying his own name,[23] you have no cause to complain about it. You are paying a just punishment for your ill will. The pious are rendered more cautious by your example, and they give thanks more eagerly as they become more aware, because of your blindness and destruction, of how much they owe to the divine kindness. Pharaoh had no cause to accuse God; he was overthrown by his own ill will, and yet his ill will made clear the glory of God among the Hebrews.

But what cause would they have for complaint if now, just as he formerly postponed the destruction of Pharaoh, he bears and endures the unbelieving and stubborn Jews for a long time and with much gentleness as if they were deserving vessels? These vessels are soon to be destroyed so that it may become more evident to all that those are worthy of destruction who, even when challenged in so many ways, cannot be corrected; and likewise, by their punishment, others may fear the omnipotent God whom we should not provoke to certain anger by constantly sinning. And also [the vessels may be destroyed] in order to show more abundantly the magnitude of his own glory toward the pious, whom he cleansed when they were filthy vessels and consecrated to honourable uses, not by the merit of circumcision or the law, but by the merit of faith. They have been admitted to this honour by the commendation of their faith alone. But those who have been admitted include not only those who are Jews like us, but also gentiles. For in this instance it is not birth but the choice of God that makes us heirs. The Jews ought not to be surprised that the gentiles, previously profane and strangers to God, are now being adopted into the number of the sons of God, since they themselves, though once spurned, rejected, and disinherited because of the sins which they had committed against God, nevertheless afterwards came to their senses, were corrected and were received into grace by the divine gentleness and clemency.

Their own prophet Hosea [1:10] testifies to these things when he says: 'Those who were not my people I will call "my people," and her who was not beloved I will call "my beloved," and her who has not obtained mercy I will call "her who has obtained mercy." And in the very place where it was said to them, "you are not my people," they will be called "sons of God."' Why do they condemn in others what they have found to be true in themselves? Why do they not rather beware that they do not become once again through their own fault what they formerly were? Why do they envy those whom they can imitate, if they did not prefer to argue rather than to obey? But if most men perish by their own stubbornness, still God will fulfil for those few who have believed what he has promised to all. And successors to this inheritance will never be lacking. Isaiah [10:22-3] did not conceal this, but he spoke in a clear voice prophesying about the Israelites: 'If the number of the sons of Israel is equal to the number of grains of sand on the beach,' and if so many should perish by their own sin, 'nevertheless some will always remain,' who will be saved by faith. No matter how great the crowds of those who fall away, it will not upset the promise of God. To break one's word in promises is characteristic of mankind; but God is one who fulfils completely whatever he has said, and in full measure - not cheating, but truly and justly. Because of this Isaiah likewise said [28:22]: 'The Lord will execute his sentence upon the earth with vigour and dispatch.' Shadows seem to have an element of deception and the law speaks at great length; it promises, foreshadows, instructs, warns, and consoles. But Christ has been sent and has fulfilled once and for all what was promised, has embodied what was foreshadowed and has reduced the lengthy list of instructions to the single precept of evangelical love. He scattered the seed of heavenly doctrine which, though it has borne no fruit among many in the nation, nevertheless has borne fruit in some men.[24] Likewise, further above he testifies[Isa 1:9]: 'If the Lord of Hosts had not left us seed, we would have fared like Sodom and been made like Gomorrah.' Consequently, even though very many Jews fall away from Christ, Christ will not permit the genuine and legitimate seed of Abraham to perish utterly.

Since all this is the case, what shall we say? Only the truth: that the gentiles who used to seem strangers to righteousness and exempt from legal ceremonies have nevertheless achieved true righteousness. This is not Jewish righteousness which held fast to corporeal things and displayed only some shadow of righteousness, but a saving and efficacious righteousness which comes, not to those who are satisfied through works under the law, but to those who submit and dedicate themselves to God through a simple faith. On the opposite side, the Jewish people, who follow eagerly and hold tenaciously onto the law of righteousness according to the flesh, have not arrived at the true law of righteousness. For they have fallen away from Christ, toward whom all the oracles of the Mosaic law aimed as toward a goal. Someone might say: 'What is the reason for such a sudden alteration of things? How has the matter been so reversed?' No doubt because God rejects the proud and gives himself to the humble and meek. And therefore he received the gentiles who acknowledged their own sickness and submitted themselves to God. On the other hand, he rejected the Jews, haughty once more, who applauded themselves for their false title of righteousness, relied on sabbaths, washing, circumcision, and similar trivial observances,[25] disdained to receive the yoke of faith, refused Christ, and handed over to death the author of life. Isaiah, who knew the future, foretold that this very thing would happen. He prophesied that Christ, whom the law had promised as a Saviour, would become the cause of ruin for them because of their unbelief; and that same rock, which would have been a trustworthy and safe defence for the pious, would be transformed into disaster for those as long as they prefer to resist and to dash themselves against God instead of finding peace in him through faith. For thus does God the Father of Christ speak in the prophet Isaiah [28:16]: 'Behold I place in Zion a stone against which they may fall and a rock against which they may run. On the other hand, whoever believes in him will not be ashamed,' deceived by his own confidence.

Chapter 10

Brothers, I speak these things with great sadness of mind, because I long in my heart to help those who are perishing, if I can. Now the one thing I can do is to pray in the daily prayers which I raise to God that they may eventually come to their senses and not persist in this blindness forever. I cannot excuse their unbelief, but nevertheless to some extent something can be alleged as a pretext for their sin. They are not totally strangers to God, as are the gentiles; so I hope all the more that what they have begun to have in part may be perfected and that they may now grasp the truth of that whose shadow they have proclaimed for so long. For although, falling into the worst impiety, they have crucified the Lord who is the fountain of all glory, nevertheless I grant one thing to them, and do not deny, that they are motivated by a certain enthusiasm and zeal for God, even though it is without judgment. They do not completely err in their feeling of piety, but they err very much in their discrimination. To have zeal[1] for religion no matter what kind, was better than having none at all, and they deserved to have some credit given to them for what they have, unless they were to adhere so stubbornly to the beginnings of piety that they reject true piety; so to cling to and insist on the shadows and semblances of truth that they reject the fountain of truth itself. For while they diligently but nevertheless foolishly defend and uphold the Mosaic law, they fall away from the whole law, fighting against that for the sake of which the law had been established. Now the sabbath, circumcision, various kinds of foods, the avoidance of dead bodies, fasting, feast days, had been established for a time with this intent, that through these crude beginnings they might train themselves for true righteousness, and might progress from a kind of human righteousness toward the highest and perfect righteousness of God. And yet the law had been given the Jews only to foreshadow something better; they were wrong to let their love and zeal for the law carry them so far as to despise and reject the very thing at which the whole law aimed. But now that the righteousness of God has been revealed, the Jews should have left behind human righteousness. Instead they do the reverse, defending and fighting for that ancient and now deadly – not to say superfluous – righteousness, so that they refuse to acknowledge the righteousness of God, and relying on their own ceremonies, they oppose the gospel of Christ to which they ought to have submitted in faith if they wished to be truly righteous.

For one ought to imagine that righteousness is twofold:[2] the author of the first was Moses and the author of the second is Christ. The former consists in ceremonies, the latter in faith and obedience. The first is a kind of groundwork and beginning of the second, just as the unchiselled slab is the beginning for a future statue, or just as a coagulation[3] of blood later grows into a living creature. However, it would be most foolish to cling to the rudimentary when you have at hand what is finished and completed. But Christ is the completion[4] of the whole Mosaic law (which by itself is rudimentary and weak), because he confers true righteousness not through circumcision but through faith. And this path to righteousness is open not only to Jews but to all who believe. Moses himself described the image of each kind of righteousness. That temporary righteousness, which had depended upon ceremonies to be observed only for a fixed time, he describes in Leviticus [18:5], saying: 'Keep my laws and commandments, for the man who has done so will live by them.' That true and lasting righteousness, which we obtain through Christ by way of a living faith, he describes in Deuteronomy [30:12] when he says: 'Do not say in your heart, "who ascends into heaven?" For this is to bring Christ down from heaven. Or let no one say: "Who descends[5] into the abyss of the earth?" For that would have been to call Christ back from the dead.' Neither of these seems to believe, since each demands proof. But one who sincerely believes is so convinced that he will never require any proof that Christ at one time descended from heaven and now is seated in heaven at the right hand of the Father, even if he does not display either of these things a second time before our eyes; likewise that Christ descended into hell and returned from hell; that he came to life again – even if he does not repeat these things a second time for men to perceive. It is enough that they have been done once. All we can do is trust those who saw them done.

And this need not be sought from far away. The Jews saw these things and they did not believe. Others have heard who have not seen and they have believed. Nor is scripture silent on this point, for shortly afterwards it reads: 'What we say is close at hand, in fact in your mouth and in your heart' [Deut 30:14]. What is that word about which scripture speaks? Doubtless the word of the gospel, which we as heralds of this righteousness preach, and which brings present salvation. You must only apply your mind through faith. But how is it 'in your mouth' and 'in your heart'? If you confess and acknowledge the Lord Jesus with your mouth and likewise truly believe from the heart that God raised him from the dead so that with him we might be

brought back to life from our sins and henceforth live in innocence, you will
be saved. For belief comes from the heart which is the door to righteousness.
On the other hand, inasmuch as we owe glory to Christ, it is not enough to
hold faith within the mind unless, as often as the matter demands, you also
confess him with your mouth. In this lies the attainment of complete
salvation.

You see that the substance of this matter does not depend on
ceremonies but on faith. Even Isaiah [28:16] testifies to this when he says
about Christ: 'Whoever believes in him will not be put to shame.' When he
says 'whoever,' does he not destroy every difference between Jew and
Greek? When he says 'believes,' but does not say 'has been circumcised,' or
something similar, does he not then render ceremonies of the law obsolete?
Faith alone is required, and faith can be common on an equal basis to all. For
God is not only the Lord of the Jews but equally of all. His kindness must not
be limited by such narrow boundaries that it should be extended to the
Hebrews alone and then exhausted. On the contrary, his abounding and
overflowing goodness is immense, not toward one or another nation, but
toward all peoples of whatever nation, provided that by sincere trust[6] in the
divine power, they implore his help. The prophet Micah[7] affirms this. He
says: 'Everyone who calls upon the name of the Lord will be saved.' The
word of the prophet excludes no human race. Whoever calls upon him with a
believing mind will attain salvation, whether Jew or Greek or barbarian. And
on the other hand, whoever does not call upon him will perish.

However, no one calls upon someone or asks his help who does not
trust him. But how can they trust one about whom they have heard nothing?
Moreover, how will they hear unless there should be one to proclaim him
who is unknown? And how will the apostles preach unless they have been
sent by him whose gospel they are preaching? Isaiah calls them to mind
when he says [52:7]: 'How beautiful are the feet of those who preach the
gospel of peace, the gospel of good things.' You hear what the heralds of
Christ are ordered to preach: not circumcision and the keeping of the
sabbath, but 'peace,' which through faith, after our sins have been
abolished,[8] welds us together by mutual love in Christ; and those 'good
things' which are always good because they are good by their own nature.
Therefore, although nothing has been neglected by God who invites all
mortals to salvation, and although there is no nation to whom the gospel has
not been preached, nevertheless not all believe in the gospel. And thus it
will come about as Isaiah predicted [53:1], speaking in the role of the apostles:
'Lord, who has believed our words?' Indeed, even among the gentiles very
few believe in the gospel if they are compared with those who do not believe.

Therefore, let us sum up what we have said. If calling upon God brings salvation, and if one who lacks faith does not call upon him, then clearly faith is required most of all, not circumcision. Moreover, faith is engendered in the mind, not through proof, but through the preaching of the apostles; that is, it is not engendered through the eyes but through the ears, through which the gospel of Christ is poured into the obedient heart.

Therefore, since the brightness of the gospel has now shone forth through all the world and the name of Christ has become known, why do you suppose that so few of the Jews believe? Can they excuse themselves because they have heard nothing about Christ? On the contrary, now we see fulfilled what David had prophesied [Psalm 19:4]: 'Their voice has gone out to all the earth and their words to the end of the world.' Therefore, since Christ was promised formerly by so many oracles of the prophets, since now he has been preached publicly in every nation through the apostles as suitable witnesses, since miracles build up confidence in the preaching,[9] can the Jews allege as a pretext that they do not know Christ? On the contrary, they have seen the light, but malice has blinded their eyes. They have heard the gospel, but envy[10] has stopped up their ears. For they prefer to envy the gentiles who have been called to salvation rather than to imitate their faith. And both these things, namely, that the Jews would reject the preaching of the gospel and that the gentiles would receive it, were prophesied both by Moses and by Isaiah. Moses prophesied first in the song in Deuteronomy [32:21], representing the Lord, offended by the unbelief of the Jews, as speaking thus: 'I shall provoke you to jealousy through a most despised nation,' which up till now in comparison with you has not been considered a nation. And since you yourselves think you are wise, 'I shall provoke you through a nation' in your judgment 'foolish and stupid,' so that envy might all the more excite you. And Isaiah followed Moses, and did not fear to testify openly that the obedience of the gentiles was more pleasing to God than the stubbornness of the Jews. For he thus speaks in the role of Christ: 'I have been found by those who did not seek me; I have shown myself openly to those who did not ask for me' [Isa 65:1]. Such a magnificent testimony of faith does he offer to the gentiles. But, to the detriment of the Israelites, who more properly should have embraced the evangelical faith, what does Isaiah say in the passage immediately following? He says [65:2]: 'All day long I have held out my hands to an unbelieving people.' I have sent prophets; they have slaughtered them. I myself have stirred them by producing so many miracles;[11] instead of giving thanks, they have said: 'He is possessed by demons, and he does these things by the help of Beelzebub the prince of demons.' They have despised humility, they have understood virtue impiously.

Chapter 11

But what is the outcome of my statements? Does my teaching imply that the gentiles have been adopted by God because of their faith, although previously they were strangers to God, while on the contrary the people previously chosen by God have now been rejected outright because of their unbelief? By no means. For it is not at all reasonable that God has now rejected a people whom he has freely acknowledged up to the present time as chosen and as peculiarly his own. For if God had rejected the whole nation, I myself would not be preaching Christ, inasmuch as I am a true Israelite by race, sprung from the stock of Abraham, belonging to the tribe of Benjamin. And although I myself formerly persecuted the pious by a misdirected zeal for the law, I have been approved to carry out the service of the gospel. Surely you recall what is written in the third book of Kings [1 Kings 19:10] where the prophet Elijah speaks to God, complaining and accusing the Jews of impiety. He says: 'Lord, they have killed your prophets, they have demolished your altars, and I alone am left, and they plot against my life.' After such impious cruelty, it rightly seemed that God would completely abandon the nation as though it were hopeless. But nevertheless what answer did Elijah receive from heaven? 'I left for myself seven thousand men who have not bowed the knee to Baal' [1 Kings 19:18]. Just as then God did not wholly cast away his people, but from so many wicked persons left a small number for himself, so the same thing is happening now. For God has not allowed the whole nation of the Jews to be separated from him. And he has not allowed the whole remaining race of mortals to die in their own sins, even though from both groups there are few who believe, compared with the many who refuse to believe. But nevertheless God preserved a few by his own kindness, not because they are Jews by race, not because they kept the law of Moses, but because out of many God chose to impart his kindness and grace to these. If this is due to generosity, not to merit, it should not now be imputed to deeds. For what is paid in return for deeds is wages, not the result of generosity; on the other hand, what is spontaneously granted to the undeserving is truly a favour. But if recompense is totalled up in return for works, then the favour ceases to be a favour and has to be called a reward.

Therefore, what happened? Surely the Israelites, due to their unbelief, failed to obtain what they had sought by trusting in the law. The only ones to obtain it have been those who qualify through election, not circumcision. Neither circumcision nor observance of the law was at all useful for the rest. But they were so blinded by malice that no matter how many portents they saw, they did not believe them. Even though they had been waiting so long for Christ, when he came they looked at him with the eyes of the body and failed to see him with the eyes of the spirit. Isaiah foresaw[1] that this too would come about; we see that it has happened, and we grieve. For because they rejected that holy and gentle Spirit of Christ, God sent upon them a spirit fierce, stinging and intractable, so that what they see with their eyes they deny as if they did not see, and what they hear with their ears moves them no more than if they did not hear it. Such were they once toward the prophets, such have they been toward Christ himself, and such are they, even to this day, toward the heralds of the gospel. David also sees these things with his prophetic eyes and he prophesies that a destruction is imminent – one that will be worthy of such stubbornness against the power of heaven. He says [Psalm 69:22–3]: 'Let their table become a snare and a trap, a pitfall and a retribution which their actions deserve. Let their eyes be darkened so that they do not see, and their backs be bent forever.' For they do not wish to enjoy the things which have been set before them, and they have turned against things which have been exhibited before their eyes and ears. They have not taken the trouble to lift their eyes to heaven and to acknowledge the kindness of the creator toward them. No, they are attached to the lowly letter of the law, and despise sublime things; they are devoted to temporal things and reject eternal things. They carry around the books of Moses,[2] though they do not understand them. They read the prophets and deny the promise given by them.

But someone will ask: 'What is the purpose of all these things? They have been blinded, they have been taken captive, they have been bowed down, they have become deaf. Have they so fallen that they have completely perished? Is there no hope that they will rise again?' Perish the thought! But on the contrary, their fall was temporary and it worked to your advantage, since it was the opportunity for your being accepted into salvation. Then in turn even the Jews, through the example of the gentiles, will be forced at the very end of the world to a zeal for true piety. And just as the desertion of the Jews from Christ opened the way for the gentiles to come to Christ, your faith may even someday goad the Jews on to belief by a kind of jealousy.[3] But if the fall of the Jews was useful as an opportunity, so that their desertion not only brought no loss but actually increased the spread of faith to many more people (for only those few fell away, but the gospel has been brought to all, and the loss of one nation has gained so many nations for Christ), how much more will the world be enriched when that nation as well is stimulated by your piety to join the others?

I address you gentiles as my disciples, inasmuch as I am the apostle of the gentiles, even though a Jew by birth. Though there is nothing I would

not do on your account, still, even more will I strive to honour the apostolic
duty committed to me, and I will strive to lure as many of you as possible into
the fellowship of Christ, then to reveal you as worthy of Christ, if somehow
in this way, I might challenge my own people – for they are my people by
blood relationship but strangers in the matter of faith – to emulate your piety,
even by a kind of envy and jealousy,[4] for the Jews are a jealous race. And if I
am not thus able to persuade everyone, at least I might save some of them.
For I know that you desire the same thing I desire. Now if the rejection of the
Jews was the opportunity for the rest of the world to be reconciled to God
(since, while the Jews were falling from grace, the gentiles were admitted to
grace), that is, if the misfortune of the Jews has worked for good in the
world, how much greater the good if these Jews who are now strangers
should, through faith, be received back as though revived from the dead, so
that the number of the faithful would be filled up, and nothing would be left
except the resurrection of the body.[5] For one must not despair of the whole
nation because of the impiety of some in that nation. If gentiles, strangers to
religion, could be drawn to the true religion through the call of God, what
prevents some from this nation, which has had pious founders and leaders,
from being called back to faith? On the contrary, it is more reasonable that the
pious should be born from the pious because the later stages of a thing
usually resemble its initial stage. If the yeast is holy, it is necessary to
consider the whole lump holy inasmuch as it has been saturated by the yeast.
And if the root of the tree is holy, then the branches which have grown from
the roots should also be holy. As the founder of their race and lineage, the
Jews have Abraham, whose faith has been approved by God. What would
prevent his descendants from reproducing the faith of their founder?[6]

But if they do not do so, they cease to be the descendants of Abraham in
the same way that the branch of the tree ceases to be nourished by the sap of
the root if it is broken off. But if we see that the branches are broken off from
their own native tree on which they first grew, how much less should we be
surprised if those grafted on to a different tree are broken? Consequently,
you see that the Jews, having grown like native branches from the holy root
of a true olive, are broken off and torn away from their own trunk because of
their unbelief in such a way that the root is not at all useful to them. You, on
the contrary, have come forth from the root of a wild olive, and you were
grafted onto the true olive not by nature but by the skill and will of God. You
have been called and accepted among the branches of that tree in such a way
that you have now been removed from the unfruitful tree and made consorts
and participants in a root alien to you. Although some branches which have
grown on that tree, when they are cut off, dry up, you are made rich and
fertile by an alien sap. But beware of being foolishly pleased with yourself on

this account and despising the branches which have been cut off. But if you have conceited thoughts, if you become insolent, if you are swollen with pride, you should remember that the root supports you and not you the root. Do not say to yourself: 'The original branches were broken off so that I might be grafted in.' Let no such thought enter your mind. They were not broken off for your sake; and yet as a consequence you have been grafted in. You say rightly, however, that they were broken off, though they grew from the root. But see why they were broken off. Without doubt, they lie ruined and are trampled on because of their unbelief; you stand firm in the tree by the support of faith. Do not rejoice in the woes of others; instead, let their misfortune teach you modesty. Learn from their calamity what you must fear if you sin in a similar way. For you see that God has not spared the natural branches and that it did not profit them that they sprang from holy fathers and belonged to the chosen people of God. There is also a danger that he will not spare you if you alienate him by arrogance and ingratitude. Learn from their fall what you should avoid. Your happiness should give you no reason to preen your feathers, but it should remind you of the divine goodness towards you. You do have cause to rejoice and to thank God, but you have no cause to gloat over those who have been rejected. They have rightly been cut off, you have been grafted on beyond what you deserve.

Weigh carefully both the goodness and the severity of God: the one should teach you gratitude, the other should teach you to forget your pride and arrogance. An example of the severity of God has been revealed in the Jews who fell from their original status into such blindness that they attacked and abused Christ even though they had been waiting for him for so many centuries. In yourself you have experienced an example of God's kindness inasmuch as you have been adopted freely to partnership in so special a happiness. This was not the reward to be expected by you members of a profane race who lived impious lives. The sins of your former life have once for all been gratuitously forgiven you. By divine favour you have once for all been chosen into the number of his sons, but you have been so chosen that, although you were adopted through no merit of your own, you can be cut off by your own sin. God will withdraw from the ungrateful what he has freely bestowed, unless you acknowledge his kindness and rightly use the divine gift. Your ingratitude will destroy what the goodness of God has given you. Arrogance will destroy what obedience has gained. Unless you are careful, you may fall away again from the olive tree into which you have been grafted. In the same way the Jews also, if they change that which alienates them from God, that is, their unbelief, will in the end be grafted back again into the place where they were cut off. And faith will restore them to the position from which their unbelief has evicted them. You are profane, born from the profane. If you have been cut from a wild olive tree, so to speak, and grafted into the olive tree, contrary to your nature, how much sooner will the Jews, sprung from pious parents, return to the character of their own race and[7] once again be grafted onto the native olive tree from which they have been cut off?

I shall reveal a certain secret to you, my brothers, which would perhaps be better hidden in silence if it were not to your advantage that I speak – to prevent you, that is, from being arrogantly pleased with yourselves because you seem to have been preferred to the Jews. This blindness came upon the Jewish people, but not upon all of them and not forever. A good many of them do acknowledge Christ, and others will persist in their own blindness only until the number of gentiles has been filled for whom the fall of the Jews has now opened an access. But when they see that the whole earth abounds in the profession of the Christian faith, that they await that messiah of theirs in vain, that their city, temple, sacred things, and people have been dispersed and scattered,[8] they will finally begin to regain their vision and to acknowledge their own error,[9] and they will understand that Christ is the true messiah. And thus all of the Israelites will be restored to salvation,[10] although now part of them have fallen away from it. For they will truly be worthy of the name of Israelite when they begin to recognize Christ as God and as the Son of God with the eyes of faith, and when, strong in faith rather than in reliance on works, they have wrung the blessing from the Lord.[11]

All the more should you believe this, inasmuch as it has also been prophesied by Isaiah. He prophesied both that they would fall away and that they would come to their senses. We see that the first has already happened, and this itself is a reason for faith in the prophecy; the other, with a similar faith, we expect to happen. We find this prophecy [Isa 59:20-1]: 'The deliverer will come from Zion, he will banish ungodliness from Jacob, and this will be my covenant with them when I take away their sins.' God formerly made a covenant with this nation, and having once sanctified that convenant he will not allow it to become null and void through the fault of some who behave themselves in a way unworthy of the promises. However, some will come forth who will play the part of the entire nation.[12] For they did not fall from the grace of God to such an extent that they cannot be reconciled. Very many of them do not accept the gospel of Christ but adhere to the letter of the law, and are thus enemies of God; and (lest you scoff at them) this has worked to your advantage, because when they rejected the gospel it was offered all the sooner to you. However, they are descended from holy men and belong to the one nation which God chose for himself from among all nations as his own; commended by these things, they are beloved of God. Consequently, they will be received more easily into grace if they recover their senses, because God has promised to their fathers what we are preaching. For God does not, in our human way, promise a gift or receive into adoption only to repent later and change his mind. He is absolutely immutable, for just as he never errs, neither does he ever need to repent. He will remember his promise as soon as they cease to reject it. Change is characteristic of all things. It is wrong to gloat over the fallen, especially if their fall has worked to your advantage. Rather we should rejoice when they come to their senses.

Now just as you were at one time what many Jews are now, that is, unbelievers in God, nevertheless he did not eternally abandon you. For now it has come about by his mercy that, while they reject faith, you have been received into the fellowship of faith. Moreover, now in turn God has allowed these people for the moment to be alienated from the fellowship of faith while the opportunity for faith is given to you, so that when they also answer God's call and repent they may obtain mercy together with you. Thus, neither should find fault with the other but rather each should rejoice with the other, since each has experienced an equal[13] mercy. For God by his unfathomable judgment is so managing and regulating human affairs that there is no human race not subject to sin. Not that he causes anyone to sin, but for a time he permits men to fall by their own evil so that they might acknowledge their error and realize that they have been saved, not by their own merit, but by the gratuitous mercy of God.[14] In this way they cannot become insolent. And in the meantime, while he does these things, he not only does not send evil upon anyone, but he even wonderfully turns the evil of others to our good by his own goodness.

But perhaps we are going deeper into the sanctuary of this secret than is right for a man to speak about among men. As I gaze upon the ineffable purpose behind the divine plan I am dumbfounded, and since I am not able to explain, I choose to cry out: O the depth of the divine wisdom most abounding! How little can the judgments of God be understood or perceived by any human mind! How little can the purpose of his plans be detected by any created intellect! For who has ever known the mind of the Lord, or who was present in his deliberation? Or who has first stirred God by his service so that what has come to him from God could seem to be a reward owed for one's work? Thus God takes thought for the salvation of mankind by a plan we cannot understand but which could not possibly be better. For he wishes his own kindness to be felt by us in such a way that we are not able to claim anything for ourselves. For whatever is evil may be imputed to our own vice. On the other hand, whatever is good proceeds from God[15] as from its source and is conferred through him as through its author. All good things are in him as the guardian and protector of his gifts, so that man can claim for himself no portion of praise from this, since beginning, middle, and end belong to God. Therefore, to him alone are owed honour, praise, and glory for all eternity. Thus it is impious for man to claim anything for himself.

Chapter 12

Therefore, now that by the gift of God you have been brought over from your former superstition to the true religion and are free from the burden of the Mosaic law, I beg and implore you, brethren, through these mercies of God which he has already bestowed on you in many ways and continues now to bestow (to whose freely given goodness you owe your entire happiness),[1] that henceforth you sacrifice victims to him worthy of this profession – not goats or sheep or oxen which are chosen as pure animals and suitable for sacrifices, for this custom belongs to the heathens and Jews. It is enough to have indulged until the present in base sacrifices of such a kind, but in the future God requires from you far different kinds of rites, another kind of worship, other victims, namely, that you offer your own bodies to him.

This should not be done by mutilating your members, but by subduing your evil desires. You should not offer dead beasts but a living, truly pure, and holy sacrifice, pleasing and acceptable to God – a rational sacrifice, in which the mind[2] rather than a brute beast is the victim.[3] As long as the law remained carnal, God allowed the bodies of beasts to be sacrificed to him. But since the law has begun to be spiritual, sacrifices must be made to God with spiritual victims. Sacrifice your disposition to pride rather than a young calf, slay your boiling anger instead of a ram, immolate your lust instead of a goat, sacrifice to God the lascivious and seductive thoughts of your mind instead of pigeons and doves. These are the sacrifices truly worthy of a Christian, these are the victims pleasing to Christ. God is spirit, and he is won over by gifts of the spirit. He demands to be worshipped not by ceremonies but by pure affections. Cut away from your heart superfluous and unbecoming desires instead of cutting away your foreskin from your body. Let the sabbath be for you a mind free from the tumult of disturbing passions. Christ has offered himself for us; it is right that we in turn should sacrifice[4] ourselves for him. And so it will come about that just as by your profession you have been separated from this world and incorporated into heaven, so in your life and your feelings you will be at variance with your former life, and you will be transformed into new persons, as it were, that is, into heavenly creatures as far as possible – if not yet by the immortality of the body, then certainly by a new state of mind. Thus henceforth you will take no pleasure in what is approved by the vulgar crowd, which is dedicated to perishable things. Rather, you will pursue nothing except what is approved by God. You will not be guided by the human precepts of the Jews; instead all your pursuits and actions will depend upon the divine approval and will which cares nothing for what is base and imperfect but rather for what is truly good and acceptable, for what is legitimate and suitable to divine worship and piety.

It is customary among those who pursue the things of the world that the fortunate despises the unfortunate, that the unfortunate envies the fortunate. Therefore, I admonish each of you individually, whoever he may be, however powerful, or however common and humble provided only that he has been incorporated into the Christian flock and freed from participation in the world: in order that no one through a haughty spirit, attribute more to himself than is right, but that each of you be sober and modest in spirit, first of all, let no one claim for himself more than he possesses; second, let him remember that God has given him what he has, not through the commendation of works, but through the commendation of faith. God has given it to him, not that he might take pride in it, but that he might use it to serve the public good. Moreover, God variously distributes his gifts so that no one may either despise another nor think that he alone is sufficient to himself. But let brotherly love make the gifts given to one common to all.

For it is not proper that the grace of Christ should have less power in us than the force of nature has in the body of any living thing. What the union of interdependent members is in the body of a living creature – this is the union of interdependent individuals who have been elected from the various sects and nations into the fellowship of Christ. For even though this visible body is one and the same, it is yet made up of many members, which do not all have the same function. The eyes perform one duty, the feet another, the stomach and hands another; and yet the eye does not see for itself alone but for the whole body, the stomach does not digest food only for itself but for all the members. Now just as there are duties for each member in the body, so there are varied gifts variously distributed among us. Therefore, just as the more outstanding members, for example the eyes, do not despise the more humble members but seek to help all by performing their own duty – so let each member strive according to his ability to make the gift allotted him, whether outstanding or mediocre, work for the advantage of the whole body, after we have once been incorporated into the head of Christ as if moulded into one spiritual body. And a Christian supports a Christian in the same way that a member supports another member of the same body.

But nevertheless, as I said, different persons have different gifts, not according to our merit, but according to the generosity of God which distributes to each whatever seems to work to the best advantage. Therefore, just because someone has received a gift, let him not be carried away with it, but rather let him use it soberly and modestly for the good of all. If one is given the gift of prophecy for explaining the mysteries of Scripture according to the measure of faith[5] (for God respects faith alone, not other merits) let him communicate his gift to others without pride, or if the opportunity of service to a brother should arise, let him modestly perform his own duty. Or if one is given the gift of teaching, let him not despise the unlearned but, without contempt, let him impart his own learning to others. If it has been given to someone to arouse others to piety and morality by preaching from sacred literature, let him use his gift modestly. Or if one has the means to supply the wants of others and bestow gifts on the needy, let him run to help others, not for glory, not with the hope that thanks will be paid to him with interest, but with a simple heart.[6] If to someone the care of others has been assigned, in order that he should be in charge of the others, and he is successful in this task, let this honour not increase his pride but rather his anxiety because of the care committed to him. Let him administer the gift given to him, not for himself, but rather for others whose care he has taken up. One who comes to the aid of the pitiful and suffering should keep sadness far from him inasmuch as it may press down the one whom he is lifting up and be a kind of reproach to his act of kindness; rather, let him double the thanks for his task by his cheerfulness. Thus, whatever you do, seem to do it unselfishly and wholeheartedly.

The services of ordinary people are generally corrupted by such evils, even if they seem to do something out of kindness. Let all deceit be far from you, but let there be mutual love among yourselves which is equally ignorant of putting on appearances and of dissimulation, and which will render everyone's service acceptable to God. Do not measure anything on the basis of your own desires as the common crowd does, but on the basis of virtue alone or of baseness, being averse to all evil, adhering to all good things. And because you are brothers daily imploring a common father and destined for a common inheritance, you should in turn be kind and well-disposed toward each other through brotherly love. Among men who belong to this world there is a rivalry for superiority of rank; you should undertake a different kind of rivalry, in which each of you attempts to give others preference over himself. No one should live for himself in a life of leisure, but each should be zealous to perform his own duty. And you should not seem sleepy and lazy and weak, as though by an infirmity of the flesh, but you should seem eager and fervent in spirit. You have ceased to be carnal, you have begun to be spiritual. It is characteristic of the flesh to be sluggish; the spirit, on the other hand, is an agile and lively thing.

You should not fight against evil, but you should serve the time,[7] accommodating yourselves to present conditions. And if something unpleasant arises, either avoid it, if you can conveniently do so, or tolerate it. And do not be dejected – for that is a characteristic of unbelievers – but in harsh situations be joyful and cheerful through a hope of future reward. In the meantime keep in mind that if you give up or relinquish something to someone you are giving this to the Lord, and he will surely pay you back with interest.[8] But if the wickedness of the impious should trouble you more seriously, do not prepare a defence, do not strive for revenge, do not run for help to human protection, but implore help from heaven by constant and persistent prayers. If other Christians are in need, he who can help them should do so, not unwillingly and unpleasantly as if he were giving a coin to a beggar, but as if he considered his own wealth to belong to them as well. And exercise this generosity not only among yourselves but also towards those who are absent. But to those who come to you from abroad you should be hospitable, so that they do not suffer want shamelessly, or are forced to turn disgracefully to the heathens. And just as you should have generous hands, so also your tongue should cause others no harm. Nor is it proper to take vengeance on or even to curse those who persecute and crush you out of hatred of Christ. You must bless even people like this, you must bless them, I say, so that they may repent. Far be it from you to curse anyone. Those whom you are not able to help with your substance, you must still wish well. There should be true friendship among you which makes cheerful and sorrowful things a common concern, so that you may be joined together both in your joys and in your sorrows and tears. A harmonious spirit and common affection should unite you in all things, whether something fortunate or something unfortunate happens to you. Do not be of a haughty and disdainful mind toward each other. But he who is greater should incline and accommodate[9] himself to the humble and to those inferior to himself. It is not your place to praise yourselves; none of you should be the one to decide that he is great or admirable. For a person who behaves this way finds it hard to yield to anyone.

If someone has by chance offended you, you should not retaliate with invective for invective or injury for injury. Granted that this is considered right among the Jews and heathens, it is impious before Christ to double evil by another evil and deliberately to imitate what you condemn in others. Contend through acts of kindness, and so contend that not only will your conscience testify that your acts are pleasing to God, but all will approve of them as well; nor will your conduct offend any weak person by appearing to be evil. And every life should be so completely free from all crime, and even, as far as possible, from all suspicion of crime, that not even evil persons will be able to slander. This will happen if, insofar as it depends upon you, you maintain peace not only with Christians but also with those who are strangers to Christ. The strength of heroic virtue is great: it forces even its enemies to love and admire it.[10] However, peace cannot be established if everyone continues to avenge his own grief. Vengeance is characteristic of heathens and Jews. When wounded by injury, do not demand vengeance, but rather yield to anger which will vanish more readily by your gentleness than if you should provoke the other more and more, each by mutual retaliation. If you have overcome by kindness someone who rages with anger, this is a gain. But if that person continues to rage, he will not fail to be punished. You should leave him to his judge who takes from us the right of avenging ourselves and who keeps it for himself, speaking thus in Deuteronomy [32:35]: 'Vengeance is mine, I will repay, says the Lord.' On the contrary, if you have been wounded, so far from returning the wound, you should actually offer kindness in return for injury. And if by chance your enemy is hungry, give him food. If he is thirsty, offer him a drink. There is scarcely any temperament so barbarous, so wild, so harsh, that it cannot be softened by kindness, since in this way even wild beasts are overcome. Overcome your enemy in this way. Having experienced such great gentleness, such great piety, perhaps he will come to his senses, be ashamed, regret, and repent of his savagery. Then perhaps, as though conquered by your love, he will be stirred to love in return. In this way feuds can be ended, whereas they go on and on by the mutual retaliation of evil. To contend through good deeds is beautiful, to conquer is most beautiful. To contend by evil deeds is most base. But even the heathens confess this. It will be your special praise if you overcome by your good deeds evil done to you, if you overcome anger by gentleness, abuse by blessing, injury by kindness. However, you must beware lest some evil person should overcome your goodness by his malice so that you begin to be unlike yourself and to imitate the very one you are condemning. Instead, let your goodness overcome his savagery so that he will be conquered and won over to your side.

Chapter 13

But if persecution by rulers and magistrates[1] should break out against you because of your profession of Christianity, it must be endured even though it did not arise from any fault of yours. But persecutions must not be provoked or invited by refusing to do what these leaders in their own right demand and what can be done without offence to God. The state stands firm through order,[2] it ought not to be disturbed under the pretext of religion. There are disgraceful desires, there are vices, in which it is not right to go along with others. On the other hand, there are things in which, because of the nature of the times, one ought to go along even with the heathen for the sake of public peace and order, lest those who ought somehow to be restrained by fear should become worse by your example. For we may divide all things into three classes. The first are those which are truly heavenly, and which, inasmuch as they are peculiar to Christ, are in every case to be preferred to all other things. The second class are things which belong wholly to this world, for example, desire and sin. These you must flee in every possible way. Between these there is a third class, which is neither good nor bad in itself,[3] but which is nevertheless necessary for protecting the order and concord of the whole state. However, I should not want you to throw into confusion what may indeed be but the shadow and outward form of justice which this world has, provided it does not plainly conflict with the righteousness of Christ. Persecution must be borne, and likewise worldly authority, even if it should be somewhat unfair,[4] so that when they persecute you they may not seem to do so on a well-founded pretext – which they could if you alone should reject the public laws which have been received by all. Christ has not sanctioned such laws, but he has not condemned them either; he gave no thought to them, as it were, because he had more important things to do. Therefore, whoever belongs to the human race should obey public laws. He should submit to magistrates who bear a sort of image of God[5] and who, through punishing evil, do the work of God in one way or another. And to that extent, certainly, the power of those men comes from God. Consequently, whoever resists a ruler or magistrate, even an impious and heathen one, who is performing his duty, resists not the one performing his duty, but God, from whom all authority derives. For just as the shadow of the Mosaic law was from God and until now was not to be disregarded, so also the justice of the law arises from God, so that it is also fitting to grant some authority to this justice for a time.

For just as God wished that there should be order among the members of his own body, about which we have just spoken, so in the whole commonwealth in which there are both good and evil, he wished that there be a certain order. And order itself is good in itself, even if someone abuses a magistracy. Consequently, those who disturb this order fight against God, its author. And those who fight against God will justly pay the penalty. But if you do not wish to be subject to laws or to magistrates, you should not think that you can achieve this by defiance, but rather by innocence. For magistrates have no power by law except over those who commit an act which is not permitted. Live rightly and the law does not concern you; there is nothing which you should fear from the magistrates. On the contrary, they provide a reward and honour for those who perform their own duty. And so, just as the magistrate is the servant of God for punishing wickedness, so also he seems to be in some way his servant, when he bestows honour on good deeds. Consequently, whoever acts rightly is more than free from laws. But if you commit some act worthy of punishment, you are at fault, so that you must now fear the magistrate. For he bears the sword in order that he may punish those who have done wrong, and in this respect also subserves divine righteousness which in punishing evil deeds uses the service even of those who are evil. Consequently, since the public order cannot be firm unless authority is granted to the magistrates, you too should obey them for the sake of the common need of the state. You should obey them not just because they would otherwise be provoked by your stubbornness and seem to have good cause to rage against you, no longer punishing you for being Christians but as fomenters of sedition; you must also obey them for the sake of your own conscience. For even if the rulers do not threaten you with any punishment, your conscience tells you that you must not disturb what God wished to be left in order.

And because in this respect they carry on affairs which are public, and what is public pertains to all, for this reason you pay a tax and tribute to them as a reward for their service. Even if they are impious, nevertheless, because they administer public justice and because God is justice, they are the ministers of God and in a way rule for him as long as they apply their efforts to the mandate given them by public authority. And so if they forbid something which in itself is a crime to carry out, obey them; they should be obeyed in what is right, even without the deterrent of fear. But if they order impious things, God must be obeyed rather than men. But if they demand, by right of office, something the payment of which does not entail the loss of piety, it is not worth it to stir them up against you for that reason. Pay to all whatever they demand as if it were owed to them. Christ himself, certainly subject to no one, paid a tax to Caesar, not because he owed it, but to avoid giving any offence. Do not act in such a way that you seem to cheat them of their due. If someone requires a tribute, pay the tribute. If someone demands a tax, pay a tax. If someone insists upon respect, without which he thinks his own authority is despised, offer to him public respect. If someone should wish to be granted honour because of his administration of a public office, grant the solemn honour to him. If they administer their own office with praise, honour is paid to God; if otherwise, this honour is conferred for the sake of public tranquillity. In order that none of these may have anything left to demand from you, fulfil your public obligations.

On the other hand, among yourselves there should be no right or debt, except of mutual love. Love does not wait for one to demand payment but of its own accord anticipates the request. If you pay them what they require you cease to owe. Even if love satisfies others, it[6] never satisfies itself but always heaps up service upon service. Therefore you should especially embrace love which in a word embraces all laws.[7] For whoever loves his neighbour with sincere and Christian love possesses the essence of the whole Mosaic law. If love is absent, no laws, however many, suffice. If love is present, there is no need for other laws, since this alone prescribes more efficaciously whatever is ordered by innumerable prescriptions of laws. The Mosaic law forbids adultery, murder, theft, false testimony, coveting the property of another, usury, and other things of this kind. And yet the essence of all these things is embraced by the brief rule of love,[8] thus: 'You shall love your neighbour as yourself.'[9] Love is, as far as possible, helpful to all, even to evil men, and it harms no one. Therefore, of what use is it to make a list of forbidden acts – 'do not harm in this way or that way' – since it is the nature of love to harm no one at all? Will the one who loves commit murder? Or will someone lie with the wife of another man when he loves that man as much as he loves himself? Will he pillage someone by theft when he is prepared to help him even with his own riches? Will he ruin another by false testimony whom he would be willing to save even at his own risk? Will he make a loan at interest to one whom he regards as the joint owner of all his property? Will he wish that a loss be suffered by one for whom he prays the same things that he prays for himself? Will he be able for any reason to harm or to sadden anyone for whom he knows that Christ has died? And so, as I said, love is the sum of all laws. Through love, one learns in brief what one must avoid and what one must follow.

To the pursuit, therefore, of love, the very consideration of the time also encourages us, that is, that we should come to our senses and awake out of the sleep and shadows of our former life. Night seems to offer freedom for sinning, because it is free from shame. On the other hand, even those who are lascivious and make fools of themselves in the night, nevertheless, as soon as day arrives get themselves ready, out of a sense of shame, to face the glances of their fellows, and as though different persons, they appear in public sober rather than intoxicated, chaste rather than lustful, restrained rather than quarrelsome, wide awake rather than half asleep. Therefore, we must seize the opportunity of the time, and if we use it rightly, our salvation is nearer than at the time when we trusted in the Mosaic law and thought that it was very near. The night of our former life has advanced far; that day is upon us which will uncover even the most hidden things. Let us measure up to our day, let us give up the habits and deeds that belong to the night and of which we are ashamed in the light. If we cover the body with more decent clothing when the sun rises lest anything should offend the eyes of others, much more now that the light of the gospel is rising should we adorn the mind with a garment of virtues which is worthy of the light and does not dread the eyes of God. Henceforth let us so arrange our whole life that we cast off the shadows of our former life and that we may be seen walking in a bright light, visible to God, to angels, and to men. Let us not yield to extravagance in feasting or to intoxicating drinking parties. Let us not serve filthy sexual desire and lust, let us not quarrel disgracefully among ourselves through contention and mutual envy. For you were subject to all of these as long as you wandered in the shadows of your former life. The soul is improperly clothed in such a style of dress. Now since you have been incorporated through baptism into Christ, put on Christ himself. Let him whom you have professed shine forth in your whole life. Imitate him whom you have drunk in. He is chastity, he is sobriety, he is peace, he is love; and a garment of such virtues[10] is fitting for this light of the gospel. Up to this point you have used certain things for pleasure; hereafter you should use them for the requirements of the body. Before you were guided by your desires to indulge yourselves shamelessly. From now on, turn to the same things soberly, only to the extent of your natural needs. The body must be so nourished that it is strong and living, not lascivious. Food and drink should prevent hunger and thirst, they should not invite and nourish lust.

Chapter 14

Those who have fully attained faith in Christ make no distinctions and have no preferences about the use of these things, provided as we said, that they use them for necessity, not for pleasure. Nevertheless, if there is someone among you, perhaps a Jew by race, who, because he has grown accustomed[1] for so long to his former practice and life, is still rather superstitious, and whose faith has not grown in him enough to enable him to exclude all observance of the former law, he must not be immediately rejected with contempt, but instead he must be attracted and encouraged by gentleness and courtesy until he too begins to advance and receive the strength of faith. This will come about more readily through goodwill than through contentious arguing. For it is not proper immediately to place the worst construction on something which may fall short of wickedness. In order that peace and concord exist everywhere among you, some things must be ignored, some endured, some interpreted with more kindness. This forebearance and sincerity has great force to produce a mutual fellowship of life. Peace will never remain firm among many unless in some things one gives way in turn to another, inasmuch as there are various opinions among people.

Now one who is free from all superstition considers that it is right for him to enjoy any kind of food at all without restriction, obviously bearing in mind here nothing other than the necessity of nature. On the other hand, one who is still rather weak and superstitious feeds on vegetables to avoid accidentally eating some kind of fish or other living creature which has either been prohibited by Jewish law or sacrificed to idols. These things ought not to be so important to you that on their account brotherly concord[2] is torn apart. He who is stronger and feeds on anything he likes should use his strength in such a way that he does not scorn the weaker person who is afraid to eat [as he does]. And again one who accommodates the weakness of his own spirit, and abstains from certain kinds of food, should not condemn and judge one who eats indiscriminately whatever has been served to him. But rather, the strong should bear the weak, interpreting his weakness thus: The error is a vestige of the long habit of his former life, and it cannot immediately be rooted out; it will gradually drop away and his superstition will disappear as true piety increases. Likewise, a somewhat superstitious person, when he sees someone eating whatever food he wishes, should think thus to himself: It does not matter at all to me what he does, it is reasonable to suppose that he is acting with a clear conscience, since the Lord has joined him to himself and has made him his own, by whose will he lives, and he sins against the Lord alone – that is, if he does sin in doing things which are not evil in themselves. But if it is a sin of arrogance to despise the superstition of the person who is weak and errs through naiveté, will it not be a sin of much more intolerable arrogance if one who is weaker in faith should judge and condemn one better than himself, according to the vulgar standard of the ignorant who think that whatever they do not do is unjust and that whatever they love is holy?[3] Is the following not said rightly to him: 'Who are you that you should judge and condemn another man's servant?' Jesus Christ alone is the Lord[4] of all. One stands before Christ if he is firm in his faith. One falls before Christ if, as you suspect, he commits sin. Not that he will fall because of those things which you mention; on the contrary, he will be made stronger and enabled to endure in the strength of his faith. For his Lord is abundantly powerful and capable of supporting his own servant lest he should waver at all.

What has been said about the choice of foods likewise must be admitted about the observance of the sabbath and new moons. For one who is weak and of imperfect faith distinguishes one day from another, as if one day were sacred, another profane, and as if it were wicked to eat foods or to do work on one day, but proper to do so on another day. On the other hand, one who is strong and of firm faith makes no distinction among days, thinking that all the time[5] of life must be sacred and set aside for the duties of piety. Christian concord should not be torn apart among you on account of things like this, but let each of you make use of his own judgment and not condemn the opinion of another, especially since both are free from sin, and the substance of true piety dwells in both. One who understands and feels within himself that every single day is equally sacred and holy, understands this for his Lord, and how he understands it is of no importance to you. Likewise, if one believes that there is some difference between one day and another, he errs for his Lord if he errs, and this does not at all concern you. Again, one who eats any foods at all without distinction does so in honour of his Lord. For he gives thanks to God whose gift he is eating and whose kindness has provided all things for our use. On the other hand, if one abstains from certain foods because of the weakness of his spirit, he abstains for his Lord, and it is of no importance to you; for while eating his vegetables, he gives thanks to the same Lord as you do. But if he approves that person's thanksgiving and considers it acceptable, why do you pronounce judgment on him? The case is different, but the point at issue is the same, the intention is the same, the Lord is the same. One gives thanks for the freedom to eat whatever he wishes, because the evangelical law distinguishes intentions, not foods. Another gives thanks for the benefit of self-control, while, because of weakness, he avoids intoxication and is restrained within the boundaries of temperance. All are equal in such matters, and no one ought to cross swords with his brother for the sake of protecting his own opinion. It is enough if the Lord approves; it is up to the Lord to judge things which either are uncertain or must be borne on account of the times.

The only claim which a Christian has on a Christian is to be useful to him. And none of us lives for himself, since all of us belong to him who has liberated us from sin [and brought us over] to godliness, from death to life. So no one lives for himself, and no one dies for himself any more than a slave under someone else's authority, whose master has the power of life and death over him. But if the slave lives, he lives for the advantage or disadvantage of his lord, not his own or anyone else's. If he dies, he dies to the profit or loss of the lord, so that he would act shamelessly should he, as a slave, get mixed up in the affairs of a fellow slave. He need satisfy only the lord. But no slave among men belongs so much to his master as we belong to Christ who has bought us, not with silver or gold, but with his own blood. Therefore, if we fall we fall for him, or if we stand we stand for him; whether we live or die, we live or die for him. Some slaves perhaps cease to belong to their lord after they have died. But for our part, whether we live or whether we die, we are the Lord's for whom all things live. Christ has authority not only over the living but also over the dead, for he paid out both his own life and his own death in order to save us. For he died, having been made a man for my sake, and likewise he rose from the dead in order that he might be the Lord equally of the dead and of the living. If we live for piety, we owe it to him. If we have died to sin, we owe that to him also. He is the Lord, he is the judge. Why does a slave claim for himself over another slave an authority which belongs to the Lord alone? You, indeed, who are superstitious, with what impudence do you judge your brother who is stronger than you, because he eats freely or makes no distinction between days? Or why do you who are more experienced reject and despise your weaker brother as if you were his Lord and not rather his fellow servant? Why does this person or that person usurp the function of the Lord and anticipate the day of judgment? One person must not judge another. He who is the one Lord of all will pronounce judgment upon all. For at some time we must all stand before the judgment seat of Christ and either be condemned or acquitted by the word of him who sees the deepest and inmost recesses of the mind. In the meantime, no fellow slave should usurp for himself lordship over another slave. For God wished this honour to be saved for himself alone, as he himself testifies in the prophet Isaiah [45:23]: 'As I live, every knee will bow to me and every tongue will confess to God.'

In the meantime, let each one strive with all his might to keep in view how he is to render an account before this judge, and let no one pass a negative judgment on another. But if one here in the meantime must judge, he ought rather to judge and determine how it may be possible to help one another and to avoid doing evil to anyone or as far as possible presenting him with an opportunity for evil. Let us raise up the spirit of the wavering, not cast it down; let us kindle a smouldering wick, not quench[6] it. Considerations of dignity used to demand that the more ignorant submit to the more experienced, but it is characteristic of Christian love that the more experienced sometimes yields to and complies with the more ignorant, not to approve of his error but to correct him or to keep him from offending too grievously. Let me take myself as an example. Moses formerly designated certain foods as impure and, in his typical fashion, he calls such food common, that is, profane, which it was forbidden to eat; he calls certain other foods clean which it was permitted to eat. Now I know and have been thoroughly persuaded by the Spirit of Christ, who wishes the carnal part of the law to be abolished completely, that nothing is impure in itself and that the choice of foods makes no difference at all. But if anything is at all impure, it is impure only for the one who so judges; that is, it is impure to the weak and the superstitious. But to one who is strong and truly Christian there is nothing impure, but all things are pure to the pure.

And yet perhaps it is better sometimes to abstain from that which is in itself not impure, not because the Mosaic law commands this, but because the brotherly love which is peculiar to Christians dictates it. For if your brother is wounded or grieved in heart because of food for your body – your brother who should be as dear to you as you are to yourself – then apparently you are living only for yourself, and you are not adequately mindful of mutual love. For you make light of and scorn a weak man's error and his offence, when it would be so easy for you to heal him. Is it asking so much to abstain for a little while from permitted foods in order to help your neighbour who is in danger? A brother, even though weaker and more ignorant than you, should not be so worthless to you that you allow him to perish for the sake of your food, when Christ died to save him. No matter what sort of person he may be, if the Lord thought so much of him you must not neglect him over such a trivial matter. Do not think it is enough simply to do what is right. Rather, you must take care that what is in itself right should not be subject to the suspicion of evil, and what is good for you be turned into evil for another, if people see that there is strife among you over food and drink, and similar things of little importance.

Now inasmuch as in the future age in the kingdom of God there will be neither food nor drink which now are the aids of our mortality, so evangelical doctrine and the truly Christian life consist neither in a choice of foods nor in a distinction between drinks, for neither of these has any importance for piety. Rather, we must practise those things which can be carried with us into that heavenly life. But what are these things? Without doubt they are justice, peace, and joy, which are not conferred by taking care in what you eat, but by the Holy Spirit. A difference of opinion about food brings forth anger, dissension, sadness, offence, and grievance. The Holy Spirit produces peace in place of dissent, joy in place of sadness, service in place of offence and injury. For just as it is characteristic of righteousness to wish to harm no one, so it is characteristic of peace to contend with no one, and it is characteristic of love to inflict pain on no one. These are spiritual things; whoever serves Christ in these things at the same time pleases God too, for he follows the things which are most pleasing to God. Moreover, he is also approved by his fellows, for by compliance he avoids all suspicion or occasion of evil. They serve the flesh who cross swords among themselves about food and days. They serve Christ with the spirit who do not guard their own prerogatives, but who make concessions to others through love and become all things to all to profit all, and adjust themselves to all, in order to please all. Therefore, we who are spiritual should abandon disputes of such a kind and pursue those things which make for peace, which promote concord, which nourish mutual love, by which, in sum, we might be rendered better, and serve and help one another, while we avoid things which might offend someone. This is the substance of our profession.

You who are stronger should not cause the work of God to be destroyed because of human food. On the contrary, it would be better that food should perish than that what God redeemed through the death of his Son should perish because of your food. Food is the concern of man, love is the concern of God. When someone is forced to a choice between one or the other, he should give up that which is more trivial, not that there is any sin in foods themselves, or that one is pure and another impure as the Jews maintain, or that there is sin in any particular food you wish to eat. The point is rather that you may be providing an opportunity for sin, not because you eat but because by eating you offend a weak brother and thus food which is pure by nature becomes impure, when you overlook the danger to a neighbour. We must not overlook this: it is more praiseworthy to abstain completely from meat and to feed on vegetables, and to drink no wine at all, than become the occasion of your brother's ruin by your eating and drinking. And do not say to me: 'Why is he afraid when there is no need to be? My conscience does not blame me. What does the weakness of another matter to me? Do you wish that I should leave my opinion to one side, betake[7] myself to the opinion of another and begin to choose between the kinds of foods?' Not at all. I do not demand that you imitate his weakness but that you make concessions to him for a time, in the hope that he also may make progress. I commend your confidence in refusing to make distinctions between foods, but conceal and hide that confidence if at any time you have observed that it is causing a brother to be endangered.

In the meantime let it be enough for you if God knows and approves the fortitude of your mind. And yet you must conceal your fortitude as long as you need to avoid giving a small offence to your neighbour, as you bend and accommodate your own strength to his weakness. And you must also see to it, when you claim to have no interest in the choice of foods, that this arises from strength of mind and not as a pretext for pleasure or luxury. Furthermore, when you despise and rebuke someone, because as a superstitious person he abstains from food, beware of being indecisive and showing yourself firm in speech rather than in faith. He is blessed who possesses such strength of faith[8] that what he approves and defends before others he does not feel his conscience protesting deeply within, and condemning silently in the depths of his heart what he approves publicly. For whoever is undecided thinking that he is not permitted to eat, is condemned by the judgment of his conscience. Why is he condemned? Because what he does, he does not do out of the strength of faith and the constancy of a mind well aware of itself, but against the resistance of his conscience. However, anything which does not come from faith is connected with sin. If a man has doubts about whether or not something is evil, and still does it, even though that particular thing is not in itself evil, he nevertheless demonstrates that he would do something genuinely evil if the opportunity arose. For true piety flees from all things which have even the appearance of evil. One who sins through evil intent deserves to be chastised, and if he shows himself incapable of correction he must even be avoided. But whenever error arises out of weakness, he who is held in the grip of error deserves to be taught and admonished; he does not deserve to be despised or ridiculed.

Chapter 15

But if we are so strong that we have no need of a teacher, we must nevertheless beware that while we attack another person's trivial error of superstition we ourselves do not fall into the graver sin of arrogance. Rather, the stronger we are the more we ought to bear the weakness of others. For those who are older or have greater physical strength do not for this reason push around or trample upon those who are younger or unequal to them in strength, as if the only reason they had received strength was to enable them to harm anyone they could. Instead, the more they excel in strength of body, the more they consider it shameless for themselves to injure one younger in age or one weak because of old age. So in our case, the stronger we are in mental judgment and learning, the more it is proper for us to accommodate ourselves to the weakness of others, instead of becoming insolent in our knowledge and pleasing ourselves, and preferring to worsen the weakness of a brother instead of bearing or healing it. Therefore, no one should take satisfaction from his own endowment, as though he had received it for the sake of pride, but rather he should take pains to despise himself and by accommodating himself to his neighbour to please him; not giving in to him in every matter, but only insofar as he can help him and make him better.

And Christ himself revealed to us this way of healing the error of another, for even though he was the source of all powers, nevertheless he did not use his abilities for his own glory as though pleasing himself. But in order that he might come to the aid of those erring and weak, he not only overlooked the glory which he deserved, but he also allowed himself to be insulted and abused; just as David also, breathed upon by the Spirit of Christ, predicted (in Psalm 68 [69:9]) would happen: 'The reproaches of those who reproached you fell on me.' This was written in the Psalms, not only that we might know, but that we might also imitate[1] and learn from his example by what gentleness our neighbour must be supported and loved until he comes of age in Christ, and ceases to be a child and feeble. Therefore, just as Christ lowered himself to our level so that he might gradually raise us to his own height, so it is proper for us to strive to imitate his example in enticing our neighbour to true piety. This example has been portrayed[2] for us in sacred literature as though in a picture, and we should have it continually before our eyes. For Christ has saved and redeemed us, not in the way common to this world, but by his forebearance, and he has advanced through humility to true glory. And similarly through gentleness, by which we bear those weaker than ourselves, and through the help of the divine books which call us to the imitation of Christ, we may trust that we also will obtain the reward which awaits those who follow in his footsteps.

The essence of your profession is peace. And so I pray to God, the author of patience, who encourages us through sacred writings to tolerance, without whose help we can do nothing at all; I pray that God may bestow one and the same mind on you all and you may be joined together in supreme harmony according to the example of Jesus Christ, who commended to us nothing so strongly as mutual love and mutual concord. And thus certainly we shall embellish the glory of God, who is the Father of Jesus Christ, if what he has taught and displayed toward us we display toward one another. And in this way people will understand that you are truly disciples of Christ if, just as you proclaim God with one mouth, so also you demonstrate by your mutual concord that you are united by the same mind.

Therefore, there should be no discord between the gentiles (who have been called to Christ from the worship of idols) and the Jews (who have been received out of the shadow of piety into true religion). But rather, receive one another with mutual compliance, and advance toward each other with your right hands outstretched, just as Christ has received you and has not counted against you the sins of your former life. He has embraced you with brotherly love in order to make clear to mankind the glory of God the Father. Hence if you too do for each other what he has done for all, the glory of God will be made clear. Moreover, Christ was a servant to both races: he was a servant to the Jews in order to demonstrate that God the Father is truthful, who fulfilled for the descendants what he had promised[3] their forefathers through oracles of the prophets. And he wished them to rejoice, since they were permitted to discover the truth of those things which the law of Moses had prefigured in types and shadows. He was also a servant to the gentiles, to whom nothing had been promised, so that they might praise the divine goodness for being admitted, beyond their merit and beyond all hope, to the common salvation by the mercy of God alone. The Jews should rejoice because they have finally received the things for which they had long waited; the gentiles should rejoice, because they now are gaining what they did not expect.

And that this would come to pass had been determined long ago by the divine plan. For Christ himself speaks to the Father in this way in the Psalms [18:49]: 'Therefore I shall celebrate your glory among the gentiles, and I shall sing a hymn of praise to your name.' Again in the song of Deuteronomy 32 [:43]: 'Rejoice, gentiles, together with his people.' And again in Psalm 116 [117:1]: 'Praise him all gentiles, and join in praising him, all peoples.' Likewise Isaiah prophesied [11:10]: 'And the root of Jesse will come in that day, and he who will rise to govern the gentiles, in him will the gentiles hope.' Moreover, I pray that God, who formed this hope in you through the oracles of the prophets, might now fulfil sufficiently what formerly he revealed he would do: that he cast aside your sadness and doubt and fill you with all joy and concord through faith; and that the hope which you have conceived from God might begin to grow daily through the confidence of a good and pure conscience, as the Holy Spirit gives you strength.

I do not say this because of a lack of trust in you. I am convinced that you yourselves by your own will are endowed with the utmost love, with the fullest knowledge, so that even without me as a counsellor, you are able to admonish one another about these things. Nevertheless I have written to some degree more intimately and more freely to you, not as one teaching the ignorant, or ordering the unwilling, but as one calling to mind what it is best to do, so that what you understand ought to be done and are already doing by your own will you may do more fully through my exhortation. At least in this respect I perform the duty entrusted to me, by the grace of God, though I did not deserve it. I submit to the will of Christ whose work I zealously perform with all my strength, so that by bringing the gospel of God to light among you gentiles, I might offer a pure sacrifice to him. However, I believe that by far the most pleasing sacrifice to him would be for me to present you to God himself as those worthy of him, like a sacrifice made pure and holy, not by carnal ceremonies, but by the Holy Spirit, who is the one and only author of true holiness.

Since I see that I have attained this very thing, to some extent I can be proud, and rightly so, not boasting about myself before men, but rejoicing before God for the happy outcome of my preaching. However, I do not attribute this to myself or my own industry but to Jesus Christ whose work I am doing and with whose help I perform the duty of preaching. For my heart does not endure to recount the exploits of others. Lest I should seem to claim for myself praise for the deeds of others, I shall mention only those things which Christ has brought about through my ministry,[4] namely, that the gentiles previously devoted to the impious worship even of idols, now submit to and obey the gospel, stimulated in part by my words and deeds, in part by the magnitude and power of signs and portents which have been produced through me to confirm the reliability of my teachings. But these things were not produced through my power or strength, but through their author, the Spirit of God, of whom I am nothing other than an instrument and a minister. Therefore, while I boast about the success of my preaching, I preach the glory of Christ, not my own. And in this way it is certainly right for me to boast, inasmuch as I attribute praise of my service to God in such a way that nevertheless I yield to no man.

For I have not preached the gospel in the usual manner, but up to this point I have preached in those provinces where the name of Christ had not yet been heard. And I have striven to gain this praise before God in order that the foundations of the Christian religion might be more broadly laid, and the boundaries of the sovereignty of Christ might be further extended. Nor did it seem right to build on top of foundations laid by other apostles. But considering that it was more difficult to establish the beginnings of religion than to protect and increase gains once they had been made, I judged that the former pertains more to the work of the gospel, especially because I understood that this was long ago prophesied by an oracle of the most holy prophet Isaiah [52:15]: 'They shall see who have never been told of him, and they shall understand who have never heard of him.'

And this zeal for extending the Christian faith has so greatly taken my attention that up to the present time I have not been able to visit you, even though for a long time now I have been most desirous of this. But every time I have attempted to come to you, affairs have hindered me – for that, I think, was what the Spirit of Christ wished.⁵ Now that I have travelled through Achaia and Macedonia, I see that there remains no place in these regions in which I have not laid the foundations of the Christian religion, and for many years now I have been moved by the desire to see you. Adequate opportunity (I hope) will be given for fulfilling my desire, so that when I set out for Spain I may see you on the way and then continue, with you escorting me, to the place to which I have determined to go, but not before I have spent some days among you and fulfilled my desire at least in part by some companionship with you. I believe that this will come to pass soon, Christ willing.

However, at the present time I have resolved to make a journey to Jerusalem in order that I might present the gifts of the Macedonians and the Achaians, which have been entrusted to me, to the Jewish Christians living there. For they decided to collect some money at random from whoever would freely offer it, in order to support the poverty of certain persons living at Jerusalem rich in religion but poor in resources. No one compelled them to do this, but it seemed best to them that they should, and in my opinion they judged rightly in this matter, because they are obligated to those at Jerusalem due to the religion which they first received from them. Consequently, since those at Jerusalem took the initiative in sharing the doctrine of Christ with the gentiles, it is proper that the gentiles in turn should share something with them from their own money, so that with something however worthless they might repay that which is most valuable of all. Those at Jerusalem have shared freely that which concerns the salvation of the soul; the gentiles now are sharing freely and willingly that which concerns the necessities of the body. Therefore, in this matter, as soon as I have performed my duty and have handed over the money (such as it is) to those for whom it was intended (for I shall hand over the money personally and under seal, lest by some trick some of it might be embezzled through others or I myself might be suspected of having nibbled at it, since I am doing the business of another without recompense), I shall set out for Spain, coming your way. And although I am hastening to proclaim the gospel in Spain, yet I shall not regret this delay and expense. For I have no doubt that when I come to you, what we find in each other will cause my arrival to lead to the greatest praise of Christ, when you receive me with an eager zeal which equals your piety and I, by the help of God, respond to your prayers in all things.

Meanwhile, I beseech you, brothers, through our common Lord Jesus Christ and through the true love which we have breathed in from his Spirit, that inasmuch as I cannot yet enjoy your presence in person, you may at least by pouring out pious prayers and vows unto the Lord, while I labour and risk such great difficulties, help free me, with God's aid, from the un-believers found in Judaea and from those who rebel against the gospel of Christ. Pray that the fruit of our preaching may not be impeded by the ill will of those, and pray that this my duty of handing over the money, which I will do in Jerusalem if no one interferes, may be pleasing and acceptable to the saints. Pray also that as soon as I have accomplished these things according to my wish, my arrival will be joyful for you if God so wills, and that I may be refreshed among you for a while after the struggles have been endured. But to end my exhortations where I began, I pray that God, the parent, author, and guardian of genuine peace and concord, may always remain among you; for God flees far and shrinks from the proud and discordant, while he is won over and retained by mutual concord.

Chapter 16

Moreover, I commend to you in this letter our sister Phoebe who has left here on a journey to you, and to whom I have given this letter to carry. She has been devoted to and has served in all ways the congregation of believers at Cenchreae.[1] I ask that you receive and treat her as a woman should be received by the saints when she deserves the best from them, and that you be of assistance to her in whatever way she feels the need of your service. For it is right that you should assist her, inasmuch as she herself has frequently assisted me as well as a great many other saints.

Greet Prisca for me, and her husband Aquila, the Jew from Pontus. When I was in danger because of the treachery of the Jews, they assisted me, so that the preaching[2] of Christ would not be impeded by the efforts of evil persons. To protect my life, they actually endangered their own lives, as though to rescue my life at the cost of theirs. For this kindness not only do I give thanks to them, but so do all the churches of the gentiles, in part because these two have earned the same gratitude from the others, in part because the others think that the kindness by which I was saved is a kindness to all. And do not greet these alone, but greet also their whole household. Greet Epaenetus, worthy of his name[3] because of his most praiseworthy way of life, and on this count especially dear to me, that he may rightly be called the first fruits of Achaia inasmuch as he was the first among all the Achaeans whom I won for Christ. Give my greetings to Mary who has contributed many services to me, not without danger and trouble. Greet Andronicus and Junias, who are not only blood relatives but also were joined to me once in the fellowship of prison, who are glorious among the apostles, and in the number of the seventy-two,[4] distinguished with the ornaments of true religion, preceding even me in this title of excellence because they were initiated into Christ before me. For if we rightly confer honour upon those who were firstborn from their parents, how much more rightly will it be conferred upon those who were first reborn in Christ. Greet Ampliatus, who by the excellence of a rare piety is especially dear to my heart. Greet Urbanus, a companion and a helper in my labours in the business of the gospel of Christ, and his wife Stachys who is very dear to me. Greet Apelles, sure and tested and approved by many afflictions suffered for Christ. Greet all those who belong to the household of Aristobulus. Greet Herodion my kinsman. Greet the members of Narcissus' family, especially those who now have been reborn in Christ. Greet Tryphaena and Tryphosa, who by their efforts and care are advancing the work of the gospel. Greet Persis, uniquely beloved of me inasmuch as she has worked very hard to spread the gospel of Christ. Greet Rufus, eminent in piety and religion, and at the same time his mother whom I consider to be mine as well as his. Greet Asyncritus, Phlegon, Hermes, Patrobas, Hermas, and the other brothers who are joined with them. Greet Philologus and his wife Julia, Nereus and his sister, and Olympas, and all the other saints who live in companionship with them. Greet one another with a kiss worthy of Christians, that is, one which is both pure and sincere and which is certain evidence of true concord. All the churches of Christ greet you, all of which I know have a most eager devotion to you.

However, I ask of you brothers that you watch out for those who sow dissension and wrangling among you, attempting to lead you into a different kind of teaching from that which you have already received, and urging that Judaism be mixed with Christianity. Recognize them so that you may avoid them. They will not be at all difficult to recognize. For they do not sincerely teach what is right, nor do they care simply for the work of Christ, but they serve their own stomach and their own gain while they seduce the minds of the simple by smooth speech and by charming rather than wholesome words. Thus they easily impose upon the simple by the outward show of feigned piety. For your obedience has been published abroad everywhere; and on that account I truly rejoice over you. For the first step toward piety is obedience. And yet you must constantly keep in mind whom to obey. Simplicity ought to be praised; and yet since it does not know how to be suspicious, it is often subject to deception. Consequently, I want you to be simple in such a way that while you do not harm or deceive anyone, you are nevertheless wise and keep your eyes open to pursue what is good and avoid things which corrupt the integrity of piety. It is not unknown to me that there are many who oppose the gospel of Christ, through whom Satan attempts to impede the salvation of mankind. Some attack by means of persecutions, others separate from Christ by a false display of religion and entice men to Moses. But persevere; God will not fail you in your efforts. With such a defender, there is nothing which you should fear. For inasmuch as he is stronger, he will crush and shatter the attacker Satan, and he will cast him conquered and prostrate under your feet by his own strength, and this shortly. May the favour of our Lord Jesus Christ always breathe upon you all.

Timothy of Derbe, my colleague in the task of preaching the gospel salutes you, and with him Lucius and Jason of Thessalonica and Sosipater, the son of Pyrrhus, of Beroea, my kinsmen. I who am called Tertius greet you. With the zeal of piety I perform my task as a writer for Paul, who is dictating this letter. Gaius greets you, one among the few to whom I have administered baptism, in whose home I am now staying. And not I alone, but also the whole congregation[5] of believers to whom he offers kind hospitality when there is need of it. Erastus, the treasurer of the city of Corinth, greets you; also, Quartus his brother.

May the favour of our Lord Jesus Christ be always present with you all; and God will bring this prayer of mine to certain fulfilment. Now to him who even without our effort can strengthen you and make you firm in that practice of life which you have accepted in accordance with my gospel through which I preach Jesus Christ – for through the gospel, the Mosaic law is not completely abolished, but the mystery which was formerly hidden for many ages is now revealed according to the oracles of the ancient prophets and made known by the radiant gospel. And this has happened by the decree and order of God, who delegated to us the duty of preaching and the task of making the secret known. Thus now that the secret of the religion of the gospel has been spread abroad among all, and through the gospel the entire worship of demons is abolished, and the ceremonies of the Mosaic law have ceased to be valid, all should obey through faith and submit themselves to God who alone is truly wise – to him we give thanks through Jesus Christ to whom belongs the glory for all eternity. Amen.[6]

PARAPHRASE ON GALATIANS

In epistolam Pauli Apostoli
ad Galatas paraphrasis

DEDICATORY LETTER

TO THE HONOURABLE COUNT ANTOINE DE LA MARCK[1]
FROM ERASMUS OF ROTTERDAM

After I had set my hand to a paraphrase on Paul's Epistle to the Galatians, I was looking round from time to time for some person to whom I could dedicate my work, since this practice has lasted from early times down to our own day. At that moment your devoted admirer Paschasius Berselius[2] brought me a letter from your Highness, which gave me a clear picture of an upright and lofty spirit, full worthy of your distinguished lineage, and of a fiery nature born for the study of that sublime philosophy which summons us to the contemplation of heavenly things and breeds contempt for those inferior objects which catch the attention of the vulgar crowd.

This gave me great pleasure, though it was no surprise, especially when I recalled the gifts of your father Robert, a warrior to be compared in military prowess with a Scipio or a Pyrrhus, and the character of your noble mother, who so resembled her excellent brother the Prince of Chimay that it is not kinship so much as rivalry in all the virtues proved her his sister; and then that incomparable prelate the Prince Bishop of Liège, your uncle, to whom I dedicated the last volume of my Paraphrase. Henceforward, surely, priests and even monks will be ashamed to spend their days in luxury and sloth, in games of chance and other sordid pleasures, when you with your exalted birth and your great fortune, in the flower of youth (for you are barely four and twenty), think nothing more important, more pleasant or more glorious than to devote your time to liberal studies and honourable accomplishments, and recall the most famous of historic princes? Well done, O noble youth; keep on your course, adding a glorious lustre by such pursuits to a lineage already distinguished in its own right, and spurring on other young men of great family to pursue honourable studies, as some of them are already inclined to do of their own accord.

Your Lordship would, I suppose, have been satisfied, had I repaid your letter with a letter of my own; and now here is a book to keep my letter company, which I will not recommend to your approval, but I hope to see all men approve it for your sake. The subject may seem somewhat remote from our own time; but in it you can see how far a wise man may praise himself sometimes without offence; how much weight we should give to human authority; how little to ceremonies, and how great the danger to true religion if men trust in ceremonies overmuch. In this Epistle is to be found the famous problem, never, I think, solved by any of the Ancients, out of which rose the well-known dispute between Jerome and Augustine about lying.[3] I have pointed out this still unsolved problem rather than explained it. Here indeed is a worthy subject for the exercise of all your mental force and power.

Farewell, noble young man. I shall count this a most fortunate omen for our friendship, if I find that you give this book a cheerful welcome and read it all through with alacrity.

THE ARGUMENT OF THE EPISTLE
OF PAUL TO THE GALATIANS

BY ERASMUS OF ROTTERDAM

The Galatians are Greeks, but they are descended from the Gauls and, according to St Jerome, 'they resembled their forebears in dullness of wit.'[1] Hilary,[2] himself a Gaul, also says in his book of hymns that the Gauls are 'slow to learn.' And Paul, in a scolding voice, calls them ἀνόητοι [foolish]. Accommodating his discourse to their character, he reproves them more sharply than he does any others in the other epistles. He rebukes more than he teaches, so authority might recall those whom reason could not persuade.

In this epistle he discusses what he discusses everywhere in his writings: he invites us to turn to the grace of the gospel and away from servitude to the law of Moses. He discusses the same thing in the Epistle to the Romans, for they also had fallen into the same error, but in a different way. For the Romans were first led into Judaism and afterwards recovered their senses. The Galatians were correctly taught by the apostle and were drawn back into Judaism through the agency of pseudo-apostles. Because of their naïveté the Romans were falsely taught, but because of their prudence they soon returned to their good senses after they had been admonished. On the other hand, the Galatians embraced Christ because of their good nature, but because they were fickle and foolish they immediately relapsed into Judaism.

Pseudo-apostles therefore had come to them, supposedly sent by Peter and James, the leading apostles. Through misrepresentation they disparaged the authority of Paul, denying his credibility by claiming that he was inconsistent: at one time, they said, he practised the ceremonies of the law, taking vows, shaving his head, and causing Timothy to be circumcised;[3] at another time, among the heathen, he disregarded and condemned the law. Those who have lived with Peter and James and who have seen the Lord Jesus in the flesh[4] should be listened to rather than Paul, who had not seen Christ and who was merely a disciple of the disciples, not of Christ. Consequently Paul, with vehemence and sharp speech (for no epistle is livelier), and with wholesome severity and gentle firmness, both cures the error of the Galatians and asserts his own authority, uncovering the fraud of the pseudo-apostles.

At the very beginning of this epistle he shows that he is equal even to the leading apostles or indeed superior to them, because he had received from heaven – from the already immortal Christ[5] – his authority for preaching the gospel. Relying on his authority, he had for some time preached Christ in Arabia and Damascus before he had indeed seen Peter and James for a few days, although even so he had received no help from them. He said that after this he was a preacher of Christ for fourteen years in Syria and Cilicia until, admonished by God, he returned to Jerusalem together with Barnabas and Titus. There he talked over his own gospel with the leading apostles, not because he had now come to doubt the preaching of so many years, but because he believed that from the approval of those whose authority was very great, others might be strengthened. But when he conferred with Peter, Peter added nothing that had anything to do with the gospel. He was so far from being compelled by Peter to impose the burden of the law on the gentiles that at Antioch when Peter was eating the common food until, overcome by fear of the Jews, he withdrew from the table, Paul publicly rebuked him to his face, teaching that the salvation of the gospel comes from faith, not from observance of a law now abrogated.

Even though he began to say this as though talking to Peter, he pursues the theme in a broader context by turning to the Galatians, demonstrating that the Mosaic law had been given for a restricted period of time only and that all things taught therein pertained to Christ alone. He states that the law is flesh, shadows, appearances, servitude; while the gospel is spirit, light, truth, freedom. He argues further that it would be truly mad for the Galatians, who had tasted better things, to fall back again to the worse. He says these things in chapters 1 through 4.

Then he strongly warns them not to receive circumcision and give themselves shamelessly over to servitude to the law. He points out that Christian liberty is not a licence for sinning but the voluntary performance of the duties of piety, which are fulfilled through the dictates of love, not the decrees of the law. Finally, he exhorts them to Christian concord, to the support of the weaker or the fallen, and to the need for rewarding well those who have taught us the faith. To deeds of this sort, since they are of the spirit, eternal rewards are owed; while for temporal ceremonies there is only a temporary glory.

In passing, Paul brings the pseudo-apostles into disfavour. They were eager for the Galatians to be circumcised, and for no other reason than that they might glory in being the authors of this evil deed. This disease those today have contracted who devise rites which are new[6] and strangely bizarre. It may be said that the disease gives rise to this class of men.

This epistle, it appears, Paul wrote entirely with his own hand in order to testify to his singular affection toward the Galatians. His other epistles, on the other hand, he usually only signs. Latin resumés testify that the letter was written from the city of Ephesus, but the Greek headings read that it was written from the city of Rome.[7]

THE PARAPHRASE ON THE EPISTLE OF PAUL THE APOSTLE TO THE GALATIANS

BY ERASMUS OF ROTTERDAM

Chapter 1

Paul an apostle, and not just any apostle, lest someone scorn me as an apostle of inferior rank or restrain me by an appeal to the authority of other apostles. For this office was not assigned to me by men, as it was to certain others who are only disciples of the apostles but behave as if they were outstanding apostles, or who force their way into the office of apostle by buying up men's favours. Not through any person, no matter how pre-eminent, is authority to preach the gospel entrusted, but through Jesus Christ himself, the Son of God. Christ ordered me to be a preacher of the gospel, not by taking a vote among men; from heaven, with his own voice, he summoned me to this calling after he had already become immortal. Surely he did so by the will and authority of God the Father who raised his Son Jesus from the dead. For he has not ceased to live just because he has ceased to be seen by us. Indeed, if they are rightly accepted as great apostles, whom Christ designated when he was still mortal, living among men and playing the role of a man, certainly I should not be regarded as inferior, since I was summoned to the apostolic service from heaven by Christ, no longer in his role as a man, but as God. For in this I am equal even to the first apostles, that I was called by the same Jesus Christ. I would be able to claim this prerogative by right, because Christ chose them at a time when he was still subject to the infirmities of the body, whereas I was the only one he called apart after he had put aside every weakness of the human condition. Therefore I, Paul, the apostle, and an apostle on this ground, write this letter to all of you who, throughout Galatia, have joined together in the teaching of Christ.

Not I alone greet you, in case you perhaps consider the authority of one man to be slight, but as many as there are here with me (of whom there is a great number), who together with me with one heart profess the name of Christ and have left behind the law of Moses to embrace the faith and teaching of the gospel. We desire for all of you first, grace, then peace and concord: grace which makes it possible that once you have been freely absolved from your former sins, you might hereafter live an innocent and pure life; concord that you may not dissent from other churches or even among yourselves. We are to hope for both things not from Moses or from any mortal, but from God the Father himself from whom all our salvation springs, as though from a fountain; and from his Son our Lord Jesus Christ, through whom he wished to bestow all things upon us freely, and to whom we should give credit for whatever evil we have escaped and whatever good we have attained. For the circumcision of the Mosaic law has not restored innocence to anyone, but Christ himself of his own accord offered himself to death to pay for our sins, so that we might thus fulfil through the grace of the gospel what could not be fulfilled through observance of the Mosaic law; that is, that freed by the kindness of him alone from the sins and harmful desires to which this world is subject, we should henceforth be slaves neither to moral baseness nor to human ceremonies. Such was the will of God our Father, by whom we were first created, and by whom now, after we had fallen back into another's power by our own sin, we have once again been claimed as his own, and as it were, reborn, for we have in a way been made heavenly creatures though formerly of the earth, and have been rendered spiritual though formerly carnal. To him therefore, from whom proceeds all our happiness, be honour and glory, not transitory, as in the case of the Mosaic law, but such as shall never have an end. Amen.

Since I recently preached this to you and you embraced it once, I wonder what has caused you to fall away, and so soon, from so kind a father. You have been alienated from God who freely forgave all your offences and called and invited you to eternal salvation, not through works of the law but through grace and the free gift of Jesus Christ. Now you have suddenly turned back to the servitude of the Mosaic law, as if it were another gospel, although there is no gospel at all except this one which we have preached. What has caused such fickleness? What has caused this frivolity, that makes you want to exchange your freedom, which was freely given to you, for a voluntary servitude? I do not choose to put the blame on your character.[1] Instead, I think the fault lies with certain pseudo-apostles who are more truly preachers of Moses than of Christ. They impose upon your simplicity and confuse you with the splendid titles of the highest apostles, striking fear and terror into your souls, as if you could not obtain salvation without the prop of circumcision. They do not so much renew the ceremonies of the old law, which now ought to have been rejected and abolished, as use them as a pretext to subvert the gospel of Christ. But since the gospel promises complete salvation through faith and piety of life to all those who wish to embrace it, it will be considered vain and deceitful if (as they attempt to teach) the path to eternal salvation is not open unless a little piece of the foreskin is cut off according to the Mosaic rite. God forbid that the authority of any man should remove you from the purity of the gospel. And let the names Peter, or James and John, however great they may be,[2] not move you in the slightest degree. For there are those who misuse these names to ensnare you in the burdens of the law. In fact, even if an angel from heaven preached to you a gospel different from the one we preached to you, not only should you not listen to him, but you should even consider him accursed and a creature to be abhorred. Lest anyone should think that these words have escaped me through resentment or a fit of temper, I repeat them again and again. Whoever it may have been, whether angel or apostle, no matter how famous, if he has preached a gospel different from the one you have received from us, let him be considered accursed and a creature to be abhorred.

For the authority of no man – no, not even an angel – ought to prevail among us, as often as it is a question of correctness of faith. One who preaches the gospel of Christ does the work of God, not of man. Why, therefore, should I fear the authority of any man? The gospel has been entrusted to me by God, not by man. Should I handle it in such a way, I ask, that I satisfy men? Or God, whom I acknowledge as the only authority and Lord? The Jews, because of a certain human tendency, desire to force their own rites upon everyone, clearly in order under this pretext to enhance their own importance. For each one wishes that the things which he himself was taught should appear as outstanding. Accordingly, certain ones earnestly desiring the favour of the Jews, urge circumcision, preach the keeping of the sabbath and the distinctions in foods, just as if they teach something special when they teach these things. But far be it from me to desire so much to please the Jews, who chase after human things more than divine, that I allow the integrity of the gospel to be spoiled by mixing it with Judaism.

At one time I was devoted to Judaism and pleased my people, persecuting in every possible way those who professed the name of Christ. But so long as I please men I displease God, who wished Moses to be set aside and Christ his Son to be brought to light. As long as I was a servant to the law, I was concerned about protecting the prescriptions of Moses, and I sought praise from man. Now God has called me to something different, and by God alone I desire to be commended. And if in the future I should strive after the same praise from men as I once did, I would cease to be a servant of Christ. For how could I appear to be a servant of Christ if I value objects of human zeal more highly than the teachings of Christ, if I fear offending the Jews more than God the Father of Christ and the author of the gospel? After I once dedicated myself to Christ, I never was slave to the ceremonies of Moses which I knew had been rejected on account of the light of Christ. For although several times, while living among the Jews, I have observed some of the rites of my fathers in order to allay a disturbance, nevertheless I have never regarded them as an aid to salvation. I accommodated myself for a time to the feelings of my own people in order to win more to Christ. But when I see that these are perversely misinterpreting my compliance and that the matter has gone so far that they are not afraid to impose observance of the law as a necessary burden on those also whom the gospel finds free from the weight of the law, then I must publicly and freely cry out against the Mosaic rites and solemnly renounce that which turns into an injury to Christ. The authority of no apostle, however famous, shall deter me. Relying on Christ as the source of my authority, I follow his teaching through every danger.

Further, in order that you may better understand that I have not rejected the Mosaic rites rashly, and that I now preach evangelical freedom with such great confidence, I want you to know, brethren, that the gospel which we have delivered to you is not subject to human authority, so that it should be changed at the whim of any man, as though it had originated from a man. As for where these preachers of circumcision got their gospel, let them decide. Certainly I did not procure my gospel from any man nor was I taught it by man, that I should be compelled either to depend on any man's authority or to follow his interpretation. Christ himself saw fit to reveal to me the mystery of the abolition of the old law, and of the introduction of the new law. Thus no one should think either that I changed rashly or that I took up the gospel I preach from a source of too little authority. Christ is a man in such a way that he is not mortal, nor subject to the affections of mortals. Christ is a man in such a way that he is at the same time God.[3] His hidden strength and inspiration changed me suddenly into a different person. Moreover, I was so devoted to the Mosaic law (for I had drunk in its veneration and religion from my forefathers), that I could not have been drawn away from it by any human persuasion, if some divine power had not inspired my soul.

I do not think that what I tell you is obscure. For I believe you know already, through my reputation, how eagerly I formerly displayed my Judaism through my love of the law, and how I abhorred the gospel of Christ, the secret of which I had not yet received. I went so far as to attack, in every possible manner, the new congregation[4] which at that time had begun to gather by the Spirit of God around the teaching of the gospel. I ravaged it with an utterly hostile mind, thinking that I was performing an honourable and pleasing service to God, while in my ignorance I was waging war against God. And certainly my endeavours were succeeding. For in Judaism, which alone at that time I judged to be holy and pious, I gained so much praise among my own people that I distinguished myself above most men of my age.

The more doggedly I clung to the traditions handed down by my forefathers, the more religious I was considered. For I erred in judgment, not in heart, and I opposed the author of the law out of zeal for the law. And God allowed this for a time by some secret plan of his. No doubt God intended that when I was soon after that suddenly changed from a great defender of the law to a preacher of the gospel, I would lead more to Christ by my example. Accordingly, when it pleased God – who had designated and selected me for this undertaking already long ago when I was still in my mother's womb – to reveal his will toward me, and when he called me (who did not deserve such an honour) to this service by his own gracious goodness, in order to use me as an instrument to make known his Son Jesus (for till then he was known to a few Jews, but to almost none of the gentiles, among whom especially he wanted me to be a preacher of the gospel), what then do you think I did? Did I cling to the regulations of my forefathers? Did I hesitate to undertake the duty assigned to me? Did I distrust this oracular command of Christ? Did I discuss[5] my gospel with any apostles of my own race? Or did I go to consult any mortal at all? Did I go to Jerusalem, so that my gospel might be supported by the authority of those who, because they were called to the apostolic rank before me, are highly esteemed? Not at all! For I did not think that it should be confirmed by the authority of man, inasmuch as it had been given to me by the order of Christ himself.

As a matter of fact, immediately after I discovered the error of my ways, after I accepted my command from heaven, I went without delay to Arabia and did not shrink from presenting the name of Christ, until then either obscure or hateful, to wild and barbarian races. And I preached the grace of the gospel with no less zeal than I formerly had preached the Mosaic law. After I left Arabia, I returned to Damascus where I had first begun to preach the name of Christ after I was baptized.[6] Then after three years I came to Jerusalem in order to visit Peter rather than to confer with him. However, I stayed with him no more than fifteen days, because he seemed to hold first place among the apostles. I was not eager to see any of the other apostles except James, surnamed the Just, who was called a brother of the Lord because of the distinguished holiness of his life. He, out of them all, was the first to be made bishop in the church at Jerusalem. I am far from despairing of my gospel and from fleeing to human aids. I do not lie. God himself is my witness, by whose command I undertook the preaching of the gospel. After these things I went into the regions of Syria and Cilicia, proclaiming everywhere the name of Christ. For in these regions also some congregations of Jews had begun to unite in the teaching of Christ. But I was little known by sight to them, even though I myself was a Jew by birth. This only had they learned from rumour, that I was the one who had suddenly been changed by the divine will from a persecutor of the Christian faith, and that I had now become a preacher of that faith; that the faith which I at one time opposed with all my might I now defended at peril to my life. For this reason they doubly glorified God who caused this change because they had been freed from the serious worry of persecution and because they had obtained such a defender of their own profession.

Chapter 2

When I had already preached the doctrine of the gospel for fourteen years, chiefly to the gentiles, I went again to Jerusalem with my associates Barnabas and Titus, whom I wanted to be witnesses to this fact. I did this, however, not out of duty as was the case earlier, but commanded by a divine oracle in order that it would be all the more clear to the Jews that salvation is no longer to be sought through circumcision, but through faith in the gospel. For they would see that so many gentiles had been called to a universal salvation without the aid of circumcision. Therefore, I discussed with them my gospel which up to now I preach among the heathen by Christ's command. But I spoke primarily to those who were most influential among the Jews, to the end that none of them who still believed in combining the Mosaic law with the gospel of Christ would publicly assert that in the race course of the gospel I had been running, or was still running, in vain. For without mentioning circumcision, I promised [the gentiles] the same salvation through the gift of faith that we who are circumcised hope for, relying on Christ. We were far from believing that the burden of circumcision ought to be imposed upon the gentiles.

In fact, while Titus was living in Jerusalem and among Jews who held doggedly onto circumcision, not even he was compelled[1] by the apostolic leaders of the Jews to be circumcised, for the very reason that he was a Greek, not a Jew. All the less ought you in your Galatia to be compelled to this by pseudo-apostles. Those who held the highest rank among the apostles did not require of us that we circumcise a Greek – no doubt because they wanted the servitude of the law gradually to be abolished and the freedom of the gospel confirmed. But certain ones had sneaked into our company who are called Christians falsely since they press for that which Christ intended to make obsolete. Deceitfully indeed they had sneaked into our company in order to spy out the freedom which the gospel of Christ brought to birth for us. They were envious of the gospel and proposed to drag us back through circumcision into servitude to the law. It was rather they who pressed us so hatefully that it seemed as though we would have to give in to avoid an uproar. However, we did not yield or comply with them even for a moment by circumcising Titus. We did this in your interest, so that you would not fall away from the truth of the gospel into Judaism and imitate voluntarily what might have been done to Titus out of necessity. But if certain men, whose authority is especially great, sometimes required or permitted circumcision of certain others, it makes no difference to me whether they acted rightly or not. It is enough that they have left behind their former opinions and now agree with me. Among men the opinion of a person has value. Before God, it is only conformity to the truth that counts. I grant that those may be more pre-eminent than I in authority. But as far as the integrity of the gospel is concerned, I gained nothing[2] from them – in fact, they gained something from me.

For after I had shared my gospel with them, they perceived that the duty of preaching the gospel among the gentiles had been entrusted to me by Christ, just as the duty of preaching it among the Jews had been delegated to Peter, and that my preaching was no less effective without the aid of circumcision than Peter's had been with circumcision. In our discussion with them, they recognized that I too had been granted an equal share of the gospel. As a result, Peter, James, and John (for they seemed to be the pillars among them) were so far from condemning our gospel that instead they extended their right hands in agreement and fellowship with Barnabas and me. We were to preach the gospel with united hearts, each in his own sphere: we among the gentiles, they among the Jews. They did not impose upon us the necessity of demanding that any of the gentiles be circumcised. They requested only that while preaching the gospel among the gentiles we remember the poor who were living in Jerusalem, in case anyone wished to collect some relief for them. We eagerly obeyed their commands, seeing that they were not inconsistent with evangelical teaching. By no means would we have obeyed if they had ordered us to circumcise the Greeks. For it is not right that the authority of any mortal should carry such weight with us that in pleasing him we neglect the work of the gospel.

And yet, at the start the situation demanded that some temporary concession be made to those who had turned from Judaism to the gospel (since they could not be completely diverted from the teachings of their ancestors, whose religion they had been fed from youth), otherwise many might have been driven away from Christ. But we had to try to teach them, hoping that eventually they would listen to our counsel and cease to use this indulgence, especially when it seemed that indulgence would result in far more danger than gain. For the number of Jews who have embraced the faith of the gospel is very small compared to the gentiles we have won to Christ. And from these too in the future a much more fertile hope smiles upon us, inasmuch as so many nations of gentiles are spread far and wide, while the race of the Jews is circumscribed by very narrow boundaries. The greater number of the gentiles were so averse to circumcision that they would have rejected Christ sooner than submit to the yoke of the odious law. There is also another danger, that if for a long time Jewish Christians make indiscriminate use of this indulgence, the free gift of salvation (which God wished to see credited to his own goodness and our faith) may appear to be owed in large part to the ceremonies of the law. If they perceive that these ceremonies are being observed by the chief apostles, those who are somewhat superstitious will conclude that without these ceremonies the faith of the gospel is not enough for attaining salvation. For everyone sees what is done, but not the spirit behind it. Mortals' minds are usually suspicious; they interpret everything in the worst sense. Thus, what those did for a time – going against their own opinions by giving in to the unconquerable superstition of some – others will conclude was due to religion, not compliance. This excusable weakness of the Jews was tolerated for a time, but they should have moved beyond it, little by little. But by no means must we allow that to be required of the gentiles which was tolerated for a time in the case of the Jews. At first the Jews were excused by the conviction which they derived from their forefathers by long usage, the strength of which is equal to nature, by the fact that God was the author of their religion, and by many other things. The gentiles, however, will be able to find no such defence if they combine Christ with Moses. But the special care of the gentiles was assigned to me, just as the special care of the Jews was assigned to Peter. And it is fitting that each be especially devoted to his own sphere.

Indeed, in this matter I intend to yield to the authority of no one. Therefore, when Peter came to Antioch, although I saw that among the apostles he was first in authority, nevertheless I was not afraid to oppose him publicly and to his face;[3] I regarded the work of the gospel as more important than his rank. And I did not hesitate to rebuke him before everyone for the fear and vacillation which he displayed,[4] since his behaviour was reprehensible[5] especially on this ground, that it was leading to the destruction of many who were misinterpreting his intention, thinking that he acted thus because of superstition, not because of his deep concern for the weakness of the Jews. For at first he took his place at a dinner with some of the gentiles who had given assent to the gospel and ate the common food together with them. But when, soon afterwards, several Jews who had been sent by James arrived, he began to withdraw from the dinner, pretending that he had not shared a common meal together with them. Doubtless he was afraid he would offend the conscience of those he suspected were still too superstitious to be able to overlook an indiscriminate choice of foods, and who thought it showed a lack of piety for a Jew actually to share a common meal with the heathen. This pretence[6] by Peter, although it arose from a pious mind, was nevertheless rather imprudent and threatened to bring about the open destruction of many. In fact, not only the other Jews who sat at our table approved Peter's pretence, but even Barnabas my colleague was so moved by the authority of Peter that he too began to withdraw together with Peter from the dinner. I had no doubt that nearly all the others would have imitated their pretence if he had not encountered a sharp and clear rebuke.

And so I saw that some were wavering,[7] accommodating themselves now to the gentiles, now to the Jews, and that they were not straightly and constantly enough proceeding towards the truth of the gospel which now had shone forth so brightly that the time had come to declare frankly and firmly this truth, that the ceremonies of the law had been set aside and contributed nothing toward the salvation offered by the gospel. To remedy the danger to everyone, I opposed Peter in the presence of all so that, after the correction of their leader, the others, seeing that Peter submitted to our admonition, would return to their senses and emulate him. I opposed him with these words: 'What are you doing Peter? With what intention are you withdrawing? Why, out of a misguided fear for your own people, are you thoughtlessly leading these people of mine into destructive superstition? For although you are by nature a Jew, you have nevertheless condemned the superstition of your people, and you live in the manner of the gentiles, considering nothing impure which is not impure to God. And since you did this formerly with Cornelius the Centurion, and recently with us, why do you act differently now and contradict yourself by withdrawing from our dinner? It is as if your former lack of concern about the choice of foods and commerce with gentiles was not really based on a definite plan and decision but on human courtesy. Do you not realize where your example leads? Not only will it confirm the Jews in their own superstition which should be abolished; but since you are first among the apostles, your example will also force those gentiles who have been joined to Christ to be weighed down by Jewish ceremonies from which Christ has wished them to be free. Christ's wish extended not only to those whom the grace of the gospel finds free from the law, but also to the Jews themselves whom the grace of the gospel finds under obligation to the law.'

We are not descended from the gentiles (all of whom the Jews consider sinful and impure, and the preaching of the gospel discovers as idolaters), but we are Jews by race, born under the law which we rightly served for a time. Nevertheless we have been taught that true righteousness does not come to anyone through the observance of the law, but rather through trust, by which we hope for salvation through the free goodness of Christ. We have lost faith in the law of our forefathers and fled to faith in Christ, by whose help we promise ourselves true righteousness, a righteousness which commends us not to men but to God, and which observance of the law was incapable of accomplishing since it was ineffective. In view of this, shall we cause the gentiles to lose faith in Christ and flee to the protection of the law, even though we have discovered by our experience that no mortal whatsoever can attain true righteousness by the help of the law? If we do this, of what use was it to pass over to the faith of the gospel? But once we have embraced the faith of the gospel, if we nevertheless still find ourselves subject to sin, and need to find still another remedy (as we did when we were under the law of Moses) and all our hopes are dashed so that we have to flee back again to the law we had abandoned, what shall we say? That Christ, whom we have believed the author of perfect righteousness, is rather the tinder of unrighteousness? That he not only failed to remove the old unrighteousness but actually took the opportunity to pile up more unrighteousness? That he not only failed to confer the salvation longed for, but in addition led us to a more severe condemnation? Through trust in Christ we have abandoned the law; if we are now compelled to return to it, it appears that we have abandoned it wrongly and inadvisedly and that Christ has given the opportunity for this evil.

But far be it from anyone to feel this way, and think that we must turn to the law of Moses to gain salvation because of some deficiency in the grace of the gospel. For after we have embraced the law of the gospel, to return again to the law of Moses amounts to a desertion of Christ and an insult to the gospel. On the contrary, anyone who does this, whether Jew or proselyte, clearly shows that he has transgressed the Mosaic law as well. For if the law had anything to do with achieving salvation, why did he abandon it? If not, why return to it? If I demolish a building and erect it again from the same foundations, do I myself not witness to my own offence by restoring what I wrongly destroyed? Therefore, now that we have embraced evangelical faith through which the kindness of Christ wished to confer perfect righteousness and salvation upon us, there is no reason for us to look to the protection of the burdensome[8] law to which we have ceased to be subject.

For just as the death of a husband or wife frees the surviving spouse from the law of marriage,[9] so I as a Jew had to do with the law as long as our mutual obligation lasted, and the law was alive to me and I alive to the law. But as soon as I was given over through the death of Christ and the sacred bath to the law of faith which is spiritual, I died – in a way – to the burdensome law.[10] Not that I ceased to live, but I began to live more happily. Formerly I was alive to Moses, now I am alive to God. For God is spirit. Just as

Christ previously lived as a mortal, carrying around a body subject to our evils, so he died to the flesh, to men; now he is alive to God the Father, free from all the vicissitudes of mortality. And I, through baptism, have been crucified together with Christ. I have died together with him and so little am I concerned with these gross things which savour of flesh rather than of spirit that I am actually dead to them. For it is not my former self which lives, a gross, carnal man, subject to human desires. Saul, that champion of the law and persecutor[11] of the gospel, has died, and yet I live better now that I have drunk in the Spirit of Christ. In fact, I myself do not live, I who of myself am nothing other than carnal; but Christ, whose Spirit guides all my deeds by his own will, lives in me. Moreover, I am not yet completely free from all the taint of mortality, but I still carry around this body, which to some extent is subject to human passions and the vicissitudes of mortality. In a way, nevertheless, I live an immortal life which has been apprehended by a sure hope.

In this I rely on the promiser, the Son of God, whose free grace has brought me the gift of faith, and through faith, righteousness. Righteousness will bring immortality, not through observance of the burdensome law but through the unprecedented love of Christ who, of his own free will, loved me though I did not deserve it, to the extent of paying the penalty for my sins on the cross. He gave himself up to death for my salvation. What he bestowed upon us is wholly free. He wanted us to owe our salvation to his kindness, not to observance of the law. Of his own accord he confers this benefit upon all; he takes away sins and bestows innocence. Would I not be the most ungrateful man, indeed would I not insult Christ, if I reject what he offers? But does he not reject it who looks back to the protection of the law after he has received baptism, as if the death of Christ was not powerful enough to abolish the sins of the whole world and confer eternal salvation on all? For if immortality is reached through innocence, what, I ask, is the cause of our hope for both? Is it trust in the law or in the goodness of Christ? If our hope is due to the goodness of Christ, why do we still depend upon the law? If our hope is due to observance of the law, Christ must have died in vain, since we do not obtain through his death that for which he was willing to die.

Chapter 3

Everywhere you have a reputation for being simple-minded and gullible. But in this instance, O truly foolish Galatians, who could ever be made to believe such an absurdity, that now that the faith of the gospel has freed the Jews from the burden of the law, you, who were born free, are voluntarily handing yourselves over to servitude? Whatever evil there is here I do not impute wholly to you. I do blame your credulity and gullibility, but I blame even more the malice of certain men who enticed you to this. If only you had preferred to follow your own inclinations rather than the pernicious counsel of others! Who was that man who envied the happiness you were enjoying until then through the liberty of the gospel and bewitched[1] you with an evil spell? Who charmed you out of your former mind which was worthy of Christ and cast upon you such a spell of madness that you seem to have lost faith in Christ, and are fleeing to the protection of the frigid law? Where now is that noble trust by which, through the death of Christ, you used to hope for perfect righteousness and salvation without the aid of the law? Jesus Christ, the one author of all salvation, had been so stamped upon your minds, and you saw him so much with the eyes of faith[2] as the one who reconciles the whole world to the Father through his cross, that it was as if he had been portrayed[3] before your eyes, or as if the event at Jerusalem had occurred before you as witnesses. You saw more than the Jews who looked upon him as he hung on the cross and denied him. In your midst he was truly crucified, and by his death you hoped for eternal salvation. You used to turn your eyes to the brass serpent fastened onto the wood, from which alone you hoped for a remedy for all your sins. Now you have suddenly been changed, and in what direction do you turn away your eyes?

    If there is still any soundness in your minds, at least weigh carefully what is yet before you and what could be clear even to a blind man, to prevent me from pleading with subtle and far-fetched arguments. You remember that recently you received the Spirit of Christ at the preaching of the gospel, through baptism and the laying on of our hands.[4] Your belief was not unfounded. Miracles[5] of tongues, prophecies, healings, and other gifts taught that this was a matter of divine power, not human delusion.[6] Did you receive this Spirit from Mosaic circumcision or from believing in the gospel of Christ through me? You were not under the Mosaic law, but thanks to your faith, Christ imparted to you his own powerful Spirit, a sure pledge of the promised happiness. Why now do you hope for salvation from another source when you have so clear an assurance of salvation? If I preached circumcision to you and if the heavenly Spirit came upon you through trust in circumcision, I do not prevent you from crediting some portion of salvation to the Mosaic law. But if you have learned nothing from me except Jesus Christ and if, after you placed your trust in him alone, you experienced the same gifts in yourselves which the Jews receive through baptism, why do you think that a burdensome and profitless Judaism ought to be summoned to insult Christ?

    It is characteristic of the wise to make progress from any sort of beginning to better things. You, on the contrary, after such a glorious beginning, are falling back to worse things. The Jews, born under servitude of the burdensome law, have left behind the ceremonies of their forefathers and commit themselves to the spiritual teaching of the gospel. You, on the contrary, although you began your profession from the gospel, are degenerating into Judaism. They are becoming Christians after having been Jews. Do you desire to become Jews after having been Christians? If the Mosaic law confers salvation, what need was there to pledge yourselves to Christ? Why do you now abandon him for whose sake you have suffered so many afflictions at the hands of those to whom the name of Christ is hateful? For whoever holds out to himself the hope of salvation through circumcision falls away from Christ. Will you then act in such a way that you appear to have suffered in vain so many evils arising from your profession of Christ? But God forbid that you have endured these things in vain. Thus far you have erred in judgment, not in heart;[7] you have vacillated due to another's influence, not because of any ill will on your part. You will come to your senses in time, and will not permit the fruit of your original faith to perish.

Does God, therefore, who imparts his own Spirit to you and demonstrates his own strength through you by the evidence of miracles, do this for you because you have won him over by your observance of the Mosaic law? Rather, is it not because you believed us when we were preaching Christ? If proselytes who are received into Judaism experience that abundance of signs when they are circumcised which you experience, you have reason to think the law must be desired. But if such signs accompany evangelical faith alone, why do you expect that the end will come from any other source than did the beginning which you see?

The originator and author of circumcision is Abraham; the Jews boast that they are his sons, and they follow his example in being circumcised. And yet not even Abraham obtained the praise of true righteousness on the basis of circumcision, but on the basis of the faith in God who was making the promises, a faith he had before he was circumcised. For we do not read in Genesis [15:6]: 'Abraham was circumcised and was made righteous,' but 'Abraham believed God and this was imputed to him as righteousness.' And so, what was formerly promised to the descendants of Abraham does not apply to those who have nothing in common with Abraham except circumcision, but to those who as true sons represent anew the faith of the parent and believe the gospel. Moreover, those who are puffed up with circumcision and display themselves in public as sons of Abraham boast in vain, since they are bastards, not legitimate sons of Abraham. For according to God those are, in the final analysis, the sons of Abraham who, following his example, believe with all their hearts, and trust God who speaks to us through the gospel, no matter to what race they trace their origin. For this relationship is not determined by affinity of blood but by emulation of mind.

But notice that this message was foreseen and indicated long ago in scripture, namely, that righteousness should be expected by all through faith, not by a few through circumcision. What today is preached to you through the gospel, God promised many ages ago to Abraham saying: 'All nations will attain praise and blessing in you' [Gen 12:3]. Now all nations could not possibly have been born from Abraham; and yet at the same time a blessing is promised to all through him, as if to his descendants, not, surely, because of blood relationship, but because of the emulation of faith. For it is characteristic of sons to be like their parents. Consequently those who trust the promises of the gospel and abandon faith in the works and [8] ceremonies of the law will receive, as true sons of Abraham, along with their parent in the faith, the blessing promised to Abraham. And those will be shut out who place their faith in the protection of circumcision, just as if they were bastards born in adultery. A curse rather than blessing is appropriate for them.

For those who depend on the observance of the Mosaic law, which, however, they do not observe, are subject to a curse. The Jews themselves cannot deny this, since it stands written in Deuteronomy [27:26]: 'Let anyone be cursed who does not persevere in all things written in the book of the law' and fulfil those things commanded by the law. Righteousness is not promised for observing the law, but a curse is pronounced for not observing it. However, who could fulfil the whole law? For it incites a desire to sin through prohibition without conferring the strength to conquer the desire of the heart. Finally, if anyone can fulfil the whole law, perhaps he will be considered righteous among men; he will not be so considered by God. If no one merits praise for righteousness before God by observing the law, then it is clear that what the prophet Habakkuk wrote [2:4] is undoubtedly true: 'The righteous lives by faith.' For just as sin is the breeding ground of death, so is innocence the source of life. However, the law does not depend on faith but on observance of prescribed ceremonies. Those who observe these will indeed obtain life, but not the eternal life which faith promises. The life given by the law is of the same kind as the righteousness which the law offers. Among men he is righteous who does not violate prescriptions of the law; among men such a person lives safe from punishment. But before God he will not be righteous nor will he live, unless he trusts in the promises of the gospel.

Christ alone of all was not subject to the curse, for he was wholly innocent and owed nothing to the law. We were guilty and for this reason accursed. But he freed the guilty from the curse, changing our guilt into innocence and our curse into a blessing. He is very far from wanting you[9] to be led into servitude to the law. How has he liberated you? Though innocent himself, he paid the penalty owed for our crimes, thus taking upon himself the curse which held us firmly in its grasp. He did this though otherwise free from the curse and a partner in the blessing. Did he not take our crimes upon himself when as a criminal among criminals he underwent the ignominious punishment of the cross to redeem us? For we read in Deuteronomy [21:23]: 'Cursed is anyone who hangs on a tree.' Why, however, did God want this to happen? Clearly in order that the curse brought by the law[10] might be removed and that the blessing through faith[11] formerly promised to Abraham might take its place. And further, that the blessing might replace the curse not only among the Jews but also among the gentiles, not through the benefit of the law which Christ wanted abolished, but through the kindness of Jesus Christ. Thus, reconciled to God and freed from the burden of the burdensome law through his death, we will obtain through faith the evangelical blessing promised to the descendants of Abraham, descendants I say,[12] not according to the flesh, but according to the Spirit. Let us have faith in a trustworthy God, for he will not deceive anyone. He will fulfil what he has promised.

So that you might better understand this, I shall bring forward a human example. For although there is no comparison between God and men, nevertheless no one rescinds the testament of a man or a covenant,[13] or adds anything beyond[14] the will of the testator once it has been approved and established. All the more should this be the case for the established covenants and promises of God. He promised a blessing to Abraham which was intended to reach all nations through his seed. Scripture says 'seed,' not 'seeds,' so that we would not hope for the promise through Moses or David or any others. But it has designated Jesus Christ that one seed, the true seed of Abraham the eternal father. We are incorporated into Christ through baptism and the communion of the Spirit, and we anticipate the same things through him which God has already fulfilled for him.

But let us consider the proposed example. This covenant which God made once with Abraham before the law was established – a covenant he wanted ratified – cannot be made null and void by the law which followed the promise. Now this would happen if the inheritance of the blessing promised to the descendants of Abraham was due to the observance of the law, since there was no stipulation about the law in the covenant. How could there have been, since the law itself did not yet exist? Moreover, even supposing that the law had not followed the promise, God would still have carried out for the descendants of Abraham the covenant which he had made with Abraham. But if the inheritance of this happiness is due to the promise, and if the promise came before the law and does not involve the condition of observing the law, why do we bar from the promise those who are strangers to the law, but are not strangers to faith? For if the inheritance is obtained with the help of the law, it seems that the covenant with God is rendered null and void inasmuch as he does not wish to fulfil the covenant without the additional stipulation of the law. It is just as if someone made an agreement with a man to give him his daughter as a wife and then, after the contract had been duly completed, he refused to give him his daughter unless the man should hand over his sister to him to marry in exchange, although at the time the agreement was made the sister had not yet been born and the pact had made no mention of a reciprocal marriage. The promise of God was free and it was established on the sole condition of faith. Anyone who fulfils this condition maintains his right to the promise.

But someone might say: 'If we were intended to hope for salvation from this source, for what reason did God afterwards add the useless law?' It was not completely useless. For even if it does not confer innocence, it restrains the licence to sin, holding back evil desires by means of ceremonies which serve as a kind of barricade. The law would not have been given if our unbridled malice had not required it. And yet it was not given to bind everyone forever, but for a time fixed beforehand by God, during which [time] it prefigured Christ by images, deterred people from sin by punishment, and invited them by promises to strive for innocence. For this purpose the law was established with God as its author, and conveyed through the angels until, after centuries had passed, that one seed should come forth through which the God of Abraham had promised salvation to all the legitimate sons of Abraham. But the law was conveyed by angels in such a way that power over all of it remained with Christ, and he, standing midway,[15] intervened between the Mosaic law and the grace of the gospel, in such a manner that he was the end of the former and the beginning of the latter. He interposed himself between God and men in such a way that he included in himself the nature of both, for he intended to reconcile the one to the other. But a conciliator who intercedes has to intercede among several parties. For no one disagrees with himself. However, God is one, and there was discord between him and the human race.[16] Consequently, a third party was necessary who would share both natures and reconcile them to each other. He would placate God by his death and lure men by his teaching to the true worship of God.

Does the law, then, oppose the promises of God? By no means! In coming after the promises of God, the law did not render them null and void, but rather made men continue in the expectation of the promises, in order to make them all the more capable of receiving evangelical grace. The law has not now ceased because it opposed the divine promises, but because a shadow rightly gives way to the real and what lacks power gives way to what has power. For if the law which was given had been of a kind which could truly bestow life, there would have been no reason to abrogate it. There would have been no need for the aid of the gospel, since righteousness would truly come to man through the law. It would have been enough, therefore, for all who sought eternal salvation to put confidence in such a law. Now, lest they should rely on their own works and neglect the grace of Christ, the law was given for the purpose of prescribing what ought to be done and what avoided. In this way, all might understand that they were guilty of sins. For although they have learned from the law what is sinful, still they do not avoid it, overcome, no doubt, by their own perverse desires. Thus recognizing their sickness, they would more eagerly embrace the remedy offered to them by the grace of the gospel. Before rules were laid down in the law, they sinned with impunity, since it appeared that they might do whatever they liked, and they had a pretext to excuse their crimes. But the law so shackled them that they could not avoid acknowledging that they deserved punishment since they were not able to deny that what the law prescribed was good. By this plan, when God had taken away from us our trust in ourselves and had placed our evil before our eyes, it was revealed that this promise – which God made to Abraham and which the Jews alone awaited as if the promise had a special reference to them as the only sons of Abraham – it was revealed, I say, that the promise pertained to all who had become true sons of Abraham by their trust in God. They became true sons, not by the merit of observing the law, but by believing with a sincere heart the gospel that through the death of Jesus Christ innocence, life, and salvation came to all.

For a time the Mosaic law also served the purpose of restraining the Jews, as if hemming them in with a wall, in part by threats of punishment, in part by the expectation of the promise, in part by foreshadowing the coming of Christ. Thus when Christ came, he would not find them fallen headlong into every kind of impiety and hence unworthy and unreceptive to the grace of the gospel. Through the promises of the law, therefore, they dreamed in one way or another about the mystery of the gospel. They were therefore dependent on the tutelage of the law only until that could be disclosed which the law had outlined in shadows, and until they could awaken and see exhibited in a bright light what previously they had awaited as through a dream.

Therefore, the law did not offer perfect righteousness, but it had been given like a pedagogue[17] to an untutored people so that if a regard for virtue could not yet hold them to their duty, the fear of punishment might restrain them from great outrages. Thus gradually making progress, they might be led to Christ, through whom alone, after they had abandoned faith in their earlier ceremonies, they could expect true righteousness. However, a pedagogue is not given to boys to be with them always, but only until they have grown up and by their own will are attracted to honourable things. Then they have no need to be restrained from crime by fear of punishment. Rather, through the encouragement of their father they are voluntarily and willingly drawn toward honourable things, and in turn they begin to issue orders to the same pedagogues whose severity, which was beneficial for a time, they used to endure. Thus a father, although he maintains a unique affection for his children, nevertheless forces them to serve for a time a pedagogue whose master they are soon to become. In the same manner, God restrained his own people by the severity of the law when they were still young and uncultivated, until, by laying hold of evangelical faith, they should be restored to him, and cease to be under the jurisdiction of a pedagogue, but instead live freely as free-born sons under the mercy of a most kind parent.

But God did not consider the Jews alone as his sons, although the pedagogue was given to them alone. On the contrary, all who are grafted through evangelical faith into the body of Jesus Christ and drink in his Spirit, are made one with Christ and thus rendered sons of God. But if this way of being joined to Christ is open to all, surely God will acknowledge all equally as sons? Through baptism, not circumcision, you have drunk in the Spirit of Christ. Therefore, as many of you as are baptized have passed over into the fellowship of Christ. In this respect, you are not at all inferior to the Jews who vaunt themselves by their privilege of circumcision. In other things, which depend on human indulgence, the distinctions of conditions and persons are maintained, but God wanted this benefit of his to be as common to all as it was freely given to all. Through baptism we are reborn and suddenly transformed as if into another creature. Whatever one was before baptism, whether Jew or Greek, slave or free, male or female, is not credited for or against him so far as this gift is concerned. Through baptism you all have passed over into the body of Christ, equally sharing in this gift, which flows, as it were, from the head to all other parts of the body. But if Christ is that seed of Abraham through which God promised his blessing to all nations, then you who are grafted into Christ must be the offspring of Abraham. If you are descendants of Abraham, you come as heirs to the right of the promise. If the name of son is given through fellowship with Christ and all are equally received into this fellowship through faith and baptism, the inheritance must belong equally to all.

Chapter 4

This legal right was long since owed because of the promise, but now at last
we are admitted into it. For, as we said before, according to human law, so
long as an heir is a minor he does not exercise his own authority; indeed, he
differs in no way from a slave, even though by birth he may be lord of all. He
is held back by fear and led by the will of others, living under guardians and
governors[1] until he reaches the adult age which the will of his father or the
law has prescribed. Likewise, when formerly we were not yet able to grasp
this gift because it requires completely heavenly minds, and our minds had
not yet gathered adequate strength, we also were confined like children, by
laws quite carnal and clearly accommodated to our weakness. For we did not
yet understand that heavenly teaching but were only impressed by things
which can be discerned with corporeal eyes. These are the kinds of things
which consist of the elements[2] of this lower world, as distinctions among
days, choices of foods, differences in ritual, animal sacrifices, marks on
the body. To all these rules we submitted for a time in the manner of slaves,
as long as we were not yet ready for a higher station. But as soon as we
ceased to be children[3] and reached the age of adulthood, when the measure
of time had passed which the eternal Father by his own secret plan had set
up for us, God did not any longer allow us to be enslaved to these too
burdensome rules but for this purpose he sent, not Moses or a prophet, but
his only Son Jesus Christ. Moreover, he sent him not in a dream or vision, but
exhibited him publicly to all our senses.[4] God wanted him born as a man from
a woman, subject to the evils of our nature,[5] so that he might in person heal
our injuries. God wanted him both to be circumcised and to endure all the
rest of the servitude to the law, so that the Jews whom he found subject to
the law he might release from its burden. In this way no one, as though a
child,[6] would still serve as if under governors, but we would all be adopted
into the freedom of sons. For slavery is inconsistent with the name of son.

 And in order that the divine goodness might teach by an infallible proof
that we have been given the liberty of sons, no longer afraid of punishments,
he poured the Spirit of his only Son into the innermost recesses of our hearts.
This Spirit is our surest witness that we are the sons of God. For the spirit of
slaves breathes and cries out one thing, the feeling of sons, another. The
former prays that it may escape from the anger of the lord, while the latter
cries out 'Abba, Father,' with great trust. And we do not doubt that God
acknowledges the appeal of piety and love, not of fear. If this were not true,
Christ would not have called his followers brothers, and he would not have
taught us to address the universal God by the name of father: 'Our Father,

who art in heaven.' Consequently, whenever God imparts the Spirit of his Son to someone, that one is no longer a slave but a son. But if he is a son through Christ, he must be an heir through Christ also. For whoever adopts someone else and gives him the name of son receives him into the right of the inheritance.

But just as the Jews were for a time confined by carnal religion – or rather, by superstition – to prevent them from completely falling away from all religion, so you at one time, when you did not know the true God, worshipped demons because of the tradition of your forefathers. Now although the demons are believed to be gods, they really are not. Yet, one who is in the grip of a false religion would seem closer to true religion than one who believes there is no deity and is affected by no religious feeling at all. It is not charged against the Jews[7] that, because of the nature of the times, they were subservient to the traditions of their forefathers, for after they were taught better things they turned away from such teachings and devoted themselves to a true zeal for piety. Nor is the worship of images charged against you. For you judged that such images had divine power and you worshipped them in error, but later, through evangelical preaching you came to know the true God, or rather, you were known by him. For God has not been discovered by you, but he himself has drawn you to himself[8] by the breath of his Spirit. Hence you love him now as a father for no other reason than that he first loved you. The first error is easily forgiven, but the disgrace is inexpiable[9] if, after having recognized the truth, you wilfully fall back again into your original error.[10] The Jews are abandoning their own ceremonies now that they have learned about the true cultivation of piety. You have been called back from the worship of idols, have been instructed thoroughly in true piety through the gospel and have received the heavenly Spirit; but now you are rushing back into servitude to Judaism. Thus, although you are free, you desire of your own accord to serve the elements of this world which do not have the power to confer righteousness and are not efficacious for salvation.

Are you not slipping back when you observe days, months, and years, and other differences of the times according to Jewish superstition? Does true salvation derive in any way from the keeping of sabbaths, new moons, feast days, and other occasions on which the Jews perform particular ceremonies, or abstain from certain things as if they were impious? Do they contribute anything to true salvation when, for Christians, all occasions are free opportunities for the cultivation of piety? If you truly trust in Christ, whence this superstition of yours? If you do not trust, I fear that I have in vain undertaken such great labour in instructing you. For indeed you do fall away from Christ if you mix in Judaism. Do not let it come about that I have laboured in vain in handing on the gospel to you through various afflictions, and that you have suffered such great evils for Christ in vain. But rather be like me. You see that I have abandoned observance of the law, trusting in Christ alone. I, too, was at one time as you are now, supposing that being circumcised, observing sabbaths, discrimination in foods, and sacrifices of animals was some kind of exceptional piety. At that time I persecuted the church of God out of zeal for these things, all of which I now disregard as useless.

Brothers, when I dispute with you so vehemently about these things, believe me, I have your interests at heart, not my own. I myself could have been satisfied with my own inner knowledge of the right. I am not angry with you because of any injury you may have inflicted on me. I pity you if you degenerate from such excellent beginnings. Be constant and always advance to better things rather than falling back to the worse. When first preaching the gospel of Jesus Christ to you, I lowered myself to your weakness, now you in turn should raise yourselves to my strength. Do not lose that splendid glory of your faith. For you know that before when I passed on the gospel to you, I put on no great display, but I exhibited the outward appearance of a humble and lowly man of no importance. What you saw was an insignificant man, subject to troubles, hateful to many on account of the name of Christ, troubled by many afflictions,[11] with a rough and simple way of speaking. I did not preach anything else to you except Jesus Christ crucified for you,[12] and so quick was the response of your faith then that you did not reject any of these things as offensive and scorn our gospel when we promised immortality on the basis of this faith.[13] On the contrary, you received me with the greatest eagerness and the greatest honour, not as Paul but as an angel of God, indeed, as Jesus Christ himself. You understood that this was not a human but a divine teaching which I introduced to you, and that I was working not for my own interests but for Jesus Christ. Therefore you worshipped God in me, Christ in me. These things show that your faith was at one time most worthy, so quick and constant that it could not be weakened by any troubles of mine or any appearance of humility.

I rejoiced with you on this account, I judged you blessed, I considered myself fortunate to have such disciples. But if you repent of your beginnings, where is that happiness of yours, of mine, in which we used to rejoice with each other? For I ought to witness to the fact that the inclination of your heart toward me was so great that you would even have plucked out your eyes and given them to me if the need had arisen. For what reason are you now estranged from us, and why do you adopt new apostles from whom you might learn Judaism? Those men are luring you by deceit and flattery and are winning you over, not by preaching things which are conducive to your salvation but by preaching things which make for their own profit and pride. Have I therefore become your enemy because I have reminded you truly and simply about things which I realized would contribute to your salvation? For my part I see, Galatians, what is going on. Certain men solicit you and, as if envious of me, entice you, but not with a sincere mind. They do not do these things out of concern for you, but rather to draw you back to Judaism, to which they themselves are subject, and to shut you off from the freedom of the gospel. For they seek to make others like themselves, so that they themselves may appear to follow as well as teach an excellent and wonderful doctrine. Do not think that anything and everything ought to be emulated.¹⁴ Only what is right should be emulated, and that constantly, not only when I am present among you, but also when I am absent. You have seen that I disregard the ceremonies of the law, that I preach nothing except Christ, and you emulated me in this when I was present. If that was right, why, now that I am absent, do you seek to emulate others in those things which are not right?

Would that you could turn your eyes into my heart. You would certainly see with how great a sadness of spirit I write these things. My little children, I once brought you to birth in Christ, not without much travail and pain. And once again, now that you are falling away from Christ, I am in travail over you, until Christ is fully formed in you. I had sown good seed, from which genuine Christians ought to have been born. But by some kind of witchcraft you are degenerating into Jews and passing over to another form. Christ is heavenly and spiritual. Do you aim to be earthly and carnal? But a letter does not adequately express the feeling of my heart. Would that I might now be among you so that what I express inadequately in a letter I might be able to communicate to you with the spoken word. My face, my tears, the ardour of my voice itself would add something. I would change myself into everything to recall you to Christ, now coaxing, now entreating, now reprimanding. I would better accommodate my speech to the varieties of your moods and to the present matter. I would try every kind of remedy, until I had recalled everyone to health. Now when I see that some of you have fallen back into Judaism, that others are very close to this danger, while others of you, I hope, are remaining constant in what you have learned from us, my mind is torn apart by different cares and fears, and I have no idea what kind of letter I could write to remedy such a great evil.

I shall specifically address those who have any desire to return to the servitude of the law. Answer me, please: If you believe so little in the gospel, and if the law of Moses¹⁵ pleases you, why do you not follow its authority? For the law of Moses itself also wishes those who are received into the fellowship of Christ to be free from servitude to the law. You accept the law and have not heard the law; or, if you have heard you do not understand, because you adhere to the shell of the letter and do not penetrate to the marrow of the spirit.[16] For it is written[17] that Abraham, who was the originator and father of those who believe, had two sons. The older named Ishmael, was born from the maidservant Hagar; the younger Isaac, from his legal wife, Sarah. But he who was born from the maidservant was born in our common human way. He was nothing other than the son of Abraham, just as are also[18] the Jews, however much[19] alienated from Christ. He, on the other hand, who was born from the free wife contrary to the usual law of nature, that is, from a barren mother and a very old father, was born according to a divine promise. Both their age and the feebleness of their bodies caused them to despair of having an heir, but the divine promise gave them a sure confidence that they would have offspring. And so the first son was the product of nature, the second of faith.

Now concealed in this story is a mystery which goes beyond the narrative of events. This is usually the case with the law of Moses;[20] just as in man the mind, as ruler of the body, lies hidden under the heavy cover of the body, so under the story something deeper and more sublime lies concealed. Therefore, let us examine what the two mothers and the two sons signify for us through allegory. Certainly the two mothers represent the two testaments, of which the first gave birth to a people subject to servitude of the law, the other to a people freed through faith from the burden of the law. For Sinai is a mountain in Arabia. In the language of the Chaldaeans, this word corresponds to the name of the maidservant Hagar.[21] Sinai borders[22] on Mt Zion, where a city is located which at one time was called Jebus; now it is called Jerusalem. Moreover, the people who dwell near the mountain of Hagar are in servitude to this day, as though representing by their situation the author of the race. But the Jerusalem which has fallen to the descendants of Isaac does not know servitude. Since this city is situated on a lofty hill, it represents that heavenly motherland into whose citizenship we have been received. It is the mother not only of the Jews, but of all of us also[23] who believe in Christ. The Mosaic law is earthly, the evangelical law is heavenly, proceeding as it does from heaven. As the body is subservient to the mind, so the heavy and corporeal is servile, while the spiritual accords with freedom. The Mosaic law was the first to produce its own offspring. The evangelical law gave birth later, but how much richer was the offspring it generated for God! The former produced only a single race, and that not so numerous. The latter comprises all the nations of the earth.

Let no one think that this happened by chance. As it happens, this was predicted by Isaiah [54:1] who, through the prophetic Spirit, foresaw the multitude of nations flocking together from every side to the gospel of Christ. He exulted in these words: 'Rejoice, you barren, who do not give birth. Break out in a joyous voice and shout, you who do not bring forth. For far more sons will be born to you who have seemed childless and sterile than to her who has a husband,' and he promised a marvellous hope of descendants from himself.[24] Judaism formerly rendered very few acceptable to God. However, the faith of the gospel reconciles many to God and will continue to do so without end. You see two mothers and two sons, founders of two races. Those who still hold doggedly onto the Mosaic law belong to Ishmael who was born from the maidservant. We, however, who have left behind our trust in the law and depend on Christ alone through a sincere faith, belong to Isaac who was born from a free woman, not according to the flesh but according to the promise of God. For we are not received into the salvation of the gospel because we were born under the law, but because God long ago promised salvation to all who through faith entered into fellowship with his Son Jesus Christ.

But the allegory corresponds beautifully, in this respect also, that each offspring reflects its origin. For in former times, Ishmael the elder, being the son of Abraham only according to the flesh, persecuted the young Isaac, who was born according to the promise of God. Even then Ishmael claimed for himself more than was fair among those with whom he played. So it is in our time. Those who cling to the carnal law regard with hostility those who embrace the spiritual law of the gospel. They try to take precedence over these, as if claiming the right of the firstborn. But this right belonged to Christ alone. By the argument of priority in age, they try to coax the sons of a free-born mother into a common servitude, clearly in order that they themselves, as older slaves, might in some way lord it over the younger. But the free-born mother does not approve of this relationship. She does not want those of different birth to be mixed together. She is indignant, and at once cries out, as Scripture says [Gen 21:10-12]: 'Throw out the maidservant and her son. For I shall not permit the son of the maidservant to be heir with Isaac my son.' The synagogue clings too closely to those who have believed in the gospel. Jews put too much pressure on Christians, whose freedom they envy. If the slave[25] mother does not wish to depart voluntarily, she should be driven away rather than corrupt my son by contact with a slave. The inheritance of eternal salvation was promised and is owed to Isaac. Let Hagar carry off if she wishes the jug of the insipid law which she so passionately loves. My Isaac, by drinking the powerful draught of evangelical teaching, shall grow up happily until he turns out a perfect man.

Consequently, my brothers, since the Jews are so stubbornly pleased by the servile law, let them keep their servitude; let them preserve the character of their mother. We were ourselves at one time also subject to the servitude of the law and like sons of the maidservant Hagar, and we persecuted the free-born sons of the church. Now we are released from our former servitude and have been admitted into the rights of the sons of Sarah. We owe this liberty to Christ, in whom we have been incorporated through faith with the result that we have entered into the common right of the promised inheritance. Christ, at his own cost, has restored us Jews[26] to this freedom, giving us back our former privileges. You gentiles[27] he has called to freedom through the gospel.

Chapter 5

Nothing remains to be said, except that you continue steadfastly in what you once attained. For what madness it would be to place your necks in the yoke of servitude, giving up the freedom which has come to you through the kind act of Christ freely done! We have endured the burden of servitude, and rejoice that we have finally obtained freedom. Are you tired of freedom and do you of your own accord strive after slavery? Perhaps you are cajoling yourselves and saying: We are not falling away from Christ, but we are combining the law with Christ, so that we may have a more certain expectation of salvation. But just as Christ wanted this entire free gift to be common to all, likewise he wanted you to credit it to him alone. He does not allow partnership in this matter.

And in order that you may understand what a risk you are running in considering Judaism, I, Paul, not unknown to you as an apostle of the gentiles, and an apostle established by Christ himself, proclaim to you publicly that if you are circumcised, Christ will be of no profit to you. For if you truly believe that through Christ perfect salvation can be offered to everyone, why do you introduce circumcision? But if you have no faith, you do not yet acknowledge the free gift of Christ. Those who lack faith cannot be partners in this gift. For it is granted to faith alone, not to the merits of works.[1] Either you must be clearly Jews and give up Christ, or clearly Christians and reject Judaism. He does not put up with those who limp on both feet. He does not want new wine poured into old bottles, or old wine poured into new. He does not allow a new patch to be sewn on an old garment, nor an old patch woven into a new one.[2] If servitude were a slight thing, perhaps it could be overlooked. If there were a great reward for servitude, the burden of the condition could be compensated by the magnitude of the reward. But aside from the fact that the burden is most troublesome, not only does it bring no profit, it leads to the greatest loss. Do not deceive yourselves with soothing words: We shall[3] not bind ourselves to the entire burden of the law, but shall inflict only some of it to avoid being complete strangers. We shall allow only circumcision; we shall not allow the sacrifice of cattle and other things of that kind.

I, on the contrary, in order to prevent you from unknowingly falling into some error, testify in a loud voice before all men:Whoever has himself circumcised, whether Jew or otherwise, makes himself subject to the observance of the entire law. For just as we are wholly dedicated to Christ through baptism, so one who is circumcised is dedicated wholly to the law. For by this as a token he is accepted into the race of the Jews. Those who have not been circumcised are permitted to extract some things from the law. But the whole law has the circumcised under obligation. For one who agrees to circumcision must agree to sacrifices, sabbaths, new moons, washings, choice of foods, appointed fasts, and other things of this kind.[4] Is it not a manifestation of a certain kind of madness to take on so great a burden voluntarily, especially when this is your reward, that for the sake of a most vexatious and useless servitude you fall away from Christ, the only author of freedom and salvation? For, as I have often said, if you expect true righteousness through the help of the law, which promises a certain kind of righteousness through trust in works, you have become strangers to the fellowship of Christ, who wanted this gift to be one of grace, not of merit. But if you depart from service with Christ, not even the law will be useful to you. On the contrary, it will bring disaster. For if it had any use prior to the evangelical light,[5] it has now lost this completely by the public proclamation of the mystery of the gospel. If the law has force among you, Christ has been rejected; if Christ holds sway, the law must be rejected.

When I say the law, I mean that burdensome and carnal part of the Mosaic law which is the only thing the Jews hold onto doggedly. From minute observances pertaining to the body, they promise themselves perfect righteousness. They think that sprinkling the blood of cattle expiates the soul from its sins, or that a bath of water washes away the filth of the mind, or that pure food cleanses or impure food contaminates the heart.We, on the other hand, have embraced the spiritual part of the law.[6] We expect the promised righteousness to come, not from the superstitious observance of such corporeal things, but from what we believe through the gospel, that true innocence and true salvation are given to us freely through the death of Christ. Moreover, it does not matter whether you come to Christ circumcised or uncircumcised, for this whole affair depends not on observance of the law but on faith. Though faith does not share in the works of the Mosaic law, it is nevertheless not idle. It adds a hidden force to all the duties of piety, not because of the precepts of the law but because of love. Love, freely and through no command, accomplishes much more than any law could extort either with threats or with punishments. When love is present, what need is there for the prescription of the law? If love is not present, to what is observance of the law conducive?[7]

You were running well in the race of the gospel, speeding directly to the prize of eternal happiness. Who has hindered your course? Why do you not continue to approve what was once pleasing? Why rescind your own resolution and vote in favour of another man's proposal? Beware lest you so greatly value the authority of some man among you that you withdraw from the course you have begun. You once believed in the truth. It is most shameful to turn away now to shadows.[8] What I have taught you I have taught with God as my authority. As for those who are trying to persuade you otherwise, who are interrupting the course of your faith to divert you to Judaism: they do not follow God as their authority (who has called you to grace through faith, not to Judaism through circumcision), they are following human desires; they are serving their own gain, their own glory, and their own tyranny. Again and again, I say, beware of their eloquence. There are few of them, but it is dangerous not to avoid these few. They will infect the whole multitude and corrupt the purity of the whole congregation. For you see that from a little yeast all the dough in which it was mixed is made sour, gradually spreading its own sourness through all the previously untainted flour. A portion of Judaism, however small, will vitiate the purity of your entire faith if mixed with the gospel. But even though now you have begun to vacillate due to the impulse of an outsider, I entertain a firm hope that you will persevere in your original purpose, confident in part because of your hearts (which I have long since examined and known) but even more because of the help of Christ. He enabled you to begin eagerly. Likewise, he will enable you to persevere firmly. For the rest, whoever is disturbing the tranquility and purity of your faith with a new teaching will not escape the judgment of God, however much he may have deceived men. For the present, for reasons of my own, I neither reveal who he is nor do I rage against him. However, God knows who he is; and God is moved by no man's authority. That man will pay the penalty before God, for he has offended God rather than me.

Let it indeed not disturb you if certain men bring forward in public that I also do not shrink back from observance of the law, for I have frequently become a Jew to Jews, and I circumcised Timothy.[9] I was compelled to do this, and though protesting continuously, I made a concession to that particular occasion on which no great danger seemed to threaten if I did it; but if I had refused there would have been a great outcry. Now different circumstances demand a different judgment. Finally, it is one thing to allow circumcision, another to preach it.[10] I allowed Timothy to be circumcised. I have never taught that circumcision was necessary. So also, while living with the Jews, I frequently abstained from food prohibited by the law; but I never dictated to anyone which foods ought to be chosen. On the contrary, I taught that it makes no difference which foods you eat provided only that you eat soberly and with thanks. There was a time when some concessions had to be made because of the unconquerable conviction of the Jews. But now that the gospel has sufficiently shone forth and the Jews with unyielding minds are attempting to drag even the gentiles into their superstition, it is neither right nor safe to vacillate. It must be freely and frankly preached that the Mosaic law has ceased and that evangelical freedom should be embraced by everyone. If what those keep saying is true, namely, that I am the champion and proclaimer of circumcision, then why do the Jews persecute me with such stubborn hatred to this day? All the hatred of their race is directed against me because I preach the gospel of Christ in such a way as to teach that the law of Moses has been abrogated. They think that they would be considered of higher value among all if they mixed the rites of the Jews together with Christ. And they are tortured with envy because, now that everyone has been admitted through faith to this grace, they themselves bear on their bodies a useless circumcision. This is the principal reason that with obstinate minds they have been plotting my destruction for a long time: I promised perfect salvation to all through the cross of Christ, without the help of circumcision. But if I still preach circumcision, as certain men slanderously claim, why do the Jews not cease persecuting me, since the reason which had caused me to be hateful to them has been removed? Believe me, Galatians, my preaching has always been and will always be the same. See to it that in the same way your faith remains the same. For I am so far from agreeing with those who teach circumcision that if they cannot be wrenched away from their own law, they should be separated completely from the fellowship of the gospel rather than weaken you and shift you away from your correct position with their persuasion. If circumcision is so tenaciously pleasing to them, may God grant that they not only be circumcised but actually be cut off completely. Thus may they get enough of what they love. It is better that those alone perish than that they draw so many others into ruin with them. Let them enjoy their own shameful servitude[11] if it is so pleasing to them.

You, brothers, have been called through the gospel not into servitude but into freedom. Nothing remains except that you beware of using this opportunity to apply the freedom you have received through the Spirit of Christ to the desires of the flesh. For servitude to the law has been abolished, and evangelical love has taken its place. This love obtains more from the willing than the law used to extort[12] from the unwilling. Moreover, there is no domination or servitude among those who love, but rather a mutual compliance. The law does not teach that you should lay down your life for that of a friend, that you should deny your natural inclination by helping a brother in need, that as a strong person you should help the weak, as a learned person the unlearned, as a better person the worse. But love does command this, and its orders are always such that you carry them out voluntarily. Moreover, what the law does not bring about by its many prescriptions and threats, love alone fulfils by a shortcut, embracing in itself the meaning and essence of the whole law.[13] For what the law with its many words attempts to bring about by innumerable precepts is fulfilled completely in a single brief sentence, which we find in Leviticus [19:18]: 'You shall love your neighbour as yourself.' Consequently, if you are welded together by mutual love, you will all be supported by mutual service to one another and sustained by mutual compliance. On the other hand, if, as is the case among the carnal, you disagree among yourselves with mutual hatred, and not only do not support one another, but also bite each other with disparagements; and if you not only bite and gnaw at each other, but also, as is characteristic of savage beasts, devour each other, insofar as you can; then you must constantly beware lest by mauling each other like wild beasts you perish as they do from mutually inflicted wounds. To such depths sink those devoid of evangelical love who cling to the carnal law as they measure all things according to their own advantages. Christian love, on the other hand, is subservient to the advantages of others.

Of the things which have been said, the principal point is this: after you have been freed from servitude to the Mosaic law which is carnal, you should live life according to the spiritual law of evangelical love. This will happen if you do not measure righteousness by Jewish ceremonies and if you abstain from carnal desires. You will not cease to be subject to the law if you continue to be subject to desires. Consequently, strive to live life according to the guidance of the Spirit. If you do this you will abstain from those things to which desires of the flesh tempt you. For just as in one person the body is heavy and corporeal, but the soul is heavenly and immortal; and as in the same law there is something carnal, which we call the letter and, on the other hand, something heavenly which we call spirit,[14] so in the same soul there is one force summoning him to honourable things, and a different force, comparable to the body and the letter, which incites us to a different life. Between these two there is a perpetual war in which the flesh opposes the spirit and the spirit the flesh. The flesh can be restrained but it cannot be completely prevented from struggling against the spirit. If the flesh wins out, it sometimes happens that although one seeks according to the spirit those things which belong to piety, still overcome as he is by the flesh, he does those things which he knows ought to be avoided. But if the Spirit of Christ impels you willingly to things which are honourable and pious, the Mosaic law has no jurisdiction over you. The spirit is invisible, and the flesh about which we are here speaking is likewise invisible. Nevertheless, it is not difficult to determine whether someone is subservient to the will of the flesh, or whether he follows the leadership of the spirit. As are the sources, so are those things which come forth from the sources. The life, manners, and deeds of a person bear witness to the character of his mind.

Let us not speak now in uncertain or obscure terms. These are the things which demonstrate publicly that one is subservient to the flesh, even if he has been baptized and escaped the servitude of the law: adultery, fornication, filth, lasciviousness, worship of images, witchcraft, enmity, lawsuits, rivalries, anger, strife, factions, jealousy, drunkenness, revels. Whoever is subject to these things, whether baptized or not, is not truly free, but is a slave of evil desires. Nor is there any cause for you to flatter yourselves on baptism or the display of miracles. When I was present among you before, I warned you, and now I declare to you again through this letter, that all those who do such things will be cut off from the inheritance of the kingdom of heaven. On the other hand, those who are truly free and are led by the will of the Spirit are recognized by fruits of this kind. For they have as companions: love, joy, peace, gentleness of mind, kindness, goodness, faith, mildness, self-control. Those who achieve these things of their own accord have no need of the spur of the law. Their own innocence renders them free from the law. Moreover, those who truly belong to Christ have crucified their own flesh along with their own sins and carnal desires, as befits those who are spiritual. For through baptism we die with Christ, and at the same time we are buried with him. It is not proper to waver in the middle between flesh and spirit. If the spirit imparts life to the body, it is right that the body be guided by the will of the spirit. If we have received life from the Spirit of Christ, not from the law, let us live according to the impulse of this same Spirit. If we have truly breathed in the Spirit of Christ, let us produce its fruits and be far removed from works of the flesh. Let us not be desirous of empty glory, for the sake of which we provoke one another to rivalry, envying one another. These vices frequently sneak up on those who profess a zeal for piety, for they are the chief plague of true piety.

Chapter 6

I have shown you, brothers, the direction in which everyone must strive who has once for all offered his name to Christ. And yet baptism does not exempt us from being human. Therefore, if someone should fall through human weakness into some sin, you who are strong in spirit and have not yielded to the desire of the flesh have the duty of restoring[1] such a one courteously and gently, encouraging him so that he rises again, not trampling him down with harsh words so that he despairs. Arrogance and harshness of such a kind are characteristic of hypocrites. The Spirit of Christ, because it longs for the salvation of all, entices men to come to their senses by gentleness. Often a gentle and brotherly reproach softens and renders humble those whom a quarrelsome severity completely alienates. The Mosaic law restrains sins in such a way that it destroys the sinner. Christian love heals defects; it does not annihilate the person. The better you are yourself, accommodate yourself the more gently to your brother's weakness. If you are moved too little by the example of Christ who endured his own people most gently until they should come to their senses, be motivated at least by the realization that you might someday be treated the same way in return. Has someone given in to a human failing? Remember that you also are human. His mistake should teach you not to trust yourself nor to strut around. Deal with his mistake as you would desire to be dealt with if something similar happened to you. For whatever is human can befall anyone. Those who vacillate through the urging of pseudo-apostles ought not to be alienated by savageness but recalled to their original firmness through love. For it might come about that after they have gained strength they in turn will come to the aid of your weakness. One who labours under a burden ought to be raised up, not cast down. Therefore, if you will in turn bear one another's burdens, then truly you will fulfil the law of love which is the special law of Christ. Christ was not subject to sin, and he did not share in the peril of sinning. Nevertheless, he himself has borne our iniquities, and he has healed us by his kindness, not condemned us by severity.

Let no one take pride in his own righteousness, and trust in it while despising a brother hindered by some sin. For this itself is a sign of false righteousness, that he thinks himself righteous. Consequently, if someone thinks he is something when he is nothing, he deceives himself. For one is not righteous simply because he considers himself superior to someone else who has fallen. And he will not be corrupted by the sin of another person if he stoops down to raise up one who has fallen. Nor is he good simply because he compares himself to someone worse. Everyone must be judged by his own deeds. However, no one ought to trust his own deeds, but he should rather consider whether what he regards as a good deed is worthy of approval by God. And if your conscience does not disturb you, take pride in your own strength, but do not boast because of the weakness of another. And you should boast privately, congratulating yourself on account of the divine gift. You should not brag among others or despise those who do not match your own strength. If you can, help him; if you cannot, leave him to his judge. His transgression will not diminish your reward. You will not be punished for the sin of another. Rather, each person will bear his own burden before God the judge.[2]

Moreover, as long as we are in this world, we ought to sustain each other by mutual service. And just as those who excel in gifts have a duty to come to the aid of a weak brother by teaching, comfort, and exhortation, so also those who are aided should remember not to show themselves ungrateful for the favours. Thus it will come about that you will share all good things[3] in common. Those whose strength lies in teaching the gospel should instruct, encourage, and support the ignorant, while the latter, in turn, share their own resources with their teachers and counsellors. Thus an exchange of duties will be effected. Moreover, those who teach should see to it that what they teach is worthy of Christ and reflects the Spirit of Christ. Otherwise, it is better not to agree with the teacher. Moreover, one who has falsely transmitted the evangelical teaching and accepts recompense from him whom he has taught, may deceive that person and even himself, but not God. Wherefore I warn you to teach honestly, for God is not mocked. But whatever seed one sows, such also is the harvest he will reap. One who hands down a carnal teaching will reap, for his carnal seed, a fruit which will perish. But one who imparts a spiritual teaching will gain from the spiritual and heavenly teaching a like reward, namely, eternal life. Let us have a perpetual zeal for doing good to all. Let us never cease benefiting others, whether or not we receive thanks for our favours or have a reward returned to us by men. For in due time we will receive from God a fruit which will never perish, and for temporary services an eternal reward will be given to us. The time for sowing will not always be at hand. A day will come when we shall be sustained by the good deeds neither of ourselves nor of others. As long as we live in this world, it is permitted us to seek God's favour by good deeds, and to help others. But on the day of judgment there will be no place for good deeds and no chance to do favours to others. Consequently, while we have the time let us use it and be zealous in well-doing to everyone, but especially to those with whom we dwell together in religion and faith. The Jew acknowledges only his own people; the Christian,[4] following the example of Christ, is eager to do good for all.

You see, Galatians, how dear this matter is to my heart. For I have written a very long epistle[5] to you with my own hand. You recognize the letters written by my own fingers. There is no reason for you to suspect that the letter is a forgery; it is wholly mine, and an indication of my disposition toward you. See that this letter carries more weight with you than the speech of the pseudo-apostles. As a matter of fact, those who consider it more important to please men than to please God – it is they who are dragging you to circumcision, for they want to make you hated by the gentiles on account of Christ and by the Jews on account of your foreskin. For they are Jews; and they fear the hatred of their own nation if they were to profess Christ without circumcision, as though they were abolishing the law. These have respect for men rather than for God, and they pursue glory from men rather than from God. They are afraid that a sincere profession of the cross of Christ will excite persecution against them by those to whom the name of Christ is hateful. They are afraid that they will not be famous enough teachers if they teach nothing except the crucifixion. For they do not do these things out of a natural zeal for the law, as I did, who at one time raged against the flock of Christ, erring out of a love for the ancestral law. Not even the Jews themselves obey the law, even though they have been circumcised like their forefathers. But they are abusing your simplicity by imposing on you the burden of circumcision, in order to show off among their own people because you accepted Judaism once again through their authority and direction. By this stratagem they try to placate the jealousy of their people, who are outraged that through the gospel of Christ the law is abolished. I am not deterred by the hatred of the Jews and the insults of the gentiles from preaching the gospel of Christ honestly.

However, far be it from me to boast of anything other than the cross of my Lord Jesus Christ. I know that the cross of Christ is scandalous among the gentiles, hateful among the Jews. But it is enough for me to place all my glory in the cross alone, for the glory of the world does not now touch me even a little. I have been incorporated into the body of Christ through baptism, and the world is dead to me and I in turn to the world. I am neither intimidated by its evils nor enticed by its privileges. I do not fear its hatred and care nothing for its approval. I do not dread disgrace or strive after glory. To me Christ is enough to assure every good and ward off every evil.

It makes no difference whether you come to the profession of Christ circumcised from Judaism or uncircumcised from the gentiles. For whoever is elected into the body of Christ through faith is so suddenly transformed into another person that he becomes a new creature and therefore is said to be born again. Therefore, let them keep making their human distinctions. Whoever professes Christ should remember only this, that he is a Christian. Let this be an unshaken rule. I pray for peace and mercy to those who have followed it. For it is fitting to pray for the same thing for these as David prayed for the Israelites, when he said in the Psalms [125:5]: 'Peace on Israel.' But there are two kinds of Israelites: Israelites according to men and Israelites according to God. He is not necessarily a true Israelite who has an amputated foreskin but rather he who has a circumcised mind and who, through faith, is steadfast for God.[6] For these Israelites, then, among whom you too are to be numbered, I desire peace and mercy.

Farewell to those falsely called Israelites who fight against the gospel of Christ with stubborn hatreds. They certainly will never move me from this opinion. I will always preach what I have preached. Thus, let no one hereafter give me trouble about this matter. There is no way in which I can be torn away from evangelical truth, either by any disgrace or by afflictions. For everywhere I carry about on my body as the signs and brand-marks[7] of my Lord Jesus Christ all the dishonour which has been branded on me because of him, such as prisons, floggings, chains and stonings, and all other evils which I have endured for the name of Christ. I display these as trophies[8] and count it to my glory that insofar as is permitted, I am deemed worthy to represent the cross of Christ which I preach.

May the favour and goodwill of our Lord Jesus Christ always be with your spirit, my brothers, so that you may continue steadfastly in the integrity of the gospel through the help of Christ. May he by whose inspiration I wrote these things bring this prayer to fulfilment.

Notes

The Paraphrases of Erasmus: Origin and Character

xi
1 Cicero *De oratore*, 1.34.154; Quintilian *Institutio oratoria*, 10.5.1–11
2 On the use of these techniques in classical education and in Renaissance education based on classical models, see Donald L. Clark *Rhetoric in Greco-Roman Education* (New York 1957) *passim*; and Donald L. Clark *John Milton at St Paul's School: A Study of Ancient Rhetoric in English Renaissance Education* (New York 1948) 178–84.

xii
3 CWE 24 303:17–27
4 CWE 24 679:15–22
5 Ep 188:64–79

xiii
6 Ep 208:12–30
7 See Albert Rabil Jr *Erasmus and the New Testament* (San Antonio 1972) 37–46; and John B. Payne 'Erasmus: Interpreter of Romans,' in Carl S. Meyer ed *Sixteenth Century Essays and Studies* (St Louis: Foundation for Reformation Research 1971) Vol 2, p 6.
8 Ep 164:41–2
9 Ep 165:8–14. Cf below p xviii.
10 Ep 181: 36–41
11 Ep 301:20–2

xiv
12 Ep 334:181
13 Ep 373:146–7
14 *Novum Instrumentum* (Basel: Froben 1516) 411. The comment is found in his annotation on Rom 1:1 ('Paul'), but disappears in the 1527 edition.
15 John Colet in June 1516: Ep 423:41; Karl Ofhuys in October 1516: Ep 480A: 30–3; Gerardus Listrius in November 1516: Ep 495:44–5
16 Ep 894:46–52
17 CWE 24 696:14. For the 1530 catalogue, see CWE 24 697–702.
18 See Rabil *Erasmus and the New Testament* 58–61.

xv

19 Ep 755:4–7

20 Ep 794:86–90

21 Cf the biography of Erasmus by Beatus Rhenanus (1540), printed in Allen I 56–71, esp 64:301–3.

22 For the evolution of Erasmus' consciousness in writing paraphrases, see Albert Rabil Jr 'Erasmus' Paraphrase of the Gospel of John' *Church History* 48 (1979) 142–4.

23 Ep 456:93–6

24 See LB IX 464C, 465A–B, written 1526.

25 Ep 710:31–3 (cf below, p2).

26 LB IX 464C

xvi

27 Allen Ep 1274:34–6

28 See LB IX 879D–E; 1115C–F; 1116C–D; Allen Ep 1255:38–9; 1333:395–7; 1381: 421–2.

29 Ep 710:51–2 (cf below, p3).

30 LB IX 883C; 445B; 462B, E

31 LB IX 462A

32 Ep 373:5–6

33 See below, p3

34 Allen Ep 1274:39

xvii

35 Allen Ep 1381:425–6; on the question of *persona* in the *Paraphrases*, see Jacques Chomarat 'Grammar and Rhetoric in the Paraphrases of the Gospels by Erasmus' *Erasmus of Rotterdam Society Yearbook One* (1981) 30–68, esp 65–8

36 LB IX, 879A

37 LB IX 800 E; 1116A; see also Ep 456:93–8.

38 LB IX 1116B

39 These have been published in *Commentaria in Aristotelem Graeca* v/1–6 (Berlin 1900–1902).

40 See G. Downey 'Themistius and the Defense of Hellenism in the Fourth Century' *Harvard Theological Review* 50 (1957) 259–74, especially 265. In the letter cited above (xvi n34), Erasmus appeals to Themistius' work to explain the nature of a paraphrase (cf lines 36–7).

41 LB IX 1115D. Juvencus' work is published in CSEL 24, ed J. Huemer.

42 Ep 456:100–1

43 LB IX 1115D. See *Lexikon für Theologie und Kirche* I.800. His works have been published in CSEL 72, ed A.P. McKinlay.

44 LB IX 1115D. The works cited were published in Paris in 1507.

xviii

45 Ep 456:105–13

46 See Allen Ep 1823, introduction. Titelmans even wrote a critique of the work of Erasmus and Lefèvre, to which Erasmus responded. See *Responsio ad*

Collationes cujusdam juvenis gerontodidascali LB IX 967–1016. This Apology is in response to Titelmans' criticism of Erasmus' translation and annotations of Romans.

47 LB IX 462A
48 Ep 165:13–14. Cf above p xiii.
49 Ep 916:450–5
50 Allen Ep 1255:106–8
51 Allen Ep 1333:389–91
52 LB IX 1115F

xix

53 In addition to our notes, see John B. Payne, 'Erasmus and Lefèvre d'Etaples as Interpreters of Paul,' *Archiv für Reformationsgeschichte* 65 (1974) 54–83.
54 For summaries of their criticisms see: Béda: LB IX 469A–72A, 475E–6D, 666F–75C, 687C–91D; Sutor: LB IX 800D–1D; Pio: LB IX 1114D–17B.

The Publication of the Latin Paraphrases

xx

1 It is a pleasure to thank Drs E. van Gulik, lately librarian of the Bibliotheek der Gemeente Rotterdam, Drs J.J.M. van de Roer-Meyers, the present curator of the Erasmus-collection in Rotterdam, and Dr David Rogers of the Bodleian Library, Oxford, for their help and encouragement. The shortcomings of this survey are my own.
2 References have been added to identify editions in the following lists of Erasmus' works: NK = W. Nijhoff and M.E. Kronenberg *Nederlandsche Bibliographie van 1500 tot 1540* (The Hague 1919–   ); R = the *Overzicht* of Erasmus editions in the Rotterdam library (Rotterdam 1936–   ); A = H.M. Adams *Catalogue of Books Printed on the Continent 1501-1600 in Cambridge Libraries* (Cambridge 1967); B = Irmgard Bezzel *Erasmusdrucke des sechzehnten Jahrhunderts in bayerischen Bibliotheken* (Stuttgart 1979). This last work, which appeared after my essay was in draft, provided a most welcome check, and also reported several editions of the *Paraphrases* which were unknown to me.

xxiii

3 The statement made under A 740 that 'the Epistles are not included in this edition' seems to be based on a misunderstanding.

xxiv

4 This was perhaps the 'small present' made to the bishop by Erasmus which Allen in his note on Ep 1331 could not identify.
5 The edition without month-date is probably earlier than those of March and April, for it makes a somewhat less economical use of paper at the end of the book, and it was not till a text could be seen in print that a fine adjustment of matter to paper became really easy.

xxv

6 The inscription in a copy of the 1523 folio *Epistles* in the Bodleian, 'Est Frobenii 1524' might suggest that the book was not published much before the end of the year 1523.

xxvi

7 So Allen, in the headnote to Ep 1414

Sixteenth-Century Translations of Erasmus' New Testament Commentaries in English

xxx

1 John Caius *A boke, or counseill against the disease commonly called the sweate* (London 1552) A4
2 William Tyndale *Doctrinal Treatises* ed Henry Walter (Cambridge 1848) 161–2
3 STC 10494; E.J. Devereux *A Checklist of English Translations of Erasmus to 1700* (Oxford 1968) c65.1–3
4 S.L. Greenslade 'English Versions of the Bible, 1525-1611' *Cambridge History of the Bible* (Cambridge 1963) 147
5 LP vii, doc 659
6 STC 10503; Devereux c66

xxxi

7 STC 10450. For the currency of public debate about the divorce see John Strype *Ecclesiastical Memorials* ii, ii (Oxford 1822) 138–40
8 This is fully treated in my article 'The Publication of the English *Paraphrases* of Erasmus' *Bulletin of the John Rylands Library* li (1969) 348–67.
9 Gardiner wrote that 'he (who it is I know not) who hath taken the labors to translate Erasmus into Englysh, hath for his parte offended some time, as apereth plainly, by ignoraunce, and sometime euidently of purpose, to put in, leaue out, and chaunge as he thought best, neuer to the better, but to the worse.' J.A. Muller *The Letters of Stephen Gardiner* (Cambridge 1933), letter 130
10 STC 16034–6 from Grafton and 16037–9 from Whitchurch. Grafton used the title and a special device with the feathers of the Prince of Wales in some other books.
11 *Calendar of Patent Rolls* (CPR) 1 Edward vi, i (London 1924) 187

xxxii

12 *Ibid* 190
13 STC 10088–93, all with the same date. There is a reprint in Edward Cardwell *Documentary Annals of the Reformed Church of England* i (Oxford 1839) 4–23.
14 CPR 2 Edward vi, ii (London 1924) 98 and 99
15 Muller 133
16 STC 2854, bibliographically divided in Devereux c67.1–c67.7
17 Statutes of the Realm, 34 & 35 Henry viii, cap i, sect vi
18 Hill was a Dutch printer denizened in London, who did much of his work for the two Bible monopolists. See F.S. Isaac *English & Scottish Printing Types*

1535–1558, 1552–1558 (London 1932) facs 50 and notes. For the earlier careers of Whitchurch and Grafton, their political and religious ties to Cromwell, and their remarkably wide experience with Bible printing, see A.W. Pollard *Records of the English Bible* (London 1911), 218–65.

xxxiii

19 See 'The Publication of the English *Paraphrases* of Erasmus' 360–2.
20 Devereux c68.1–2
21 Devereux c67.8 and 68.3
22 I have never been quite satisfied on this point and have been unable to find any evidence that the book was banned. Philip Hughes claims that copies were destroyed, in *The Reformation in England* ii (London 1954) 243, and more recently C.R. Thompson has written that 'We may be sure the *Paraphrases* did not escape official attention' ('Erasmus and Tudor England' *Actes du Congrès Erasme* [Amsterdam 1971] 55). But I cannot find any record that such attention was given by Gardiner, who had more urgent matters on his mind. The Marian *Interrogatories* (STC 10117) inquire after 'hereticall, noughtye, or sedicious erronious … bookes, especially english testamentes or Bible falsely translated,' but do not name the *Paraphrases* or say what to do with the books.
23 Muller 130, 133, 135, 136

xxxiv

24 All Souls Bursar Rolls, All Saints 1547 to 1548
25 Edward Arber *A Transcript of the Register of the Company of Stationers of London, 1554–1640* ii (London 1875) 781

Translators' Note

xxxv

1 See Allen Epp 1672:148–53, 1804:71–2. In 1529 Erasmus published a list of emendations to his editions of Jerome, the *Annotations* and the *Paraphrases* on the New Testament, which is contained in 29 octavo pages appended to the second edition of his *Apologia ad monachos Hispanos* (Basel: Froben 1529). The *Apologia* is printed (under its 1528 title [first edition]) in LB IX 1015–94, but since the corrections listed in the *Apologia* were made in the later editions of the works concerned, they were not subsequently published separately, and do not, therefore, appear with the *Apologia* in LB IX. See Allen Ep 2095.
2 See Albert Rabil *Erasmus and the New Testament* 136–9 and John B. Payne 'The Significance of Lutheranizing Changes in Erasmus' Interpretation of Paul's Letters to the Romans and the Galatians in his Annotations (1527) and Paraphrases (1532)' in *Histoire de l'exégèse au XVIe siècle*, ed Pierre Fraenkel and Olivier Fatio (Geneva 1978) 312–30. Cf James D. Tracy *Erasmus: The Growth of a Mind* (Geneva 1972) 182.

xxxvi

3 LB IX 880A; cf IX 137C. For a detailed study of rhetoric in the *Paraphrases*, see

Jacques Chomarat *Grammaire et rhétorique chez Erasme* Paris 1981 I 587–710.
4 Marjorie O'Rourke Boyle *Language and Method in Theology* (Toronto 1977) offers a careful study of the theological significance of language as such, while as noted above (n2), other studies have attempted to trace developments in some key theological words in Erasmus, particularly in response to the Reformation; but we do not yet have a systematic study of the theological language of Erasmus.

xxxvii
5 See the annotation on Rom 1:5 'grace and apostleship.' For the paraphrase on Rom 1:7 see below 'For all of you at Rome' and on Rom 8:28 'We need not fear.'
6 See the annotation on Rom 1:17 'from faith to faith.'
7 Paraphrase on Rom 1:5 'Through him I have obtained'; Rom 3:2 'As far as the grace'; Gal 1:2-3 'Not I alone ... good we have attained'; and Gal 2:10 'They did not impose.'
8 Paraphrase on Rom 4:10 'It is clear'
9 Paraphrase on Rom 4:24 'Holy Scripture is also'
10 Paraphrase on Rom 4:3 'My words would have.' For one other instance of a change from *fides* to *fiducia* see paraphrase on Rom 10:12 'When he says "whoever."' It is not at all clear why in these two cases alone Erasmus chose in 1521 to make this change, since he must have been able to discover many other instances in his paraphrases in which *fides* has or could have the meaning of *fiducia*.

PARAPHRASE ON ROMANS

Dedicatory Letter

2
1 TO THE MOST REVEREND] The translation of this letter, dated 13 Nov 1517, and of that to Antoine de la Marck (below pp 92–3) is by R.A.B. Mynors. They appear in the Correspondence as Ep 710 (CWE 5 195–9) and Ep 956 (CWE 6 333–6) respectively.
2 Grimani] Grimani (1461–1523) was a member of a distinguished Venetian family and son of the general Antonio, who, though formerly exiled, was doge from 1521 to 1523. Domenico was created cardinal in 1493 and patriarch of Aquileia in 1497, and was later promoted to the cardinal-bishoprics of Albano, Tusculum, and Porto. He was a friend of Julius II and a munificent patron of arts and letters. With Cardinal Riario he was one of Erasmus' most influential patrons in Rome, and his personal interest in letters was recorded by the rich manuscript collections of his library.
3 Lucilius] Cicero *De finibus* 1.3.9: he should have said not the Greek *chaere*, but a proper Roman 'good day to you.'
4 Juvenal] 3.60–1
5 serving the time] Cf Ep 740:4n. Erasmus discusses the phrase in his annota-

tion on Rom 12:11 ('serving the Lord'), and elsewhere used the phrase to justify Paul's reluctance to explain the 'mysteries' to the Romans who were still novices in the faith, a point which elicited the criticism of Nöel Béda (LB IX 467A–B and 656D–9C).

3

6 commentary] For the differences between paraphrase and commentary, see 'The Paraphrases of Erasmus: Origin and Character' above, pp xv–xvi.

7 best and greatest] In ancient Rome the title 'best and greatest' was applied to Jove for whom there was a temple on the Capitoline.

8 Hadrian's ... Domitian's] It is unlikely that Erasmus has specific antiquities in mind.

9 vultures] Cf Apuleius who refers to the corrupt judges of his day as *togati vulturii* (vultures wearing togas) *Metamorphoses* x 33.

10 prophets] Cf Horace *Odes* 3.30.8; Vergil *Aeneid* 9.448.

4

11 Judaism] In the *Paraphrases* on Romans and Galatians Erasmus will draw a highly negative picture of Judaism which he believes embodies ceremonialism. For his attitude to the Jews, cf Ep 694 intro; also Heiko A. Oberman *Wurzeln des Antisemitismus: Christenangst und Judenplage im Zeitalter vom Humanismus und Reformation* (Berlin 1981) 48–51.

12 Jerome] *Commentarii in epistolam ad Galatas II* (Gal 3:8–9) PL 26.381A; summarized in NPNF (Series 2) 6.497

13 nod] *Adagia* IV ix 39

Argument of the Epistle

6

1 to make ... epistle] Added in 1519, but as a subheading; placed in the text in 1532. This 'argument,' originally composed along with other Arguments of the Apostle's letters when Erasmus was translating these letters in 1506, was first published in Nov 1517 together with the *Paraphrase on Romans*. On the subsequent history of these Arguments, see Ep 894 intro.

2 Jerome] *Commentarii in epistolam ad Philemonem* PL 26:640A–1A

3 Acts 13] Acts 13:7–12

4 Saul ... Spirit] Acts 13:9

5 The Holy ... Barnabas] Acts 13:2

6 Origen] *Commentariorum in epistolam ad Romanos praefatio* PG 14:836B–8A

7 Jedidiah] 'beloved of Yahweh.' Solomon is so referred to by the prophet Nathan, 2 Sam 12:24–25.

8 Uzziah] Used in 2 Kings 15:32–34; Isa 7:1; Hosea 1:1; Amos 1:1; Zech 14:5. Azariah is found in 2 Kings 14:21; 15:1, 6–8, 17, 23–27; 1 Chron 3:12.

9 Levi] Luke 5:27

10 gospel] Matt 10:3

11 Saulus ... Josephus] See Jerome PL 26:639B.

12 Jerome] PL 26:641A

7

13 Ambrose] Ambrosiaster *Commentarius in epistolam ad Romanos* CSEL 81 (1)
8:14–15, 9:10–11. Although in his annotations Erasmus always refers to this
writer as 'Ambrosius,' in his preface to the fourth volume of his edition of
Ambrose (1527) which contained the commentaries, he raises a doubt concerning the authenticity of the Ambrosian authorship. He says: '… in the
commentaries themselves [of the letters to the Romans, Corinthians, and
Galatians] some passages seem to have been added, others to have been
mutilated.' Modern scholars reject the genuineness altogether of the Pauline
commentaries which came down through the Middle Ages under the name of
Ambrose. On Ambrosiaster see A. Souter *A Study of Ambrosiaster*
(Cambridge 1905), and *The Earliest Latin Commentaries on the Epistles of St Paul*
(Oxford 1927) 39ff; W. Mundle *Die Exegese der paulinischen Briefe im Kommentar
des Ambrosiasters* (Marburg in Hessen 1919); CSEL 81(1) (ed H.J. Vogels) ixff.
14 but … Σαῦλος] Added in 1532. In his annotation on Rom 1:1 ('Paul'), Erasmus
related σαῦλος to σάλος interpreting the latter as 'motion or disturbance
of the sea and waves.' This derivation, when contrasted with παῦλα ('rest')
accounts for Erasmus' comment in the opening of the paraphrase on 1:1.
15 Cenchreae … Corinth] See Rom 16:1 and Acts 18:18. Recent excavations by
the American School have revealed something of the life of this port in
antiquity (see R. Scranton et al *Kenchreai: Eastern Port of Corinth* 5 vols. Leiden
1978–81). The remains of what appears to have been a 'temple' of Isis have
been uncovered (cf Scranton vol 1 53–78). In the 2nd century AD Pausanias
found there a temple of Aphrodite and 'sanctuaries' to Asclepius and Isis
(*Description of Greece* 2.2.3). For a contemporary account of the worship of
Isis in the 2nd century AD, see Apuleius *Metamorphoses* XI.
16 Peter] Gal 2:10. The request to remember the poor, according to Paul in this
passage, came from James and John as well as Peter.
17 Rome] Cf Rom 15:22–29.
18 not … hostile] Added in 1532. Earlier editions read 'Peter was also of this
opinion.'
19 centurion] Acts 10:9–48

8

20 three … abolished] Elsewhere Erasmus likes to refer to the apostolic decree
as an example of an ecclesiastical law which had only temporary authority and
suggests that there is no reason why other laws which are detrimental to
the salvation of mankind could not likewise be so regarded and therefore
abolished or at least modified because of changing times and circumstances
– such as the law on divorce (cf note on 1 Cor 7:39 [1519] LB VI 696A–E) and the
law concerning confession (*Responsio ad annotationes Eduardi Lei in Erasmum
novas* [1520] LB IX 255E). See Payne 123, 184.
21 at least … fathers] Added in 1521
22 James] In Acts 21:20, however, the speech is represented as that of the elders
present.

9

23 So great … Jew] Probably an allusion to Vergil *Aeneid* 1.33: 'So great was

the task of founding the Roman nation.' For other anti-Jewish sentiments of Erasmus aroused in part, at least, by his scorn for Johann Pfefferkorn, the Jewish convert to Christianity, see Epp 694, 798:20–30, Allen Ep 1006:139–43. See also above p4 n11.

24 *Jewish Antiquities*] This sentiment, as Erasmus intimates, is found throughout Josephus. See, for example, *Jewish Antiquities* 17.158–60.

25 commonly] Added in 1523

26 He ... Judaism] See Gal 2:14–21; 3:10–14; 5:1–7.

27 Pompey] The Roman general captured Jerusalem in 63 BC. Erasmus' source here is probably Josephus *Jewish Antiquities* 14.1–79.

28 Juvenal ... Seneca] Horace *Satires* 1.5.100; 1.9.69–71; Juvenal 3.13–14; 6.546–7; 14.96–104. The superstition of the Jews is referred to in a fragment of Seneca's *Dialogue on Superstition* which is mentioned by Augustine in the *City of God* where Erasmus probably discovered it. See Seneca *Fragmenta. De superstitione dialogus* 41–2, *Opera* ed Hasse (Leipzig 1872) 3.427; Augustine *City of God* 6.11 (CSEL 40 (1) 298; NPNF [Series 1] 2.120–1). See also Ep 325:65–6.

10

29 (which ... flesh)] Added in 1532

30 The internal ... passions] On Erasmus' Platonizing of the Pauline flesh-spirit dichotomy, see J.B. Payne 'Toward the Hermeneutics of Erasmus' *Scrinium Erasmianum* ed J. Coppens (Leiden 1969) II 17–23.

11

31 two parts ... law] See below p45 n2.

12

32 and ... men] Added in 1532

33 But ... utility] Noël Béda, theologian of the Sorbonne (Allen Ep 1571 intro), apparently criticized Erasmus for vilifying the apostle and sacred scripture in his remarks here on Paul's lack of eloquence and the obscurities of his language. Erasmus defended himself by pointing out that Origen and Jerome likewise noted the obscurities of the Pauline language. *Divinationes ad notata Bedae* [1526] LB IX 467B–F. Cf *Supputatio errorum Bedae* [1527] LB IX 659C–66E.

34 Origen] See, for example, Origen's opening comment in the *Praefatio* PG 14:833A. Erasmus returns to this lack of eloquence in Paul again and again, usually citing Jerome and Origen to back up his contention. See his annotation on 1 Cor 4:3 (LB VI 673E–4D), his apology to John Eck in 1518 (Ep 844:98–9), and his apology against the calumnies of Luther (LB X 1543). In a preface to the fourth and fifth editions of the New Testament, he comments that 'if the language of the apostles is not grammatical, there is no reason to add to the solecism' (*Contra morosos* LB VI **4^r). See W. Schwarz *Principles and Problems of Biblical Translation* (Cambridge 1955) 154.

35 cross] 1 Cor 2:1–5

36 Origen] PG 14:1059C

37 Jerome] Ep 121.10.5 (CSEL 56:42–3)

38 Augustine] *De doctrina christiana* 4.7.11–13 (PL 34:93–5; NPNF [Series 1] 2.577–9)

39 polished phrases] *flosculos*, literally 'little flowers,' a technical term applied to the phrases of rhetoricians to stress variation. See Cicero *De oratore* 3.25.96 and H. Lausberg *Handbuch der literarischen Rhetorik* (Munich 1973) I 540.8.

13

40 speech] Cf, for example, the speeches in Acts 17:22–31; 20:18–35; 22:3–21; and 26:2–23, all of which evoke strong responses from Paul's audience.

41 1 Corinthians] Cf 1 Cor 14:18.

42 Jerome] An allusion possibly to Jerome's *Commentarii in epistolam ad Galatas* II (Gal 3:8–9) (PL 26:379–80). Cf Ep 844:71n.

43 of riches] Added in 1521

44 things ... unlawful] 2 Cor 12:4

45 solid food] 1 Cor 3:2

46 Peter ... God] Acts 2:22–36. Erasmus defends this statement against Luther, LB X 1543 E–F.

47 Origen] PG 14:1008A–B

48 letter] 2 Pet 3:15–16

Chapter 1

15

1 I am Paul ... restless] This interpretation rests largely on Ambrosiaster. For Ambrosiaster see above, p 7 n 13. However, in his annotation on Rom 1:1 ('Paul') and in the Argument (cf above p6), Erasmus shows his preference for the interpretation of Origen, who believed that Paul used both names even after his conversion, the one among the Jews, and the other among the Greeks and the Romans. Cf Origen PG 14:837A–8A. Jacques Lefèvre d'Étaples likewise adopts the Origenistic explanation (*Epistolae* 67 recto).

2 learned] See Acts 22:3–5; 23:6.

3 pharisee] As Erasmus points out in his annotation, the very word 'pharisee' means 'set apart.' See annotation on Rom 1:1 'separated unto the gospel of God.'

4 proofs] In his long annotation on Rom 1:3 ('by the resurrection of the dead of Jesus Christ') in which he describes several possible interpretations of this phrase, Erasmus indicates as proofs the descent from the family of David, 'then the death preceding the resurrection, then the resurrection from the dead, which is the pivot on which our entire faith turns.' He excludes as one of the proofs that Paul has in mind here the resurrection of the saints mentioned in Matt 27:51–53, an interpretation held by Origen (PG 14:852C) and Jerome (*Commentarius in evangelium Matthaei* PL 26:222). In the annotation on 'who was predestined,' he mentions as proofs the oracles of the prophets, innumerable signs, and especially his resurrection from the dead. On these proofs and others see Chrysostom, PG 60:397; NPNF (Series 1) 11:340.

5 duties ... apostle] In his annotation on 1:5 ('grace and apostleship') Erasmus says he translates 'performance of the apostolic duties' so no one will think that Paul means dignity.

6 philosophers] See Erasmus' annotation on 1:5 ('to the obeying of the faith').

16

7 grace and ... Christ] So read first in the 1532 edition. Earlier editions read: 'grace and peace, not the peace for which this world is accustomed to pray in its usual way, but a true and a new peace which proceeds from the Father and our Lord Jesus Christ.'

8 worship] *Colo.* Erasmus also translates the Greek λατρεύω *colo* not *servio* ('serve') as does the Vulgate.

9 gross] *Crassus,* an ambiguous word in Latin just as 'gross' is in English, which can have the meaning of 'heavy' or 'thick' as well as 'crude' or 'uncultivated.' Erasmus seems to intend both 'heavy' or 'thick' (characteristic of the 'flesh') as over against 'light' or 'airy' (characteristic of the 'spirit') *and* 'crude' as over against 'cultivated.' Cf below p106 n8.

10 now ... Moses] Added in 1532

11 by ... prefigured] Added in 1532

17

12 and ... conscience] Added in 1532

13 as the Lord ... Britons] The 1517 edition reads: 'It has been propagated first among Jews and Greeks.' The change was made in 1532. Chrysostom refers also to Scythians. Cf PG 60:408; NPNF (Series 1) 11:349.

14 faith] Erasmus' 1527 annotation on Rom 1:17 ('from faith to faith') is a long and important discourse on the various meanings of πίστις ('faith').

15 Habakkuk] Hab 2:4

16 shall live] Erasmus stresses in his annotation on Rom 1:17 ('lives by faith') that the Greek is in the future tense, in contrast to the Vulgate where the verb is in the present tense.

18

17 even ... world] Added in 1532

18 impiety] Cf Ambrosiaster CSEL 81 (1) 40:16–17, 41:17–18, 'So that their impiety could not at all be excused ... '

19 women ... males] Notice that Erasmus reverses Paul's order here in 1:27 and puts men before women as having adopted unnatural relations with one another. Women sinned by the example of men.

20 allowed] The Latin here is *passus est* which Erasmus had used three successive times in the last verses of this chapter to interpret the Greek, παρέδωκεν ('gave up' or 'handed over'). Whereas in his *Novum Testamentum* he had correctly translated this verb as *tradidit,* he interprets it in the paraphrase in such a way as to avoid making God the author of sin and to allow for the freedom of the will. This interpretation follows that of most of the Fathers, for example, Origen, Chrysostom, and Ambrosiaster. See Schelkle 68ff. Cf Ambrosiaster CSEL 81 (1) 46:20–1, 47:21: 'To hand over, however, is to allow, not to arouse or to incite.'

21 extremely] Added in 1532

Chapter 2

19

1 Nor is it ... to it] Added in 1532

20

2 obstinate mind] Theophylact PG 124:364D. For the importance of this verse as a
proof of free will in Origen, Chrysostom, and other Fathers, see Schelkle
73. For the distinction in Erasmus' theology between sin as weakness deserving forgiveness and sin as obstinacy deserving punishment, see Payne 43.

3 to better things] Added in 1521

4 rely ... and] Added in 1532

5 advantages ... body] In place of this passage the 1517 edition reads: 'rewards,
but true glory, honour and immortality.' The change was made in 1532.

6 through faith] Added in 1532. It is clear that in his original paraphrase of
1517 Erasmus interprets Paul as meaning here in 2:6–13 that good works are
necessary in order to receive the eternal reward. He does not indicate
there or in his annotations that he detects a contradiction between these
verses and 3:20. In an addition to his note in 1522 he even stresses that the
reward is offered to those who strive after it with good deeds. See Erasmus'
annotation on 2:7 ('to those seeking [eternal] life'). However, in these
additions of 1532 to the paraphrase (see n 4 above) he seemingly tries to
reconcile these verses of chapter 2 with 3:20 and shows that he had adopted
the exegesis of Origen and Chrysostom, which applies these verses also to
Christians who are judged on the basis not only of faith, but of works. See
Schelkle 74.

7 finally ... barbarians] Added in 1532

21

8 Lord and] Added in 1521

9 under ... gospel] Added in 1532

10 Ez 20.39; cf Is 52.5.

22

11 trusts and] Added in 1532

12 cry out ... and thus] Added in 1532

13 Christ ... law] This Christological interpretation of the end and substance of
the law in the paraphrase on verse 27 here, as well as on verse 26, was
probably influenced by Ambrosiaster. Cf CSEL 81 (1) 90:3–12, 91:3–11. Cf
below p60 n4.

14 flesh ... sin] Erasmus follows here the allegorizing and moralizing exegesis of
Origen which insists that the true circumcision is not that outward one of
the flesh, but the inner one of the mind in which the blemishes of sin have
been removed. See PG 14:907B.

Chapter 3

23

1 As far as ... respects] Added in 1532

2 law ... gospel] Here Erasmus suggests that the Jews by virtue of the law are more prepared for the gospel than the heathen. But cf his answer to Luther's *On the Bondage of the Will*, the *Hyperaspistes ii* (1527), where he holds that the heathen on the basis of the law of nature are equally prepared for the grace of the gospel (LB X 1530A–B). Cf also Lefèvre d'Étaples who maintains that human righteousness whether based on the written law or the law of nature is by no means to be identified with, but does prepare for, divine righteousness (*Epistolae* 74 verso).

3 faithfulness] It is clear from this paraphrase that Erasmus correctly understands πίστις τοῦ θεοῦ as a subjective genitive, 'God's faithfulness' not an objective genitive, 'faith in God.' Origen or his translator, Rufinus, holds both interpretations as possible but prefers the latter (PG 14:918A).

4 God ... promised] For very similar language see Ambrosiaster CSEL 81 (1) 96:2ff, 97:2ff.

5 Psalm of David] Psalm 51:4 (Vulg 50:6). Erasmus' expansion on this verse of the Psalm presupposes, possibly correctly, that Paul has in mind here God's faithfulness in spite of David's flagrant sin. The Pauline text is an almost exact quotation of the Septuagint, Psalm 50:6b. See Cranfield I 182–3.

24

6 Jews ... witness] Here Erasmus departs from his favourite, Origen, who applies this Psalm specifically to both Jews and gentiles and adopts rather the exegesis of Chrysostom, Ambrosiaster and Pelagius who all think that these words are directed to the Jews. See Schelkle 102ff.

7 Psalm 13] When Erasmus quotes from the Psalms, he usually gives the chapter number according to the Vulgate. In our text, the chapter reference according to modern versions, where it differs from the Vulgate, is included in the square brackets.

8 more] Added in 1532

9 when ... letter] Added in 1532

10 To understand ... health] A frequently expressed idea in Erasmus' writings. See *Paraphrasis in evangelium Matthaei* 9:12, LB VII 54C; *Paraphrasis in evangelium Marci* 1:5, LB VII 159C.

25

11 Righteousness ... Jews] Likewise for Ambrosiaster and Pelagius the law which is negated by the righteousness of faith is the ceremonial law. Cf CSEL 81 (1) 116:14ff; 117:12ff; and Souter 32:4–6.

12 and trust] Added in 1532

13 means of propitiation] *Propitiatorium*, the term in the Latin Bible (Greek Septuagint, ἱλαστήριον) for the *kapporeth* ('propitiatory' in DV, 'mercy seat' in RSV) which was a cover for the ark of the covenant (Ex 25:17). It received its name because of its function in the cult of Israel as the place where the sins of

Israel were propitiated when the blood of sacrificial animals was sprinkled on the cover of the ark (Lev 16:2, 13–15). Erasmus follows Origen who was the first of the Fathers to make explicit the connexion between Rom 3:25 and Ex 25:17 and to see the *propitiatorium* of Ex 25:17 as the type of Christ. See PG 14:946ff, and Schelkle 115–16. Contemporary scholars disagree as to whether the ἱλαστήριον of Rom 3:25 is to be strictly identified with the *kapporeth* of Ex 25:17. See Cranfield I 214ff.

14 through the Son] Added in 1532
15 He does ... promised] Added in 1532. Similarly, Ambrosiaster stresses the divine promise. Cf CSEL 81 (1) 120:8ff, 121:11ff.
16 your] This word which is present in the Vulgate is absent from the Greek text, as Erasmus points out in his annotation (3:27 'where is therefore'). He therefore omits it in his translation, but retains it here so that again Paul's reprimand applies especially to the Jews. Cf Lefèvre (75 recto-verso) who understands this verse to mean that boasting has been removed from Jew and gentile.
17 ceremonies] Erasmus' exegesis again agrees with the interpretation of Ambrosiaster and Pelagius that the works of the law which Paul has in mind here are ceremonies. See CSEL 81 (1) 122:19ff, 123:17ff and Souter 34:15ff.
18 in ... God] Added in 1532
19 through faith] Added in 1532
20 of the gospel] Added in 1532

26
21 which ... Saviour] Added in 1532
22 which ... the promise] Added in 1532. Like Ambrosiaster (CSEL 81 (1) 124:12ff, 125:10ff) Erasmus here connects faith with the promise.
23 accomplished] Erasmus again follows Ambrosiaster in judging that faith does not destroy the law but fulfils it, because what was promised as future has now through faith taken place (CSEL 81 (1) 124:22–4, 125:20–2).

Chapter 4

1 Because ... himself] Erasmus follows Origen who contrasts sharply the justi-fication by works which wins praises from men and the justification by faith 'which deservedly has praise in God's eyes alone' (PG 14:960C). Ambrosiaster holds a similar view (CSEL 81 (1) 128:3–11, 129:3–10).

27
2 trust] *Fiduciae* which represents a change in 1521 from *fidei* (faith)
3 faith alone] Cf Ambrosiaster CSEL 81 (1) 130:9ff, 131:9ff: 'How can the Jews think that by the justification of Abraham they are justified through the works of the law, since they see that Abraham was justified not through the works of the law, but by faith alone.' So also Pelagius (Souter 36:15).
4 compelled ... Christ] Cf Ambrosiaster CSEL 81 (1) 128:28ff, 129:25ff: 'To

believe or not to believe is a matter of the will. No one can be forced to believe what is not evident, but only invited.'

29

5 This ... mind] For the same sentiment see Erasmus' annotation on Rom 4:11 ('seal'). In this annotation he discusses the Pauline terms σημεῖον (sign) and σφραγίς (seal) and like Origen he notes that the carnal circumcision is the 'sign' of a spiritual circumcision and that it was also a 'seal' 'because for a time it concealed the mystery which was to be opened up later.' See PG 14:968B–C.

6 Isaac ... Son of God] Cf Ambrosiaster CSEL 81 (1) 136:3ff, 137:5ff: 'For not in Isaac are all the nations blessed, but in Christ ...' See also Schelkle 141.

7 imitation ... Christ] For a similar idea in Colet see Lupton I 9 (English), 141 (Latin).

8 faith ... man] Erasmus follows Origen in attributing merit to faith. See PG 14:970C.

30

9 circumcision ... washing] For a quite similar list of Jewish ceremonies which are now at an end, see Ambrosiaster CSEL 81 (1) 140:5ff, 141:5ff.

10 friend ... promise] Cf Origen PG 14:970D: '... the law of nature ... is not equal to the law of faith, by which Abraham believed God, and deserved to be called a friend of God.'

11 as if ... something] Erasmus interprets similarly in his translation. He translates ὡς ὄντα not *tamquam ea, quae sunt* ('as those that are') (Vulgate) but *tanquam sint* ('as if they were'). So, similarly, Chrysostom: 'For if he could "quicken the dead" and bring in "those things that were not as though they were," then could he also make those who were born of him to be his children' (PG 60:460; NPNF [Series 1] 11:390). He does not seem to take into account the widespread interpretation among the Fathers and the one generally accepted by modern scholars that the phrase of 17b refers to God's creative power. See Schelkle 137–8 and Cranfield I 244–5.

31

12 For after ... innumerable] Gen 15:5

13 one hundredth year] Gen 17:17

14 model] Erasmus here follows Origen who on the basis of the phrase 'But for the sake of us also' points out that what is spoken of Abraham applies to us also. Abraham and the other patriarchs supply for us a model for imitation. Likewise Ambrosiaster and Pelagius stress the exemplary character of Abraham's faith. See PG 14:987A–8A; CSEL 81 (1) 148:11–12, 149:16–17; Souter 40:22–3.

15 absolutely no] *Nec* changed to *nequaquam* in 1532.

32

16 through faith] Added in 1532

17 henceforth for righteousness] Cf Origen PG 14:985C–6D. Like Origen and

other Fathers, Erasmus understands Paul as viewing very seriously post-baptismal sins.

Chapter 5

1 made our peace] See Erasmus' annotation on 5:1 ('let us have peace toward God') where Erasmus runs counter to the majority of the Fathers in defending ἔχομεν ('we have [peace]') rather than ἔχωμεν ('let us have [peace]') as the correct Pauline reading on the ground that it better renders the Pauline sense. See Schelkle 150–1.
2 eager and resolute] For the idiom *alacres et erecti* ('eager and resolute'), see Cicero *De senectute* 20.75.

33
3 deceive ... ashamed] In this sentence Erasmus evidently strove to draw out the implications of the Greek verb καταισχύνειν in the active, 'to put to shame' (here, by hope deceiving and forsaking us); in the passive, 'to be ashamed.' In his translation and note he rejects the Vulgate translation, *confundit* ('confounds,' ie, 'puts to shame') and adopts *pudefacit* ('makes ashamed'). See annotation on 5:5 ('does not confound').
4 love of God ... in return] Erasmus does not decide here between a subjective genitive for ἀγάπη τοῦ θεοῦ, 'God's love for us,' and an objective genitive, 'our love for God,' but rather combines both meanings. Cf Schelkle 156–7 for the discussion among the Fathers on this point; cf also Colet whose interpretation is very close to that of Erasmus (Lupton I 11–12 [English], 143 [Latin]).
5 time ... weak] In his annotation on 'according to the time' Erasmus states that κατὰ καιρόν can be connected with either 'weak' or 'died.' He says that if the words 'refer to those who are weak, they mitigate what has been said, as though their weakness were to be imputed to the time when the grace of the gospel had not yet appeared. But if they refer to the phrase "he died" [that is, to Christ's death] you will understand that [Christ] encountered death at the fitting time, a time appointed by the Father.' He adds: 'Each reading has a pious sense.'
6 honest ... friend] In contrast to his annotation which understands δικαίου and ἀγαθοῦ as neuters, 'righteousness' and 'goodness,' Erasmus here considers them as masculines, 'righteous man' and 'good man.' See annotation on 5:7 ('dies for a righteous man').
7 reformed] *emendatis*. LB has here an alternate reading, *emundatis* ('thoroughly cleansed'), for which we find no textual support.

34
8 His death ... us] Note Erasmus' modification of Ambrosiaster on this verse: '... just as his death rescued us from the devil, so also his life will deliver us from the day of God's judgment' (CSEL 81 (1) 160:22–3, 161:23–4).
9 or] LB gives *ac* (and) rather than *aut* (or) as the preferred reading, but *aut* is clearly the better attested one.

10 and his only Son] Added in 1532
11 death ... soul] See below n17.
12 And so ... parent] Erasmus follows Pelagius who interprets Adam's sin as
   an example which has been imitated (Souter 45:11–15). The interpretation of
   the Greek text ἐφ' ᾧ πάντες ἥμαρτον had, however, a lively history. The
   Vulgate translation had been in quo omnes peccaverunt ('in whom all sinned').
   Augustine had supported his doctrine of original sin as an inherited de-
   pravity with this translation. Erasmus was the first in the history of Western
   exegesis to understand the ἐπί here as having a causal sense ('because all
   have sinned'). In a very lengthy annotation expanded over several editions
   Erasmus defended his translation and interpretation of Rom 5:12 as referring
   not to original sin in the Augustinian sense of an inherited guilt, but rather to
   personal sins committed in free imitation of the sin of Adam. Against the
   criticism of Béda concerning the paraphrase, Erasmus stated that Jerome (ie,
   pseudo-Jerome — he does not indicate to his Sorbonne critic any doubt as
   to the authenticity of the commentaries ascribed to Jerome), Origen, Ambrose
   (Ambrosiaster), and Theophylact all favour his interpretation here (Divinationes ad notata Bedae [LB IX 469A–C]). See Payne 'Erasmus: Interpreter of
   Romans' 12ff. For Augustine see Schelkle 177–8, and J. Freundorfer Erbsünde
   und Erbtod beim Apostel Paulus (Münster i W 1927) 139–46; and for Erasmus'
   significance with respect to the exegesis of this verse, see Freundorfer 158–9.
   On Origen's view, see PG 14:1018B–C: 'For all who are born in this world
   are not only nourished by parents, but also instructed, and they are not only
   sons of sinners, but disciples.'
13 Now just ... wrong] For the same point see Origen PG 14:1014A–C.

35
14 destruction ... guilty] As Erasmus points out in his 1535 annotation on Rom
   5:12, he provides here a vague expression of support for the Augustinian
   exegesis, but one which is definitely outweighed by his explicit adoption
   three times in the paraphrase on this chapter of the view that sin spread
   through mankind because all sinned in imitation of the first parent (cf paraphrase on 5:12 ['And so it happened'], 5:17 ['But if the one sin of one']; 5:19
   ['For just as one man, Adam']).
15 first parent ... righteousness] Cf Pelagius '... Adam created only the model of
   transgression, but Christ both freely remitted sins and furnished the example
   of righteousness' (Souter 47:19–20).
16 very many] Erasmus is here interpreting οἱ πολλοί as plurimos ('very many')
   though he translates it as multi ('many') with the Vulgate and though in
   the annotation on vs 15 ('pattern of him who was to come') he had pointed out
   that Origen regarded οἱ πολλοί as equivalent to πάντες ('all') because it
   better corresponds to 'one' in the clause, 'For if many died through one man's
   trespass ...' See PG 14:1006C–D, 1023C. Erasmus is saying here that 'very
   many' but not 'all' sinned according to the example of Adam. The explanation
   for his interpretation is that he is simply following patristic exegesis. Even
   Origen interprets οἱ πολλοί in vs 19 as 'many' and he is followed by
   Ambrosiaster, Pelagius and the majority of Greek exegetes. See PG 14:1030;
   CSEL 81 (1) 184:1–4, 185:2–6; Souter 48:5–8; and Schelkle 190–1.

36

17 of our souls ... death] Added in 1532. With this addition Erasmus makes
explicit his agreement with Pelagius and other Fathers, including Origen in
several passages, who interpret 'death' in 5:12–21 as spiritual not corporeal
death. See Schelkle 180–1. Cf above n11.

Chapter 6

1 to such an extent] Added in 1521
2 dead to the devil] For the identification of sin with the devil here see
Ambrosiaster CSEL 81 (1) 190:13, 191:10–11.

37

3 baptism ... denotes] Erasmus' language here hesitates between a causal and
symbolic view of Christian baptism. See the following passages in which
he clearly adopts a symbolic understanding: *Paraphrasis in acta apostolorum*
(1524) 11:17 (LB VII 713D); *Paraphrasis in evangelium Marci* (1523) 16:16 (LB VII
271C–2A). Cf Payne 163ff.
4 always ... virtue] For the same thought see Origen PG 14:1042A–B.
5 who are ... body] Added in 1521
6 imitate Christ's death] For a similar stress upon the imitation of Christ see
Origen PG 14:1044A.
7 two men in us] In his lectures on Romans 6 Colet had said: 'And herein,
that the Apostle's language may be better understood, we must observe that
— man consisting of a *soul* (which St Paul calls the *inner man*) and *a sentient
body* (which may be termed, in Plotinus' words, the *animal part* of man) —
from Adam's transgression ... this animal part of man ... has borne sway in
man's estate ...' (Lupton I 16–17 [English], 146 [Latin]). On the reference to
Plotinus see Lupton I 16 n3.

38

8 Just as ... death] Like the Fathers and Colet, Erasmus interprets this text as
stressing the obligation of no post-baptismal sins. Cf Schelkle 215ff; F.J.
Dölger *Sphragis. Eine altkirchliche Taufbezeichnung in ihren Beziehungen zur
profanen und religiösen Kultur des Altertums* (Paderborn 1911) 133ff; Lupton I
13ff (English), 144ff (Latin).
9 army] The military language here is suggested by the word ὅπλα in the
biblical text which, like the Latin *arma* (as it is translated both in the Vulgate
and by Erasmus), may mean either 'instruments' or 'weapons.' For an
extended elaboration of this military metaphor, see Chrysostom PG 60:487;
NPNF (Series 1) 11.411.

39

10 left ... embrace] Cf Origen PG 14:1059C: '... each has it in his own hands
and in the power of his will whether he be a slave of sin or a slave of
righteousness.' See Schelkle 218–19 for a listing of other Fathers who likewise
interpret Rom 6:12–20 as supporting free will.

11 freely] Cf Chrysostom PG 60:489; NPNF (Series 1) 11.412: 'You were neither forced nor pressed, but you came over of your own accord, with a willing mind.'
12 voluntarily] Cf Origen PG 14:1063C–D who also interprets this verse as teaching that whether we serve sin or righteousness is dependent on our free will.

40
13 but the most ... all] Added in 1532
14 death] Cf Origen PG 14:1068B who connects 'death' in this verse with the devil.

Chapter 7

41
1 so ... lives] In keeping with his interpretation (see Erasmus' annotation 'the law has dominion over a man as long as it [or "he"] lives') which follows Origen, Erasmus also translates 'as long as it [the law] lives.' Modern scholars, rejecting the Origenistic allegory, translate simply, 'as long as he lives.' See Cranfield I 334.
2 *immortal* bridegroom] Cf Lefèvre d'Étaples 83 verso: 'This bridegroom is immortal and makes the bride immortal.'

42
3 revealer of sin] *Index peccati*. Cf Ambrosiaster CSEL 81 (1) 222:2, 223:2: 'The law is therefore not sin, but the revealer of sin (*index peccati*).'
4 desires] In a letter to Colet from Louvain 23 April 1518 Erasmus indicates that Colet was displeased with his interpretation of chapter 7 of Romans. He says: '... it may be that what I took to refer to the affections, you preferred to apply to the Mosaic Law. But in that passage St Paul is so slippery that he looks first one way then another, so that in explaining all this Origen works himself into a lather' (Ep 825:13–16). Since these remarks are so general and since the letter from Colet expressing his reaction to Erasmus' paraphrase is lost, we cannot at all be sure of the point at issue. Neither does a comparison with Colet's earlier interpretation in his lectures on Romans help to answer the question.
5 human nature ... prohibited] It was a common view among the Fathers that 'those things which are prohibited are desired all the more passionately' (Origen PG 14:1081C). Cf Ambrosiaster CSEL 81 (1) 228:5ff, 229:5ff, and Chrysostom PG 60:500; NPNF (Series 1) 11.421.

43
6 devil] For the connexion of sin with the devil in this verse, see Origen PG 14:1083C, and Ambrosiaster CSEL 81 (1) 228:3–9, 229:2–8.
7 habit of sinning] Cf Origen PG 14:1087B–8A; Pelagius, Souter 58:12–13, 59:6. Like Origen and Pelagius, Erasmus interprets Paul as teaching that sin is more a matter of custom than of nature.

44

8 still subject] Whereas above in his interpretation of verse 14 ('The law is spiritual') Erasmus seems to think that this section of chapter 7 is applicable to Paul himself, here he appears to apply Paul's language to pre-Christian man in general. The history of the exegesis of Rom 7 has divided over whether the verses concern Paul himself, man in general, or both, and over whether they concern pre-Christian or Christian man. For the different views of the Fathers, see Schelkle 242ff, and for the history of the exegesis of Rom 7:7–25 in general, see Kuss II 462ff.

9 carnal] On the probable fusion of a Pauline with a Platonic anthropology here, see Payne 'Erasmus: Interpreter of Romans' 10.

10 habit ... sin] See the close parallels in Ambrosiaster CSEL 81 (1) 242:12ff, 243:10ff, and Pelagius, Souter 59:12–13.

Chapter 8

45

1 they will ... Christ] Erasmus' paraphrase depends in part on a phrase omitted from the best manuscripts but included in the Greek manuscripts he knew: 'Through Christ Jesus, who walk not according to the flesh but according to the Spirit.' The Vulgate has only the first part of the clause, 'who walk not according to the flesh.' Likewise the Fathers, whether they knew this reading or not, stressed here the importance of moral endeavour. Cf Schelkle 259ff.

2 two laws] Cf above p11; also the paraphrases on Gal 4:24 ('Now concealed') and Gal 5:16 ('For just as in one person'). Erasmus follows Origen with this division of the law into two parts, the fleshly and the spiritual. Cf PG 14:1094A. Erasmus defends himself twice against Béda who apparently charged him with blasphemy for making the one law into two laws: *Divinationes ad notata Bedae* LB IX 470B–C; *Supputatio errorum Bedae* LB IX 668F–9B. For differing evaluations of the similar statement in the Galatians paraphrase see Alfons Auer *Die vollkommene Frömmigkeit des Christen* (Düsseldorf 1954) 171 and 247 n 329, and Ernst-Wilhelm Kohls *Die Theologie des Erasmus* (Basel 1966) II 116 n501. Kohls rejects out of hand Auer's suggestion of an anthropological base of Erasmus' understanding of law.

3 sinners] Erasmus' understanding of this passage as signifying the identity of Christ's flesh with that of sinful humanity contrasts sharply with Lefèvre's interpretation which shrinks from such an understanding. See *Epistolae* 85 recto-verso; and Payne 'Erasmus and Lefèvre d'Étaples as Interpreters of Paul' *Archiv für Reformationsgeschichte* 65 (1974) 77–8.

46

4 when ... letter] Added in 1532

5 provided] The conditional conjunction, *si tamen*, Erasmus rejects in his note on the Vulgate text but retains in his own paraphrase. See the annotation on Rom 8:9 ('if nevertheless the Spirit of God').

6 merely baptized] For the same perspective on baptism, see *Enchiridion* Holborn 74ff, 78ff (Himelick 110ff, 116ff).

7 if Christ ... virtues] Cf *Enchiridion* Holborn 63:11–15 (Himelick 94): 'Think of Christ not as an empty word, but as nothing other than love, candor, patience, purity — in brief, whatever he taught.' Note the similar language of Pelagius: 'The Spirit of Christ is the spirit of humility, of patience, and of all the virtues ...' (Souter 63:7–8). Cf below p77 n10.

8 We imitate Christ] Cf Pelagius who likewise refers here to the imitation of Christ (Souter 63:10–11).

9 spirit ... righteousness] Cf Aristotle *Nichomachean Ethics* I 1102b 14–16 (*Aristotle: The Nicomachean Ethics* tr H.G. Apostle [Dordrecht Holland 1975] 17): 'For we praise reason or that part of the soul which has reason in the continent and the incontinent man, since it urges them rightly to what is best.' Cf also Cicero *De finibus* 5.48: 'So great is our love of learning and knowledge ... that human nature is carried away to these things (*ad eas rapiatur*) without any promise of reward.' Erasmus' expression here is *melior pars nostri ... ad ea quae sunt justitiae impetu suo rapiens.*

47

10 God ... you] Unlike the Fathers Erasmus does not read in verse 11 ('And so if the Spirit') the promise of a bodily resurrection. See Schelkle 271ff.

48

11 earth ... bodies] The basic four elements out of which the world was made according to Greek philosophy. For Plato see *Timaeus* 31B–2C.

12 angels] Cf Origen PG 14:1111C–13A. Erasmus seems to be combining two patristic interpretations of κτίσις here, one which thinks of it as the visible, sensible world (represented by Chrysostom among others), the other which understands it as especially the world endowed with intelligence, that is, the angels (represented by Origen and Pelagius among others). See Schelkle 294ff and Kuss II 623. Cf also Lefèvre d'Étaples folio 88 verso, who adopts the first interpretation and in so doing explicitly rejects Origen's exegesis. In answer to a criticism of Béda concerning his interpretation of this term, Erasmus states that when he included angels as part of the meaning he was following the opinion of Jerome, ie pseudo-Jerome, but he does not inform Béda that he has any doubt concerning the authenticity of the work traditionally ascribed to Jerome (*Divinationes ad notata Bedae* LB IX 470E–1C). For the interpretation of 'angels' by pseudo-Jerome (Pelagius), see Souter 65:18–19, 66:13–16.

49

13 whole cosmos] *rerum natura*, a phrase recalling Lucretius' poem by that name

14 after ... Saviour] Added in 1532

15 precisely ... faith] Added in 1532

16 because ... it] Added in 1532. See 2 Cor 12:7–9.

17 wish] LB gives *vocem* (voice) as the reading of the text, but the alternate reading, *votum* ('wish' or 'prayer') is the better attested one.

18 acting ... ways] Added in 1532

19 groans] Béda apparently accused Erasmus of demeaning the Holy Spirit in this sentence of his paraphrase. Erasmus answers that he is simply following the language of the Fathers, especially Ambrose (Ambrosiaster) who does not shrink from applying human emotions in a figurative manner to the Holy Spirit (see CSEL 81 [1] 288:1–8, 289:1–8). He acknowledges that there were some Fathers (Chrysostom and Theophylact) who refused to interpret πνεῦμα as the Holy Spirit, but chose rather to refer the term to the spirit of man who is renewed by the gifts of the Spirit, an interpretation which Béda evidently favours. However, Erasmus cites correctly Origen, Augustine, Ambrosiaster, and Thomas Aquinas as all favouring the identification here of πνεῦμα with the Holy Spirit (*Supputatio errorum Bedae* LB IX 673–4). For the Fathers' views see Schelkle 305ff. Probably because of Béda's critique, Erasmus adds in 1532 lines which interpret it also as the 'spirit of man.'

50
20 Sometimes ... beatitude] Added in 1532. See preceding note.
21 Ours ... God] In his annotation on Rom 8:28 ('according to a purpose') Erasmus correctly describes the ambiguity of Origen's and Ambrosiaster's interpretation which refers πρόθεσιν to both the divine and the human will. See Origen PG 14:1125D–6B; Ambrosiaster CSEL 81 (1) 288:21ff, 289:20ff. Other Fathers, in order to stress human responsibility even more, interpreted the term exclusively as meaning the human will (Schelkle 309ff). Erasmus clearly understands it in his annotation as the divine will, but in his paraphrase adopts the ambiguous interpretation of Origen and Ambrosiaster.
22 unalterable decision] See annotation 8:29 ('whom he foreknew') in which he likewise understands προορίζειν as meaning a decision which is made public and therefore unchangeable. By his translation (*praefinivit* 'predetermined' rather than *praedestinavit* 'predestined') and by his annotation, Erasmus seems to undercut speculation concerning the mystery of predestination based on this passage. He prefers to construe it in a more general sense as referring to the divine decree of election made manifest in the history of salvation.

51
23 God ... respect] For a very similar expression see Ambrosiaster CSEL 81 (1) 294:27–8, 297:4. In other passages Erasmus moves in the direction of an Origenistic subordinationism. See the annotation on Col 1:15 (1522) (LB VI 884E–5C) and on 1 Tim 1:17 (1519) (LB VI 930F). See also *Ecclesiastes* (1535) LB V 939A. He was even accused of Arianism, but unjustly. See Payne 56ff.

52
24 principalities and] Added in 1532
25 even ... hell threaten us] Added in 1532

Chapter 9

1 through faith] Changed from *fide* ('by faith') to *per fidem* in 1521.

53

2 But Christ ... God] Likewise in his translation Erasmus identified Christ with God: 'Theirs are the patriarchs, and from them is the Christ, as far as the flesh is concerned, who is in all things God, to be praised forever. Amen.' But see his annotation on Rom 9:5 ('who is over all things God') which raises questions about whether 'Christ' should be identified with 'God' in this verse.

3 and a God ... eternity] The 1517 edition reads: 'protecting all, to whom alone praise is owed for all eternity.' The change was made in 1532.

4 All ... through the Son] Added in 1532

5 Only ... with God] The 1517 edition reads: 'only those who see with the eye of faith truly fit the name of Israel.' In 1521 the passage was changed to read as it is translated in our text, except that the final words, 'that is, of one powerful with God,' were added in 1523.

54

6 Through ... named] Gen 21:12

7 power ... flesh] For a similar sentiment see Origen PG 14:1142B–C.

8 through ... God] For a nearly identical expression, see Origen PG 14:1142A; and Pelagius, Souter 74:4–6.

9 About ... son] Gen 18:10

10 Jacob ... hated] Mal 1:2–3

11 The elder ... younger] Gen 25:23

55

12 not at all] *nequaquam*, changed from *nihil* in 1521

13 no impious person] Cf Origen PG 14:1144A–B. Following Origen and a number of the Fathers after him, Erasmus, in his early editions, understands 9:14–16 ('And let no ... guilty of nothing') as the objection of an imagined opponent. The 1532 revisions obscure this *persona*.

14 So then] *quum* (literally 'since'), revised in 1532. The 1517 edition reads in place of *quum*, *quasi* ('as if').

15 However ... many] In place of this passage the 1517 edition reads: 'Or rather, some part of it depends on our own will and effort, although this part is so minor that it seems like nothing at all in comparison with the free kindness of God.' The change was made in 1532. For a similar view, see Origen PG 14:1145B–C; and *Erasmus: On the Freedom of the Will*, in E.G. Rupp and P.S. Watson trs and eds *Luther and Erasmus: Free Will and Salvation* Library of Christian Classics 17 (Philadelphia 1969) 66. See also the letter to Marcus Laurinus (1523), Allen Ep 1342:926ff, where Erasmus states that he was following Origen and Jerome in ascribing a certain minimum to free will. For a discussion of these and other changes in the 1532 edition, see John B. Payne, 'The Significance of Lutheranizing Changes in Erasmus' Interpretation of Paul's Letters to the Romans and the Galatians in his *Annotationes* (1527) and *Paraphrases* (1532),' in Olivier Fatio and Pierre Fraenkel eds *Histoire de l'exégèse au XVIe siècle* 312–30; and Albert Rabil Jr *Erasmus and the New Testament* 136–9.

16 if ... mercy] Added in 1532

17 if ... obduracy] Added in 1532

56

18 He did not harden ... glory] Cf *Erasmus: On the Freedom of the Will* (Rupp and Watson) 65–6. See also Origen PG 14:1146C–7A and *De principiis* 3.1.10 (G.W. Butterworth ed *Origen on First Principles* [New York 1966] 172–3).

19 Isaiah] Isa 29:16; 45:9

20 The clay ... no guilt] Added in 1532

21 dream of them] Like the Fathers Erasmus discourses here on the mysterious wisdom and power of God. See Origen PG 14:1147B–8A; Chrysostom PG 60:559–60; NPNF (Series 1) 11.467–8; Schelkle 346.

22 God ... purposes] Cf *Erasmus: On the Freedom of the Will* 70–1 where Erasmus notes the contrast between Rom 9:21 and 2 Tim 2:20–21, just as does Origen *De principiis* 3.1.24 (Butterworth 209–10).

23 if ... name] In editions up to 1521, Erasmus represents God as speaking in his own person in this clause: 'If I through my own wisdom make use ....'

58

24 Shadows ... men] Added in 1532

25 sabbaths ... observances] For a similar list of observances opposed to faith, see Ambrosiaster CSEL 81 (1) 338:2ff; 339:2ff.

Chapter 10

59

1 To have zeal] For a similar view see Origen PG 14:1160A.

60

2 twofold] Likewise Origen refers here to a twofold righteousness (PG 14:1160C).

3 coagulation] A tenet of Galen, who argued that flesh and bone were both formed out of a coagulation of blood (*On the Natural Faculties* 1.10.21)

4 completion] *Perfectio*. Cf Origen PG 14:1160B: 'For the end of the law is Christ, that is, completion (*perfectio*) of the law ...' Likewise in his annotation on Rom 10:4 ('the end of the law is Christ') Erasmus interprets τέλος as *perfectio* or *consummatio*, not as *interitus* ('annihilation'). Cf above p22 n13, and below p90 n6.

5 descends] Whereas the Greek and Latin texts place the verbs 'ascend' and 'descend' in the future tense, Erasmus puts them in the present tense.

61

6 trust] *Fiducia* changed from *fides* ('faith') in 1521.

7 Micah] The quotation is from Joel 2:32.

8 through faith ... abolished] Added in 1532

62

9 since miracles ... preaching] Added in 1532

10 malice ... envy] Ambrosiaster refers here also to the envy and malice of the Jews (CSEL 81 [1] 358:9–13; 359:12–15).

11 miracles] Pelagius also speaks of miracles which failed to produce faith
(Souter 84:23–85:1).

Chapter 11

64

1 foresaw] Cf Isa 6.9–10.
2 books of Moses] Erasmus shows here his acceptance of the allegory which
originated with Origen who interprets τράπεζα ('feast' or 'table') as the writings of the Old Testament, though Erasmus' allegorization is far simpler. See
PG 14:1181–4A, and Schelkle 386ff.
3 jealousy] *Aemulatione*, which can also mean 'by emulation.' The Vulgate
translates εἰς τὸ παραζηλῶσαι αὐτούς ambiguously as *ut illos aemulentur*.
Although the verb παραζηλόω in its classical sense can mean 'emulate,' here it
clearly means 'provoke to jealousy,' as Erasmus points out in his annotation. See annotation on Rom 11:11 ('that they may emulate them').

65

4 emulate ... jealousy] Erasmus here combines in his paraphrase both meanings of παραζηλόω (*aemulor*).
5 as though ... body] Erasmus' paraphrase combines both possible senses of
'life from the dead': a spiritual rebirth and a bodily resurrection. See Schelkle
393ff for the division of witness among the fathers.
6 founder] Erasmus is following the interpretation of Chrysostom and the
Antiochene school which understands the dough and the root as Abraham,
and the remaining patriarchs, the first fruits and the branches, as the
descendants in faith of the founder (PG 60:588; NPNF [Series 1] 11:490) rather
than that of Origen and the Alexandrian school which sees the root and
the first fruits as Christ (PG 14:1193B). Cf Schelkle 395ff.

67

7 and] LB gives as an alternate reading, *ut* ('in order to'), but *et* ('and') is the
much better attested reading.
8 scattered] Erasmus follows here a view which goes back to the early Fathers
that the destruction of Jerusalem and dispersal of the Jews were signs of the
Messianic age. Cf Justin Martyr *Dialogue with Trypho* 16 (PG 6:509AB) and
Tertullian *Adversus Judaeos* 3 (CCL 2.3.3–4).
9 error] Cf Ambrosiaster who ascribes the future correction and salvation of the
Jews to the fact that their unbelief was due to error rather than obstinacy
(CSEL 81 [1] 382:8–10, 383:9–10).
10 all ... salvation] Unlike most of the Fathers except for Ambrosiaster and
Augustine, Erasmus interprets the text as teaching without qualification that
the entire people of Israel will be saved. See Schelkle 401ff.
11 and when ... Lord] Added in 1532
12 play ... nation] That is, 'undertake the duty to carry out the covenant.' The
Latin involves a stage metaphor: *qui totius generis personam sustineant*. For this
idiom see Cicero *Against Piso* 11.24.

68

13 equal] *Parem*. The reading in LB is *parum* ('little'), but *parem* is the reading of all the editions during Erasmus' lifetime.

14 not ... God] Like Origen and other Fathers, Erasmus makes sure to point out that verse 32 ('For God by his') does not undercut human freedom and responsibility. See PG 14:1200. For Fathers with a similar view, see Schelkle 404ff.

15 God] Erasmus gives no Trinitarian explanation of verse 36 ('Thus God takes thought') as do some of the Fathers. See Schelkle 408ff.

Chapter 12

69

1 which ... happiness] Added in 1532. Earlier editions read: 'through the mercy of God to whom you owe your entire happiness.'

2 mind] Added in 1521

3 victim] Added in 1521. The 1517 edition read simply, 'a rational sacrifice, not [that] of a brute beast.'

4 sacrifice] The entire exegesis of verse 1 ('Therefore ... sacrifice ourselves for him') which distinguishes sharply between a carnal and a spiritual sacrifice has been much influenced by Origen. See PG 14:1203–4.

71

5 measure of faith] Erasmus follows the translator of Origen (Rufinus) in taking issue with the Vulgate translation of ἀναλογίαν by *rationem*. In his annotation ('according to the rule of faith') he says that the Greek word really means 'a proportionate measure.' Cf Origen PG 14:1213A.

6 Or if one has ... heart] This entire sentence is a paraphrase of the Greek phrase ὁ μεταδιδοὺς ἐν ἁπλότητι. The paraphrase explicates the double meaning of 'generosity' and 'simplicity' in ἁπλότης. In his translation, however, Erasmus adheres to the Vulgate rendering, 'simplicity.'

72

7 serve the time] Erasmus translates 'serving the time' rather than 'serving the Lord' on the basis of his textual witnesses which give a western reading, and on the basis of his understanding of the sense. See his annotation ('serving the Lord'). Modern interpreters are divided as to the more probable correct reading. See Ernst Käsemann *Commentary on Romans* tr and ed Geoffrey W. Bromiley (Grand Rapids, Michigan 1980) 346.

8 In the meantime ... interest] Added in 1532

9 accommodate] Following Origen Erasmus frequently points to 'accommodation' as a prominent principle in Paul's writings and in scripture as a whole. See his annotation on 12:16 ('but consenting with the humble') as well as the paraphrase on 14:20–15:2 ('You who are stronger ... make him better'), and cf Origen PG 14:1257–60. Like Origen Erasmus applies the principle not only to the conduct of the Christian life, but also to scripture, incarnation and

the sacraments. See Payne 55, 55–64, 89–91, 101–3, and E.W. Kohls *Die Theologie des Erasmus* I 176–7; II 126–7, notes 706, 707. On Origen's use of the theme see Jean Daniélou, *Origène* (Paris 1948) 257; and Rolf Gögler *Zur Theologie des biblischen Wortes* (Düsseldorf 1963) 307ff, 381ff.

73

10 The strength ... admire it] Added in 1532

Chapter 13

1 rulers and magistrates] Erasmus wrote this paraphrase of Paul's famous passage on the Christian's stance toward governmental authority in the next year after he had completed his most important work on statecraft, the *Institutio principis christiani*, published at Basel in May 1516. Although in this treatise he writes primarily about the responsibilities of Christian princes rather than about the duties of Christian subjects, he does touch on this passage in one place: *Institutio principis christiani*, O. Herding ed ASD IV-1 166:960–70; *Education of a Christian Prince* L.K. Born ed and tr (New York 1968) 178. On Erasmus' political theory see, besides the introductions of Herding and Born, F. Geldner *Die Staatsauffassung und Fürstenlehre des Erasmus von Rotterdam* (Berlin 1930); E. von Koerber *Die Staatstheorie des Erasmus von Rotterdam* (Berlin 1967).

2 order] 'Order,' which is a conspicuous term in Erasmus' exegesis of Rom 13:1–7, is also prominent in Augustine's exposition of 13:1, as indeed it is prominent in his political thought in general. See *Expositio quarumdam propositionum ex epistola ad Romanos* PL 35:2083–4; Werner Affeldt *Die weltliche Gewalt in der Paulus Exegese Röm 13:1–7 in den Römerbriefkommentaren der lateinischen Kirche bis zum Ende des 13. Jahrhunderts* (Göttingen 1969) 88ff.

74

3 Between ... itself] Cf for the division of things into good, bad, and neutral or indifferent, *Enchiridion* Holborn 63:30ff; Himelick 95ff; and Alfons Auer *Die vollkommene Frömmigkeit des Christen* 100. Auer (233 n 20) points to Jerome as Erasmus' model for this distinction: Ep 112.16 (PL 22:926); *Commentariorum in Isaiam libri* XIV 52, XV 55 (PL 24:500B, 530C).

4 Persecution ... unfair] See Erasmus' annotation on Rom 13:1 ('but which are from God'): 'Paul was aware that some Christians, under the pretext of religion, were refusing to carry out the orders of rulers, and that the result would be a confusion of established order with everything turned upside down. Thus he taught that they should obey anyone entrusted with public authority when faith and piety permitted such obedience. True, these very rulers are heathen and evil; but order is good, and for the sake of order, the pious must sometimes endure even evil rulers.'

5 image of God] In his comment on Rom 13:3, Ambrosiaster describes kings as having the 'image of God' (CSEL 81 [1] 418:21, 419:23). For the significance of this designation in Ambrosiaster, see Affeldt (op cit p73 n2) 62ff.

76

6 it] *Ipsa*. LB gives as an alternate reading *ipsi* (they), for which we find no textual support.

7 Therefore ... all laws] The same idea is expressed elsewhere: *Paraphrasis in epistolam Pauli I ad Timotheum* 1:5 (LB VII 1036E); *Ratio* (Holborn ed 244:30– 245:10).

8 essence ... love] For a similar opinion, see Origen PG 14:1231B.

9 You ... yourself] Lev 19:18; Matt 19:19

77

10 chastity ... virtues] For a similar expression see Origen PG 14:1234B, and Pelagius, Souter 105:18. See above p46 n7 and n8.

Chapter 14

1 accustomed] For a similar view see Origen PG 14:1235A.

78

2 concord] Origen likewise interprets Paul in verse 3 ('These things') as con- cerned with maintaining concord in the church, but whereas Erasmus uses the expressions 'the strong' and 'the weak' he uses the terms 'the perfect' and 'the imperfect' (PG 14:1236B).

3 and ... holy] Added in 1532

4 Lord] Cf Origen PG 14:1237A: '... there is one and only Lord Jesus Christ, who is Lord of all, rich in all things.' See Rom 10:12.

5 all the time] In his annotation on verse 5 Erasmus makes the same point and takes the opportunity to attack 'piling up holy days on various pretexts.'

80

6 quench] Cf Isa 42:3.

82

7 betake] *Pedibus ire*. This term was used of registering one's opinion in the Roman Senate, that is, of voting (cf Livy 9.8.13), when a senator 'walked over' to the side occupied by those with whom he agreed. See Frank F. Abbot *A History and Description of Roman Political Institutions* 3rd ed (Boston 1911) 229.

8 faith] In his annotation on 14:22 ('you have the faith that you have') Erasmus says: 'But Chrysostom indicates that "faith" is not to be taken here to mean faith in dogma, but rather the assurance of one's conscience, which is being contrasted with weakness and fear.' See Chrysostom PG 60:640; NPNF (Series 1) 11.531. This portion of the annotation was added in 1535.

Chapter 15

83

1 imitate] In his annotation on 15:4 ('for whatever were written') Erasmus makes much of the prefix in the Greek προεγράφη which, however, is ignored in the Vulgate translation. In a part of the annotation added in 1519 he says: 'Thus it would not be absurd to take *praescripta* in the sense of something set forward to be imitated; by a "prescription" we mean an example set up for imitation.' For exactly this sense see Theophylact PG 124:536B–C. This rather lengthy annotation is an interesting discourse on hermeneutics which describes in what sense Old Testament passages are suitable for our instruction and imitation.

2 portrayed] Here Erasmus picks up another meaning of προγράφω and as in his annotation, alludes to Gal 3:1 where this verb is used in this sense. Cf below p108 n3.

84

3 promised] In his annotation on 15:8 ('for confirming the promises of the Fathers') Erasmus, like Ambrosiaster and Chrysostom, distinguishes sharply between 'promise' here in verse 8 ('Moreover Christ') and 'mercy' in the next verse ('He was also'). 'Therefore Paul made an antithesis between "mercy" and "promises," because mercy is pure good will, while something appears [to be expected] in a promise. For if you promise something to someone, he has the right to demand it if you do not fulfil it; but a benefit which comes contrary to every expectation brings with it both more pleasure and more praise.' Cf Ambrosiaster CSEL 81 (1) 458, 459; and Chrysostom PG 60:650; NPNF (Series 1) 11. 538–9.

85

4 Lest … ministry] Erasmus follows the interpretation of Origen which he describes in his annotation ('Of those things which [Christ] has not worked by me'). He says he prefers this interpretation to that of Ambrose (Ambrosiaster) which he thinks is less modest and less true to the Greek text. Cf Origen PG 14:1269B–C and Ambrosiaster CSEL 81 (1) 466:1–4, 6–10; 467:1–4, 7–11.

86

5 for … wished] Added in 1532

Chapter 16

87

1 Cenchreae] See above p 7 n15.

88

2 preaching] *praedicatio.* LB has here a misprint, *praedicario.*

3 worthy of his name] *Epaenetus* in Greek means 'praiseworthy.'
4 seventy-two] See Luke 10:1. In some manuscripts this was the number of
  emissaries sent out by Jesus in addition to the twelve. Other manuscripts read
  'seventy.' Origen also refers to the 'seventy-two' who were distinguished
  among the apostles before Paul (PG 14:1280A–B).

89

5 congregation] *Congregatio*

90

6 Now ... Amen] The paraphrase of these last three verses is one long, con-
  voluted sentence which is difficult to render in English. In it Erasmus re-
  affirms his interpretation that the gospel as preached by Paul negates, to be
  sure, the ceremonies of the Mosaic law, but it does not abolish the law
  altogether since the moral aspect of the law finds its fulfilment in Christ. See
  above p60 n4 and below p116 n10.

PARAPHRASE ON GALATIANS

Dedicatory Letter

92

1 de la Marck] In this letter, written about the end of April 1519 and addressed
  to the young Antoine, Erasmus honours the de la Marck family, several
  members of whom he mentions in this dedication. The de la Marcks were a
  powerful family with lands on both sides of the French-Burgundian border,
  and endeavoured to enrich themselves by playing on the rivalry between
  the French king and the German emperor. Antoine's father, Robert (d 1536),
  was head of the house. He was gradually detached from his allegiance to the
  French, and in 1518, along with his brother Erard, signed a secret treaty
  with Maximilian. He reverted to the French in 1521, however, and was
  crippled, though not crushed, by the Burgundians. Erard (1472-1538) became
  Bishop of Liège in 1505. Unlike his brother, Robert, he remained faithful
  to Burgundy after the treaty of 1518. He was thought at first to be favourable
  to the reform movement, and though he became a determined opponent of
  heresy after he had received a cardinal's hat in 1520, he continued to urge
  reform within the church. Beginning in 1517 Erasmus and Erard became
  correspondents and Erasmus dedicated his *Paraphrase* on Corinthians to him.
  Antoine's maternal uncle, Charles de Croy, Prince of Chimay (d 1527),
  became godfather and mentor to Prince Charles. As the prince's mentor, he
  played an important part in the government of the Netherlands until 1509
  when he was succeeded as mentor by his cousin. Though he partially retired
  at this time, he nevertheless participated in a treaty of 1518 between the
  Netherlands and the principality of Liège. Antoine himself (c 1495-1528)
  began to acquire preferment at an early age. In 1507 he received the Cluniac

Abbey of Beaulieu-en-Argonne, in 1508 was made canon of Liège, and subsequently archdeacon of Brabant and Chartres. He followed his father's
political moves, but broke away from the French in 1525 to support the
Hapsburg alliance. He undertook a campaign into Champagne in 1527 and
the French, in return, stormed his abbey and Antoine was killed. Allen
writes, 'As Abbot, the rapacity of his officials and his own licentious conduct
soon made him odious to his neighbours.' He is said to have died at the
hands of a neighbour whose wife he had wronged. Erasmus suppressed this
preface after 1522. In the later collections including the Leclerc edition, this
Paraphrase was printed without any dedication. See also Allen Epp 738 intro,
748 25n, and CWE 738 intro and 956 intro.
2 Berselius] Paschasius Berselius (d May 1535), born near Liège, became a
Benedictine at St Laurent's near Liège in 1501. He enjoyed the confidence of
Erard de la Marck, became a correspondent of Erasmus at least as early as
1517 and visited Louvain in 1518 where he returned to study Greek in 1519.
Later he became estranged from Erasmus but toward the end of his life
sought reconciliation. See Allen Ep 674 and CWE Ep 674.

93
3 lying] Erasmus describes this dispute in his long annotation on Gal 2:11 ('I
opposed him to his face'). Whereas Augustine considered Peter to have
been guilty of a serious offence which deserved the rebuke of Paul, Jerome
could not admit that the chief of the apostles had committed an act that was
truly deserving of censure. Erasmus sides with Jerome in this debate. See
below p104 n3 and n5.

Argument

94
1 wit] Jerome PL 26:380C. Erasmus gives here not an exact quotation but a paraphrase of Jerome's meaning. This 'Argument' of the Epistle to the Galatians
had already been published in 1518 (cf above p6 n1).
2 Hilary] Erasmus derives this reference to Hilary from Jerome. Cf PL 26:380C.
3 circumcised] Acts 18:18; 16:3
4 in the flesh] Added in 1532

95
5 Christ] In 1519 the text read: 'Christ the already immortal God.' The change
appeared in 1521.

96
6 forms ... new] *cultus novos. Cultus* is normally used of worship, but sometimes
in the sense of 'ritual' or 'practice.' See *Enarratio Psalmi* XIV LB V 308–9.
7 Latin ... Rome] Cf Lightfoot 36–7.

Chapter 1

98

1 character] Described in the Argument as dull and frivolous. See above p94.

99

2 great ... be] See Erasmus' annotation on Gal 1:6 ('into the grace of Christ').

100

3 Christ ... God] Erasmus' comment here is prompted by Jerome who argues that the implication of Paul's statement runs counter to the Ebionite and Photinian opinion that Christ is only a man. Cf PL 26:346C.

4 congregation] See Erasmus' annotation on Gal 1:13 ('and wasted'), where Erasmus explains that Paul uses *ecclesia* here to refer to 'that little assembly of Christians which he utterly ravaged.' Cf p89 n5.

101

5 discuss] See Erasmus' annotation on Gal 1:16 ('I did not acquiesce') where Erasmus points out that what Paul says here seems to be in conflict with the account in Acts 9 which describes Paul after his conversion as having been brought by Barnabas to the apostles in Jerusalem. However, he does not discuss this discrepancy; rather he is content to make reference to Jerome's treatment of it.

6 baptized] Paul himself does not refer to his baptism, though it is mentioned in Acts 9:18 and in Jerome's exposition of Gal 1:17 (PL 26:353A).

Chapter 2

102

1 compelled] LB gives as a variant reading in place of *compulsus* ('compelled'), *iussus* ('commanded'), for which, however, we find no textual support.

103

2 gained nothing] See Erasmus' annotation on Gal 2:6 ('they conferred nothing') where he makes the same point.

104

3 publicly ... face] Erasmus combines here two possible meanings of κατὰ πρόσωπον, whereas in his annotation he shows a distinct preference for the first meaning, 'publicly.' See Erasmus' annotation on Gal 2:11 ('I opposed him to his face'), which has a very long discussion of the debate between Augustine and Jerome as to the interpretation of this passage.

4 which he displayed] Added in 1532

5 rebuke ... reprehensible] Though Erasmus objects in his annotation on Gal 2:11 ('because he was blameworthy') to the Vulgate's *reprehensibilis erat* (was blameworthy), on the ground that it is an inappropriate translation of the

Greek κατεγνωσμένος ἦν — (was rebuked), he employs the word *reprehen-sibilis* here in his *Paraphrase* – in a sense not inconsistent, however, with his annotation. In his annotation he argues that Peter 'was rebuked and con-demned' by those who had previously judged (wrongly) that he should not eat with Gentiles. As a result, Peter was now preparing to withdraw from the table to avoid trouble. Foreseeing the consequences of Peter's vacillation, Paul rebuked him to strengthen others who were vacillating. Thus, while Peter was 'reprehensible' for his ill-considered action, Paul did not regard him as truly culpable.

In maintaining this view, Erasmus adopted the position of Jerome who argued that Paul had rebuked Peter only in pretence as a way to encourage gentile Christians, without any intention of imputing guilt. Augustine opposed Jerome's interpretation on the ground that to ascribe pretence to Paul was to make him guilty of a lie; Paul's rebuke must therefore have been genuine and Peter deserving of it. For Jerome's interpretation see PL 26:363–6, esp 364B–C; and Augustine's PL 35:2113–14. Augustine and Jerome exchanged twelve letters concerning the correct interpretation of the conflict between Peter and Paul in Gal 2:11. For a brief account of this controversy in the context of other patristic views see Lightfoot 128–32. For a longer treatment see Georg Grützmacher *Hieronymus* III (Berlin 1908) 114–37.

105

6 pretence] Here too, Erasmus' paraphrase follows Jerome's interpretation. In his annotation on 2:13 ('by them into that dissimulation') Erasmus supports the Vulgate's *in simulationem* (his text) for the Greek τῇ ὑποκρίσει — 'hypocrisy' or 'feigning.' In the annotation on 2:14 ('walked uprightly') Erasmus dis-tinguishes Peter's role from that of the other Jews. Peter 'dissembled' rather than 'pretended' in order not to offend his own people, the others dis-sembled through fear of transgression.

7 wavering] As in his annotation on Gal 2:14 ('walked uprightly') Erasmus takes the view that the verb ὀρθοποδοῦσιν means not 'walk uprightly' in a moral sense but 'walk in a straight line.' The Galatians were not guilty of moral turpitude, but vacillation. The meaning of this verb, a New Testament *hapax legomenon*, is disputed. For a summary of the patristic evidence see G.D. Kilpatrick, 'Gal 2:14 ὀρθοποδοῦσιν' in *Neutestamentliche Studien für Rudolf Bultmann* (Berlin 1957) 269–74, whose interpretation agrees with Erasmus that the verb does not have here a moral sense.

106

8 burdensome] *crassus*. In the *Paraphrase* on Galatians, Erasmus uses this word with the primary connotation of 'heavy' (cf above p 16 n 9); hence here 'the burdensome law.'

9 death ... marriage] Cf Rom 7:1–3.

10 faith ... law] Jerome similarly distinguishes here sharply between the old law of the letter and the new spiritual law. See PL 26:370A–B.

107

11 champion ... persecutor] For a similar idea see Jerome PL 26:370D.

Chapter 3

108

1 envied ... bewitched] Erasmus here combines two possible meanings of βασκαίνειν, 'envy' and 'bewitch,' as he points out in his annotation on Gal 3:1 ('who has bewitched you').

2 eyes of faith] Cf Chrysostom PG 61:648; NPNF (Series 1) 13.24: 'He says not "crucified," but "openly set forth crucified," signifying that by the eye of faith they saw more distinctly than some who were present as spectators.' See also Theophylact PG 124:984B.

3 portrayed] As he states in his annotation ('before whose eyes'), Erasmus agrees with Chrysostom and Theophylact that προεγράφη here means 'depicted' or 'portrayed.' See Chrysostom PG 61:648–9; NPNF (Series 1) 13.24; Theophylact PG 124:984A–B. Cf above p83 nn1 and 2.

4 baptism ... hands] Erasmus here reads 'baptism' and 'laying on of hands' into the text. Paul does not mention the conjunction of baptism and laying on of hands. But see Acts 8:16; 19:5–6.

5 Miracles] Chrysostom likewise mentions these miracles in his exegesis of this text. See PG 61:649; NPNF (Series 1) 13.25.

6 delusion] *Praestigii*. LB has an alternate reading, *praesidii* ('aid') for which we find no textual support.

109

7 erred ... heart] For a similar view see Jerome PL 26:376C.

110

8 works and] Added in 1532

111

9 you] LB gives as an alternate reading *nos* ('us') but *vos* ('you') is clearly the better attested one.

10 brought by the law] Added in 1532

11 through faith] Added in 1532

12 descendants I say] Added in 1532

13 or a covenant] Added in 1532

14 beyond] Reading *praeter* which LB gives as an alternate reading, but which is the only one to be found in the several editions consulted. LB has *propter* 'on account of' in the text.

112

15 midway] In this sentence and in the next Erasmus gives two interpretations of Christ as mediator. Whereas most of the Fathers held the view that the 'mediator' here is Christ, modern scholars generally agree that the mediator must be Moses. See Schlier 159; Hans Dieter Betz *Galatians* (Philadelphia 1979) 170; and Lightfoot 146 who reports on the patristic views.

16 conciliator ... race] Cf Chrysostom: 'Now a new mediator, says he, is between two parties; of whom then is Christ the mediator? Plainly of God and men'

(PG 61:655; NPNF [Series 1] 13.28). Lightfoot (146) says: 'The number of interpretations of this passage is said to mount up to 250 or 300.'

113
17 pedagogue] *Paedagogus* (Greek παιδαγωγός). The *paedagogus* was the slave
who acted as preceptor or governor of a child in the Graeco-Roman world.

Chapter 4

115
1 guardians and governors] *tutoribus et actoribus*. See Erasmus' annotation on
Gal 4:2 ('guardians and governors') in which Erasmus shows a preference
for a different translation, 'trustees' (*curatoribus*) and 'managers' (*dispensatori-
bus*). He notes that *tutores* were given to wards, *curatores* to minors; while *actor*
was ambiguous, *dispensator* referred to one who managed property and
possessions. However, both his own translation and his paraphrase retain
the Vulgate rendering.
2 elements] See Erasmus' annotation on Gal 4:3 ('we were serving under the
elements of the world'). Erasmus' interpretation of στοιχεῖα ('elements of the
world') is closest to that of Ambrosiaster who thinks that Paul by that term
is signifying new moons and sabbaths which the Jews observe and which
were adapted to them as children (CSEL 81 [3] 43:4–10). Jerome cites two
interpretations: (1) that the 'elements of the world' are the angels which pre-
side over the four elements of the world — earth, air, fire, and water; (2)
that the term refers to the law of Moses and the words of the prophets as
having provided a rudimentary instruction appropriate for children (PL
26:397). Erasmus adopts the second of these interpretations as the simpler,
except that with Ambrosiaster he clearly limits law to ceremonies. Contemporary interpreters are still disagreed as to whether στοιχεῖα means here and
in Col 2:8 the rudimentary forms of religion (so Erasmus) or the elemental
spirits of the universe or the heavenly bodies. See Arndt and Gingrich 776;
Schlier 190ff; Betz 204–5 notes 30 and 31.
3 children] *impuberes*, 'persons below the age of puberty.' In the first edition
Erasmus had written *minorennes*, 'minors.'
4 exhibited ... senses] Added in 1532
5 our nature] See above paraphrase on Rom 8:3 and n3.
6 child] *impubes*; first edition, *minorennis*

116
7 Jews] Erasmus is here evidently referring to Christian Jews.
8 For God ... to himself] Cf Chrysostom PG 61:658, NPNF (Series 1) 13.31: 'It was
not by your own effort that you found out God, but while you continued
in error, He drew you to Himself.'
9 inexpiable] Reading *inexpiabilis*, which is clearly the better attested reading
but which LB lists as a variant. The reading of the LB text is *inexpugnabile*
('unconquerable').

10 error] The paraphrase on verse 8 ('But just as the Jews') and verse 9 to this point came under attack from his critic at the Sorbonne, Béda, to which Erasmus gave answer. See *Divinationes ad notata Bedae* LB IX 475E–6B; *Supputatio errorum Bedae* LB IX 687C–90D. Among other things, Béda apparently accused Erasmus of undermining the entire law when he talked about the 'gross' or 'false' religion of the Jews. Erasmus replies that he does not interpret Paul as rejecting the whole law but only the ceremonial part. See above p90 n6.

117
11 afflictions] See Erasmus' annotation on Gal 4:14 ('your temptation') where in agreement with the paraphrase, he prefers to interpret Paul's affliction, which was a trial or temptation to the Galatians, not as a physical malady, but as persecutions that he endured. Jerome provides both interpretations (PL 26:407). Augustine (PL 35:2131) and Chrysostom (PG 61:659; NPNF [Series 1 13.32) give only the latter one.
12 for you] Added in 1532
13 on … faith] Revised in 1532. Earlier editions read: 'on the basis of these things.'

118
14 emulated] See Erasmus' annotation on 4:18 ('But emulate the good in the good'): 'It is good to wish to imitate others; but only in a good thing, not in all things.' The Vulgate translates the three instances of ζηλοῦν in verses 17 and 18 consistently by *aemulari*. Erasmus, however, as both his translations of and annotations on verses 17 and 18 reveal, thought that in the first case, the verb was used in the sense of the Latin *ambire*, to solicit; in the other two cases, in the sense of the Latin *imitari*, to imitate. In his paraphrase here, he reflects this distinction by using first the verb *ambire* (certain men solicit you), then by two phrases suggesting imitation: *alios sui similes reddere* (to make others like themselves) and *aemulandum esse* (should be emulated). Modern interpreters reject a difference in the meaning of ζηλοῦν in these two verses. The word means 'to seek after zealously' in all three instances. See Lightfoot 176–7; and Schlier 212–13.
15 law of Moses] Erasmus here anticipates Paul's discussion in the next verses. The law of Moses itself contains in the story of Abraham and Sarah, according to Paul's allegorical interpretation, the promise of freedom through faith from the burden of the law. See paraphrase on Gal 4:24 ('Now concealed in this story').

119
16 because … spirit] Added in 1532. Cf Jerome PL 26:414BC: 'He does not hear the law who, like the Galatians, follows only the external shell.'
17 written] Gen 16:15; 21:2–3
18 also] Added in 1532
19 however much] Added in 1532
20 law of Moses] See paraphrase on Rom 8:3 ('The law of Moses') and n2.
21 Hagar] See Erasmus' annotation on 4:24 ('the one on Mount Sinai') where Erasmus gives the opinion of Theophylact (PG 124:1005C), an opinion derived

from Chrysostom (cf PG 61:662; NPNF [Series 1] 13.34, that in Arabic 'Sinai' is
called 'Hagar'; but this is rejected by most modern scholars. See Lightfoot
193ff and Schlier 219ff.
22 borders] *Confinis est.* This is likewise Erasmus' translation for συστοιχεῖν
which, as Erasmus correctly interprets in his lengthy annotation ('which has
affinity to that Jerusalem which now is'), means literally 'belongs to the
same series or line,' but then also 'corresponds to.' Sinai is, indeed, far distant
from Jerusalem, but, he argues, things which have corresponding similarities
are said to be *confinia*, contiguous. Jerome interprets *confinis est* (PL 26:417B)
whereas the Vulgate translates *conjunctus est* ('is joined to').
23 also] Added in 1532

120

24 from himself] *De se.* Erasmus here seems to be alluding to Isa 54:3–8 in which
Israel, represented as the wife of God, her maker and husband, is promised
descendants, so that this posterity can be regarded as 'from' God Himself.
The prophet is thus interpreted as speaking in the *persona* of God. It is
possible to construe the *de se* as meaning 'concerning' or 'on account of himself' which would fit with a major theme of Isa 40–55 that God redeems Israel
'for his name's sake.' See Isa 48:9; 43:7.
25 slave] Added in 1532

121
26 Jews] Added in 1532
27 gentiles] Added in 1532

Chapter 5

1 of works] Added in 1532. This addition was probably made because of
Béda's criticism that Erasmus was here agreeing with Luther. In his response
to Béda, Erasmus utterly rejects that suggestion and states: 'I do not say
that there is no merit of faith working through love, but that grace is not given
to merits, but to faith alone' (*Divinationes ad notata Bedae* LB IX 476C). Cf
Supputatio errorum Bedae LB IX 690D–E: 'If this proposition is Lutheran, Paul is
Lutheran in many passages. I speak there concerning those who are ap-
proaching the gospel and concerning the observance of the ceremonies of the
law. On this basis the Jews ascribe salvation to their merits and obscure the
grace of the gospel.'
2 new one] Matt 9:16–17. Ambrosiaster also makes reference to this passage in
his exegesis of Gal 5:2 (CSEL 81 [3] 54:9–16).
3 We shall] These are the soothing words with which the Galatians are
represented as deceiving themselves.

122
4 For one … this kind] Cf Chrysostom PG 61:665; NPNF (Series 1) 13.37;
Theophylact PG 124:1009C–D.

5 evangelical light] Cf Jerome PL 26:424B: 'There is shadow in the old law, until the day dawns, and the shadows are removed; there is truth in the Gospel of Christ.'

6 spiritual ... law] In his exegesis of verse 3, Jerome refers to the spiritual law that Christians follow which contrasts sharply with the ceremonial law. Cf PL 26:423C.

123

7 When love ... conducive] Erasmus expresses the same sentiment elsewhere: cf *Paraphrasis in epistolam Pauli I ad Timotheum* 1:5 (1520) LB VII 1036E; *Enarratio Psalmi* I (1515) LB V 181B–E.

8 shadows] Jerome uses the same image in his exegesis of this verse (PL 26:429A).

9 Timothy] Jerome also mentions here Paul's becoming a Jew to Jews (1 Cor 9:20) and the circumcision of Timothy (Acts 16:3) (PL 26:432A).

10 preach it] Cf Theophylact PG 124:1013B: 'It is however one thing to circumcise, another to preach circumcision.'

124

11 shameful servitude] *Fruantur sua pudenda servitute*, perhaps a deliberately ambiguous statement. It could also mean 'let their genital organs enjoy servitude.' Here in the last three sentences of his paraphrase on verse 12, Erasmus reflects the ambiguity he sees in the Greek ἀποκόψονται (cut off). In his annotation on the Vulgate's *abscindantur* (his text), he suggests two possible senses: that those who teach circumcision should be cut off from grace and become anathema, or that they be not merely circumcised but castrated. He says that Ambrose (Ambrosiaster), Chrysostom, and Theophylact prefer the latter sense, but he thinks the former more worthy of apostolic dignity.

12 used to extort] *Exculpebat*, the reading of the LB text. LB lists as an alternate reading, *exigebat* ('used to require'), but we find no textual support for such a reading.

125

13 love ... law] For a similar expression see *Paraphrasis in epistolam Pauli I ad Timotheum* 1:5 LB VII 1036E.

14 and ... spirit] Added in 1521. See above, paraphrase on Rom 8:3 ('The law of Moses') and n2.

Chapter 6

127

1 restoring] See his annotation on this verse, 'instruct such a one,' where he takes issue with the Vulgate translation of καταρτίζετε as *instruite* ('instruct') and argues correctly that it should be 'restore,' and then comments: 'We are too little mindful of what Paul admonishes us here, as do other sacred teachers. If some sin must be reproved, with what haughtiness, with what

wrath we instantly rage! This has alienated many excellent persons from the communion of the church ...'

128

2 God the judge] Cf Jerome who says here: 'When we come before the tribunal of Christ ...' (PL 26:458A).

3 good things] Like Jerome, Erasmus understands these goods as spiritual goods. Cf PL 26:459A.

4 Jew ... Christian] For a similar sentiment see Chrysostom PG 61:677; NPNF (Series 1) 13.45.

5 epistle] See Erasmus' annotation on this verse ('with what kind of letters') where he expresses his opinion against his favourite, Jerome, that γράμμασιν here means 'epistle' not the letters of the alphabet. See Jerome PL 26:463C–D.

130

6 is steadfast for God] Revised in 1521 from 'discerns God'

7 brand-marks] Removed in 1521 and replaced in 1523. In his annotation, Erasmus explains stigmata from the image of slaves who were branded to mark them as the possession of their master. So Paul, as a slave of Christ, had been branded by the wounds he had received, carrying on his body the marks of the cross of Christ. Jerome, too, understood 'stigmata' here as the marks of the sufferings Paul endured for Christ (cf PL 26.467A).

8 trophies] Added in 1521

WORKS FREQUENTLY CITED

Allen P.S. Allen, H.M. Allen, and H.W. Garrod eds *Opus epistolarum Des. Erasmi Roterodami* (Oxford, 1906–47) 11 vols, plus index volume by B. Flower and E. Rosenbaum (Oxford 1958)

Arndt and W.F. Arndt and F.W. Gingrich *A Greek–English Lexicon of the New Testa-*
Gingrich *ment and other Early Christian Literature* (Chicago 1957)

ASD *Opera omnia Desiderii Erasmi Roterodami: Recognita et adnotatione critica instructa notisque illustrata* (Amsterdam 1969–)

CCL *Corpus Christianorum, Series Latina* (Turnhout 1953–)

Cranfield C.E.B. Cranfield *Epistle to the Romans* International Critical Commentary (Naperville, Illinois 1975) Vol I

CSEL *Corpus Scriptorum Ecclesiasticorum Latinorum* (Vienna 1866–)

CWE *Collected Works of Erasmus* (Toronto 1974–)

Himelick Raymond Himelick ed *The Enchiridion of Erasmus* (Bloomington, Indiana 1963)

Holborn Annemarie and Hajo Holborn eds *Desiderius Erasmus Roterodamus. Ausgewählte Werke* (Munich 1933)

Kuss Otto Kuss *Der Römerbrief* (Regensburg 2nd ed 1963) 2 vols

LB J. Leclerc ed *Desiderii Erasmi Roterodami opera omnia* (Leiden 1703–6) 10 vols

LCL *Loeb Classical Library* (London and Cambridge, Mass 1912–)

Lefèvre Jacques Lefèvre d'Étaples *Epistolae divi Apostoli, cum commentariis, praeclarissimi Jacobi Fabri Stapulensis* (Paris 1512)

Lightfoot J.B. Lightfoot *The Epistle of Paul to the Galatians* (Grand Rapids, Michigan, 3rd ed 1962)

LP *Letters and Papers, Foreign and Domestic, of the Reign of Henry VIII* ed J.S. Brewer, J. Gairdner, R.H. Brodie (London 1862–1932) 21 vols

Lupton I J.H. Lupton ed and tr *Ioannis Coleti enarratio in epistolas S. Pauli ad Romanos* (London 1873)

Lupton II J.H. Lupton ed *Ioannis Coleti opuscula quaedam theologica* (London 1873) [includes *Epistolae S. Pauli ad Romanos expositio literalis*]

NPNF   *Nicene and Post-Nicene Fathers* Series I and II (Grand Rapids 1886–89)
            28 vols

Payne   John B. Payne *Erasmus: His Theology of the Sacraments* (Richmond,
            Virginia 1970)

PG   J.P. Migne ed *Patrologiae cursus completus ...series Graeca* (Paris 1857–86)
            162 vols

PL   J.P. Migne ed *Patrologiae cursus completus ...series latina* (Paris 1844–66)
            221 vols. All references are from this first edition except those to volume
            26 (second edition). For page equivalents between the two editions,
            see E. Dekkers *Clavis Patrum Latinorum* (Bruges and the Hague 2nd ed
            1961) xxvii and 587–607.

Schelkle   Karl Hermann Schelkle *Paulus Lehrer der Väter. Die altkirchliche
            Auslegung von Römer 1–11* (Düsseldorf 1956)

Schlier   Heinrich Schlier *Der Brief an die Galater. Kritisch-exegetischer Kommentar
            über das Neue Testament* (Göttingen, 11th rev ed 1951)

Souter   A. Souter *Pelagius' Exposition of Thirteen Epistles of St Paul: Texts and
            Studies*, Vol IX (Cambridge 1922)

STC   A.W. Pollard and G.R. Redgrave *A Short-Title Catalogue of Books Printed
            in England, Scotland, and Ireland and of English Books Printed Abroad
            1475-1640* (London 1926)

THE SEQUENCE AND DATES OF THE PUBLICATION OF THE PARAPHRASES

A **The Epistles**

Romans	November 1517
Corinthians 1 and 2	February 1519
Galatians	May 1519
Timothy 1 and 2, Titus, Philemon	November/December 1519
Ephesians, Philippians, Colossians and Thessalonians 1 and 2	January/February 1520
Peter 1 and 2, Jude	June/July 1520
James	December 1520
John 1-3, Hebrews	January 1521

B **Gospels and Acts**

Matthew	March 1522
John	February 1523
Luke	August 1523
Mark	December 1523/February 1524
Acts	February 1524

The Epistles were originally published by Thierry Martens in Louvain, except for Timothy, Titus, and Philemon published by Michael Hillen in Antwerp. The Gospels and Acts were all originally published by Johann Froben in Basel.

INDEXES

GENERAL INDEX

INDEX OF THEOLOGICAL TERMS

INDEX OF GREEK WORDS CITED

INDEX OF LATIN WORDS CITED

The indexes refer to the introductory essays, notes,
dedicatory letters, and arguments of the epistles.
An index of the names and theological terms in
the *Paraphrases* themselves is beyond the scope
of this volume.

General Index

Aa, Peter van der. *See* Printers and Publishers

Abbot, Frank F., on the Roman Senate 82 n7

accommodation, principle of. *See* Index of Theological Terms

Affeldt, Werner, on Erasmus' political theory 73 n2, 74 n5

Albutius, in Lucilius 2

allegory. *See* Index of Theological Terms

All Souls College, purchased *Paraphrases* xxxiii

ambiguity. *See* Erasmus, language of

Ambrose, St, Erasmus seeks commentary of xiii; identified as Ambrosiaster 7 n13

Ambrosiaster, influenced *Paraphrases* xviii, xxxvi

– citations, reflecting influence and parallels: on sin 18 nn18,20, 34 n12, 36 n2, 42 n3, 43 n6, 44 n10; on Jews 24 n6, 62 n10, 67 nn9,10; on ceremonies and the law 25 nn11,17, 30 n9, 58 n25, 115 n2; on Christ 22 n13, 29 n6, 34 n8, 51 n23; on promise and faith 23 n4, 25 n15, 26 nn21,22 23, 27 n3, 84 n3; on other topics 7, 7 n13, 15 n1, 27 n4, 31 n14, 35 n16, 42 n5, 49 n19, 50 n21, 74 n5, 121 n2, 124 n11

– interpretation rejected 85 n4

angels. *See* Index of Theological Terms

Anshelm, Thomas. *See* Printers and Publishers

anthropology. *See* Index of Theological Terms

Aphrodite, Temple at Cenchreae 7 n15

Apuleius, corrupt judges in *Met* 3 n9; on Isis worship 7 n15

Aquinas, St Thomas, no influence on *Paraphrases* xix; understands πνεῦμα as Holy Spirit 49 n19

Arator, paraphraser of scripture xvii

Arianism, Erasmus accused of 51 n23

Aristotle, sophistries of xvii; paraphrased by Themistius xvii; parallel in Erasmus 46 n9

Arndt, W.F. and F.W. Gingrich, meaning of 'elements' 115 n2

Asclepius, sanctuary at Cenchreae 7 n15

Auer, Alfons, on Erasmus' view of the law 45 n2; on division into 'good, bad, indifferent' 74 n3

Augustine, St, Erasmus seeks commentary of xiii; paraphraser of scripture xvii; little influence on Erasmus xviii; on superstition of Jews 9 n28; on the language of St Paul 12

– comments on: Rom 5:12 (original sin) 34 n12; Rom 8:26 (Holy Spirit) 49 n19; Rom 11:25 (all Israel saved) 67 n10; Rom 13:1-7 (political order) 73 n2; Gal 2:11 (Peter-Paul controversy) 92 and 104 nn3,5; Gal 4:14 (persecution) 117 n11

Averroes, sophistries of xvii

Index of Theological Terms

Abraham. *See* example, faith

accommodation, principle of 8 n20,
72 n9

allegory. *See* scripture

angels, as creatures 48 n12, as elements 115 n2

anthropology, soul-body dichotomy
37 n7, Platonist influence 37 n7, 44
n9; base for law 45 n2

baptism, two kinds 11; symbolic 37
n3; not sufficient 46 n6; assumed
101 n6, 108 n4

ceremonies, identified with Judaism
and Law xxxvi, 4 n11, 25 n17,
115 n2; temporary 95; obsolete 9, 30
n9; opposed to faith 58 n25, 78
n5, 90 n6, 121 n1, 122 nn4, 6; ceremonial law distinguished from moral
90 n6, 116 n10

circumcision, two kinds 11; spiritual
22 n14, 29 n5; *see also* ceremonies

confession. *See* accommodation

Christ, in relation to God 15 n4, 34
n10, 51 n23, 53 n2, 68 n15, 95 n5,
100 n3; incarnation of 45 n3, 72 n9;
death of 33 n5, 34 n8, 35 n15;
Lord and Judge 78 n4, 128 n2;
Mediator 112 n15; as the virtues 46
n7, 77 n10; as end of Law 22 n13,
60 n4; as first fruits 65 n6; peace
proceeds from 16 n7; types of 25
n13, 29 n6; *see also* spirit

Church, concord in 78 n2; as congregation 100 n4

death, spiritual not corporeal 36 n17;
and devil 40 n14

devil, and sin 36 n2, 40 n14, 43 n6

divorce, tract on xxx; debate on xxx
n7; *see also* accommodation

example, sin by example (ie by imitation) 18 n19, 34 n12, 35 nn14, 15;
Abraham an example 31 n14; Christ
an example for imitation 29 n7, 31
n14, 37 n6, 46 n8; imitate example
of others 118 n14; OT prescriptions
for imitation 83 n1

faith, as theme in Rom, 10, meaning
of xxxvii, 15 n6, 17 n14; and law 25
n11, 26 n23, 58 n25, 118 n15; and
works 20 n6, 26 n1, 27 n3, 121 n1;
and merit 29 n8, 30 n10; and
promise 26 n22, 54 n8; and miracles
62 n11; and conscience 82 n8; 'faith
alone' xxxvi, 10, 27 n3; of gospel
23 n2; of God 23 nn3, 5; of Abraham
65 n6; measure of 71 n5; law of 106
n10; eyes of 108 n2

flesh, opposed to spirit 10 n30, 45 n1,
69 n4; and law 45 n2, 95; and
circumcision 22 n14; did not bear
Isaac 54 n7; of Christ 45 n3; Christ
according to 53 n2

free will, theme in Rom, 10; Erasmus

Index of Greek Words Cited

Index of Latin Words Cited